The
Discarded Army

the
discarded

by Paul Starr

with assistance from
James F. Henry & Raymond P. Bonner

CHARTERHOUSE
New York

army ★ ★ ★ ★ ★ ★ ★

Veterans After Vietnam

The Nader Report on Vietnam Veterans
and the Veterans Administration

THE DISCARDED ARMY: Veterans After Vietnam
COPYRIGHT © 1973 BY
Center for Study of Responsive Law

Portions of this book have appeared in different
form in *The Washington Monthly*.

ISBN 0-088327-024-2
LIBRARY OF CONGRESS CATALOG CARD NUMBER: 73-84084
MANUFACTURED IN THE UNITED STATES OF AMERICA

Preface

Work on this report began in June 1971 and was essentially completed toward the end of January 1973, within a few days of the announcement of a cease-fire and the signing of the Paris accords. Looking back over that time, I can recall many difficult moments. I think of sitting opposite a young quadriplegic in a VA hospital and trying to make conversation as he struggled with every gesture. Or confronting twelve formerly addicted veterans in a drug program and trying to cope with the very hard questions I had asked them and they had thrown back at me. Or talking with unemployed veterans in West Virginia and the South Bronx in New York and the east side of Milwaukee—different men in different places, but with similar problems and the same frustrations. In the end, one came away with a sense not only of how deeply some men had been hurt, but of their resilience, vitality, and good humor under trying circumstances. I can never presume to speak for them, but I certainly learned a great deal from speaking with them. Had they not been willing to share their experiences and thoughts, this report would have suffered enormously.

I also benefited a great deal from discussions with government officials in Washington and with Veterans Administration employees at hospitals and offices around the country. They were almost always generous of their time and often surprisingly candid about the problems they encountered in their work. There was, of course, the usual quota of evasiveness and irrelevance from some officials in government and private organizations, but these were to be expected and were never more than minor irritations. Even when uninformative, they were unfailingly polite.

In this book, there is almost no attention to particular personalities or administrators. Our concerns are rather directed toward the more structured aspects of government—laws and policies, usages and practices, patterns of organization and behavior. There is, nonetheless, a certain tension. Part of the book is about Vietnam veterans and part about the Veterans Administration. At the beginning I assumed that these could be readily worked together into a single study, but the task proved much more difficult as it became evident how little the agency and the men have to do with each other. This in itself was a principal aspect of the problem at hand.

All quotations of veterans in the text that have not been footnoted come from interviews conducted for the report. Names have been changed and identifiable references omitted. I am much indebted to Jim Henry (Harvard College and Harvard Law School) for the use of interviews that he did, initially as part of his own research and later in conjunction with the report. Jim collaborated on the first chapter and is also the principal author of Chapter 8.

A great many other people gave their assistance. In the summer of 1972, Warren Oster (George Washington Law School) and Holly Meyers (Brown University) did research for the project. Ron Plesser of the Center for Study of Responsive Law offered invaluable legal assistance in extracting data from the Department of Defense. Dr. Sidney Wolfe of the Health Research Group gave us good counsel on medical policy. Ray Bonner, formerly a Marine Corps lawyer and more recently of the Public Citizen Litigation Group, has been an excellent critic throughout. He also collaborated on Chapter 6.

In addition, I must thank Professor Michael Useem of Harvard University for his help with military and Selective Service policy; Dr. Norman Zinberg of Cambridge, Mass., for examining the chapter on drug abuse; Jerome Karabel of Harvard, Dr. John Mallan of the American Association of Junior Colleges, and Guy McMichael, counsel to the Senate Veterans Affairs Committee, for critically examining the chapter on education. Numerous other friends and colleagues read over sections of the report and offered their reactions—literary, political, and professional.

Also greatly appreciated were the efforts of Mrs. Janice Fineman of Newton, Mass., and Ms. Elayne Butwinick of Washington, D.C., who volunteered to type much of the report. Cathy Crockford, Lynn Pease, and Jill Greenberg also shared in the work. I owe a great deal to Theodore Jacobs of the Center for Study of Responsive Law and to the Center's other stalwarts and mainstays—Connie Jo

Smith, Theo Page, Estelle Goor, Dave Moe, and especially Ruth Fort.

Finally, I have a special obligation to Ralph Nader, whose idea this book was and whose support was essential in seeing it through.

Paul Starr
Cambridge, Massachusetts
April 1973

Contents

x   Contents

Introduction

The return of nearly three million Vietnam veterans in recent years has not focused the necessary attention on the government's programs that are designed to diminish wartime afflictions and dislocations. These include hospital care, drug rehabilitation, disability, and educational payments. This book strives to do just that. Through painstaking interviewing and scrutiny of documents and hearings, Paul Starr and his associates have provided the broader context of these veterans' assistance programs as well as a specific analysis of what they actually do as compared with what they are supposed to do.

Central to the waste, injustice, insensitivity, and failings of these programs is the Veterans Administration. Little studied, an object of boredom to Congress and the media, the VA remains the federal government's third largest agency in budget and second largest in employees. Administering payments for wars fought over a century ago to the present, the VA has benefited men long out of service and lacking any service-connected injury far more than those with recent combat or service-connected harms. It has poured billions into educational training without seeing that career, correspondence, or other schools adhere to standards worthy of the young veterans. Its medical programs are geared primarily to handle the chronic illnesses of older veterans, often along the lines of an impersonal nursing-home mentality, which does not facilitate the treatment and rehabilitation of recently injured soldiers. It has presided without objection over a congressionally mandated program that requires Vietnam veterans to drop their low-cost term service insurance or convert it to high-premium, low-benefit cash value insurance that enriches private companies to the detriment of these young ex-servicemen. In its simplest functions—those of getting the checks out and deciding claims in a reasonable time—the VA generates record complaints to members of Congress.

Looking at the largest hospital system in the country or the largest program of direct educational aid (both administered by the VA) required several hundred interviews with VA officials, knowledgeable observers in and out of government, and Vietnam veterans. This is not a report of statistics shorn of any human misery. Mr. Starr records the feelings, impressions, and often acute insights of the veterans themselves. In so doing, he makes one of the main points of the study—that Vietnam veterans are quite different from veterans of earlier wars. And the nation's response has also been different.

What other war of such length and intensity was undeclared? What other war found its official rationale changing with the frequency of the Book of the Month? What other war witnessed Americans not knowing the names of their generals and not caring to? What other war witnessed such moral dissent by soldiers and new veterans? What other war drove thousands of young men abroad to escape the dragnet to the war zone? What other war provoked so many successful challenges by soldiers exerting their constitutional rights? What other war involved vast, official profiteering in the drugging of American soldiers? What other war involved such brutal military devastation of civilians, land, and future generations in so small a country? What other war induced such inchoate shame in Washington that words had to be recast, from "invasion" to "incursion," from "chemical warfare" to "defoliation," and on and on in a lexicon of deception? In what other war did lies become official explanations whose exposure only produced bigger lies? What other war displayed the utter weakness of our democracy to control a runaway, obstinate leadership in the Executive and an abdicating, cowering obeisance in Congress? In what other foreign war did millions of Americans repeatedly protest and millions more voice their objections through the polls or through their breath? In what other war have the thousands of dead and wounded received less public attention and Presidential concern than several hundred POW officers?

It is into this environment that many Vietnam veterans returned, already cynical about the battle, its methods, and its purposes. They were not seen as the returning heroes of the "Johnny Comes Marching Home" cadence; if they were seen in imagery at all, it was as broken drug addicts or demoralized unemployed. The VA behaved as if their needs were an intrusion, and the leadership of the large veterans' organizations saw no urgency for leaning on the VA to do otherwise. As a result of these neglects, the seeds for continued anguish, deprivation, and bitterness are being sown among the young men who were caught, often because of their very poverty, in America's most miserable quagmire.

The recommendations in this study, including self-help initiatives by veterans and new directions, priorities, and efficiencies, could use a healthy dose of Congressional inquiry and media interest. But just as important is the need for a continuing presence of advocates representing the rights of these veterans in Washington by monitoring the VA and other government programs. Such an effort would see how much of the present VA budget, which goes to phantom disabilities, nonservice-connected claims, bureaucratic waste, and business frauds, could partly be saved and partly redirected to the real needs of young Vietnam veterans.

Ralph Nader
Washington, D.C.

part one ★ ★ ★ ★ ★
Men and Institutions

The smoke of pipes and cigars fills the room. Desires, thoughts, ambitions in seething confusion. God only knows what will come of them. A hundred young soldiers, eighteen lieutenants, thirty warrant officers and noncoms, all sitting here, wanting to start to live. Any man of them could take a company under fire across No Man's Land with hardly a casualty. There is not one who would hesitate for an instant to do the right thing when the cry "They are coming!" was yelled down into his dugout. Every man has been tempered through countless, pitiless days; every man is a complete soldier, no more and no less.

But for peace? Are we suitable? Are we fit now for anything but soldiering?

Erich Maria Remarque,
The Road Back

1
Different War, Indifferent Peace

For nearly a decade the Vietnam conflict has occupied center stage in the theater of American politics. Crowds have marched demanding that the nation "support our boys," and even larger crowds have marched demanding "Bring them home—NOW."

Now they are home. The crowds have disappeared, the turmoil is gone, and the men who were the subject of great concern *in absentia* are paid little attention upon return. Like so many accidental figures of political history, they learn bitterly with time that all the fuss was not really about their lives in particular, but about "larger" issues. Quietly they go back home, those that live, and live out, each in his own way, part of the war's unfinished history.

Willie lies in his bed at a veterans' hospital where he has been waiting for weeks to find out whether the surgeons will finally decide to saw off his leg. It was at the end of an ambush three years ago in Tay Ninh province, after nearly all the fighting had died down, that he caught a lone sniper's last bullet in his hip. The wound left him with a permanent limp and an infection of the bone marrow that may ultimately force an amputation. "It rots the bone and the tissue surrounding it," he explains in a matter-of-fact way. "There's really not much that can be done for it. It's a constantly recurring thing, so since I got out of the Army, I really haven't been able to make any long-term plans, because you know you're always going to wind up back here. Right now, I've got my goals set on just getting out of school, pick up the ball from there.

"I've had to work a little bit along the way. I keep going to school full-time, but I don't work steady. And it's hard, you know, finding a summer job. I've done everything since I've been out. I've been a security guard, I was a janitor, and my latest endeavor was a clerical job for a mutual fund company. I've been getting jobs, but there's a difference between jobs and careers. From what I can see, there are a lot of people that like to give a vet a break, but the feeling is—I don't know, maybe I'm a little self-conscious—but a disabled vet, I think people are willing to give you the janitor's job, give you a clerk job, but look, I walk with an exaggerated limp, and I usually notice that people are a little tense when they talk to you. And a lot of guys I know that really have physical problems, they run into a lot of trouble. You know, people are uncomfortable when they're around them. And companies can't put him in a position of prominence, I guess, if it's going to offend anyone else.

"The war's the big disillusionment in my life. I went in in sixty-seven. The attitude was a little different then. Everyone was hearing about Vietnam, but I'd say the greater segment of the population still agreed with backing the government. That's the way I felt about it. But now . . . No way in hell anybody should ever have gone there.

"I remember a guy came one day on a supply chopper, and he got off the chopper and he screamed, 'Hey, the war's over.' Everyone started screaming. They were ecstatic. So finally someone got around to asking, 'Who won?' The guy told them they [the VC] did. Everyone was still happy. They didn't care . . . As far as I'm concerned, we lost. If one guy got killed over there for no reason, we lost.

"You hate to forget about it. You're forgetting about a lot of people that shouldn't be forgotten. You just put it out of your mind, and this bullshit is going to go on forever. That's the problem. A guy sits home and watches the war on television. He shuts it off at eleven o'clock, but the guys that are in it can't. . . . I walk around with it every day. I've got a bad leg, so every time I take a step, I remember it. A lot of guys with shrapnel have scars all over them. Every time they take a shower, they remember."

The war in Indochina has been America's longest agony abroad, and none of us has known that agony more closely or paid for it more dearly than the men who were sent to fight it. They have not only borne the sacrifices of life and good health that war inevitably exacts, but also faced more keenly than others the moral burdens and conflicting social pressures that the struggle has generated. And on their return home, the veterans of Vietnam have found themselves once again shouldering the burdens of the war—this time because of its social costs and economic repercussions. Jobs have been hard to find, good jobs even harder; housing is expensive; medical care suffers from shortages and maldistribution of personnel. These problems affect all Americans; they acutely affect returning soldiers because of their immediate needs for jobs, housing, and medical attention.

The material problems veterans confront are the more onerous for the context in which they occur. Men are willing to bear great discomfort and pain, even death, if they believe their actions have a legitimate and important purpose, that others have also done their part, and that their own sacrifices will be respected, or at least remembered. To most men these rewards are much more important than any material compensation. But when those private and personal satisfactions are not forthcoming, then the material problems stand out, and the inequities of sacrifice are less easily accepted.

The litany of the war's costs is familiar, but the facts bear repetition. Before the cease-fire at the end of January 1973, 56,244 men were killed in Vietnam and more than 300,000 wounded (half of them seriously), making this the third major armed conflict in American history after the Civil War and World War II.[1] Add to that an indeterminate number, well into the thousands, who have become addicted to heroin while in Southeast Asia. This only accounts for the more concrete and immediate kinds of harm. Beyond that lies the personal disorientation caused by war, which is susceptible neither to measurement nor to compensation. There are also thousands of men who had a rough time in the army—some because they resisted the military system, refused orders they thought unjust, responded to racist treatment, or just didn't know how to handle a strange environment away from home—and ended up with less than honorable discharges, which now follow them around through life, depriving them of jobs and government services that otherwise might have been theirs.

Yet the way the war has been managed administratively has been such that public concern for the new veterans has been minimized. Americans at home have been spared any direct sacrifices, such as rationing of important commodities, which might have served as a continuing reminder of the war. There has been no sudden return of large contingents from Vietnam, accompanied by parades and official proclamations, and if there were, they would necessarily be interpreted as partisan efforts in favor of the war. The only large assembly of Vietnam veterans themselves (the demonstrations in Washington in April 1971 known as Dewey Canyon III) has been decidedly unofficial and antiwar. Even then, the gathering was more an act of penance and of protest than a plea for just rewards.

Our subject is the response that the federal government has made to the men it sent to Vietnam. But before we look at that response, we need to know more about the veterans themselves and what they have been through.

★ *Going In*

At least 8 million men will have passed through the military by the end of the "Vietnam Era," which, for the purposes of law and veterans' benefits, officially began on August 4, 1964, the day Congress approved the Tonkin Gulf resolution. More than 6 million of those soldiers are now veterans, and just under half of them served in Vietnam itself. Any group that large, from a nation as diverse as the United States, defies easy characterization, and we shall try to resist the temptation to draw a simplified composite portrait of them.

Nonetheless, the soldiers who fought in Vietnam were not drawn at random from the American population, nor were their experiences in the military entirely dissimilar. Our purpose in the next few pages is to describe some aspects of their prewar background and their experience during the conflict and on their return home.

Between 50 and 60 percent of the men who served in the military during the war were drafted or enlisted because of the threat of conscription.[2] The draft struck American society very unevenly. As a result of the post-World War II baby boom, the reservoir of men available for military service was considerably larger than the number the military actually needed during the Sixties. The nation, therefore, had a far wider choice as to which men would serve than it had during World War II or Korea, but it was a choice that narrowed as the war in Vietnam deepened. At the inception of the conflict, Selective Service policy worked to exclude two groups. On the one hand, it was government policy to defer young men who were pursuing higher education and entering occupations defined to be in the national interest. These were the sons primarily of upper- and upper middle-class families. On the other hand, it was also government policy to exclude young men who could not meet certain minimum mental and physical standards. Those excluded on these criteria were disproportionately from lower-class and minority backgrounds. And so it was the middle of the class structure that carried the heaviest load of the draft—in the words of one sociologist, "the economically more secure sectors of the blue-collar working class and lower reaches of the white-collar occupations." [3]

Data on the social incidence of conscription are rather meager, but the basic pattern emerges clearly from a study that gives the probability of reluctant participation (draftees plus draft-motivated volunteers) by years of school. Setting the probability for young men with eight years or less of education arbitrarily at 1.0, the relative probability for those having nine to eleven years rose to 2.8 and peaked for high school graduates at 3.7. For youth with some college it dropped to 2.8 and for college graduates it sank to 0.8. In other words, the probability of being drafted or enlisting under pressure was more than four times as great for high school graduates as for college graduates.[4]

This pattern of unequal susceptibility to the draft was magnified by the system of occupational assignments within the military. Men with less education were far more likely to wind up on the front lines and on the casualty rolls. They also stood much less chance of acquiring skills that could be transferred to civilian life. The military has often been seen as a social equalizer. But, to a large extent, motivated by its own need to fill the more technical occupations with the better educated, it merely recapitulated and multiplied pre-existing civilian inequalities.

As the war intensified, the government faced a choice as to where it would obtain the additional manpower needed to fight in Vietnam. There were two possibilities: the upper middle-class youth receiving student and occupational deferments or the lower class and minority youth disqualified primarily on mental grounds. Which choice the Johnson administration made, how it justified that decision, and what its outcome was are the subject of a separate chapter.°

If draftees came predominantly from the families of blue-collar workers and lower white-collar employees, volunteers were no different. The data on educational background, in fact, suggest that enlistees were, on the average, slightly lower in socio-economic status than draftees.[5] Typically they were young men who had just finished high school and were not going on to college, either because they had done poorly in school or on their college boards or because college just wasn't an economic possibility for their family. The military seemed to offer them a way out, a way to redeem themselves.

° See Chapter 7.

"I had nothing better to do. I was a failure, you know? And I knew it, coming out of this high school, you know? I took the business course in high school when I should have took the college course. So that was maybe my real goof. So I was like two weeks out of high school I was in the service. . . . I was out of high school, I had no job or nothing. So the Air Force recruiter says come back in two months. So I walked in the next door. The next door happened to be the Marine Corps. And they take anything that walks in. . . ."

The military held some positive attractions as well. It offered some men a more secure standard of living than they could achieve in civilian life. For those who made rank, the middle of military society compared favorably with the bottom of civilian society. Many thought they might learn a trade there; how few actually did we shall see later. For others, it was a way to gain autonomy, prestige, and self-confidence; for some, a chance to prove, once and for all, that they were really men.

"I was pressured a little by my desire to get away from home. You know, like every young kid, just can't hack his parents, and just to do something, see something on my own."

"I know one thing. Before I went in, my brother could kick my ass, but now he can't. I was always the little brother. You know, 'Get out of here, you pest.' I always looked up to him. Real big guy. He ain't nothing no more."

Working-class veterans that we interviewed who had volunteered for military service did so largely because they believed it would provide personal benefits. Enlistment was a logical extension of their civilian activities and needs. They sought relief from depressing community routines as well as some measure of self-respect and a chance to see the world. Enlistment was an act of dissatisfaction with the opportunities for self-direction and advancement available at home. Ideological considerations were largely irrelevant.

To get away from a dead-end existence, to escape the tedium, to be able to give orders as well as take them; to walk down the street in your uniform, knowing that all the kids are staring; to dish it out and take it, without having to stay after school or talk to a judge; to drink and smoke and fight and not have to ask your father for the car; to be treated like a man. There is nothing particularly unusual or wicked about these desires. To some extent they are present in us all. The only difference is that some people have the chance to satisfy them in other ways. Status, redemption, opportunity, escape, companionship—why else do men make fateful decisions?

One other possible motive for enlistment might be a strong belief in the importance of winning the war. But surveys taken through the Sixties, some of them sponsored by the Defense Department, consistently showed that few young men joined the army for that reason, and consequently the military never appealed to potential recruits on that basis.[6] The men who enlisted generally had not given the conflict serious thought before they became engulfed by it.

"I was never, like I never read the newspapers before I went in. The only thing I used to read was sports. I never really hooked up to it that much. So I didn't have any feelings one way or the other. I figured it was more or less right, because why would I be going if it wasn't right?"

"I knew almost nothing about it. The war I thought was like they taught us in high school, you know, you're fighting communism, you know, it was just the good guys against the bad guys."

"I didn't know too much about it. I just figured North Vietnam was against South Vietnam, and we were supposed to help the South."

The American soldier was not an ideological soldier. If he enlisted, he enlisted primarily for personal reasons. But beneath his lack of a specific commitment to the aims of the war lay a basic faith in the legitimacy of American institutions and a deeply ingrained sense of obligation. Although he typically knew very little and cared less about Vietnam beforehand, he took it on trust that he would be fighting with the "good guys" against the "bad guys." This trust sustained most of the drafted men as well as the enlistees. And it was this basic trust that would be severely tested, and in many cases shaken, by the war experience.

If enlistments depended primarily on personal benefits rather than ideological commitment, they rested on fragile ground, for when the war escalated the military's ability to offer those benefits declined. As the American public turned sour on the conflict, it became less possible for young men to win status or prestige through military service. High school students also began hearing stories from older friends and relatives who had been to Vietnam and who now told them it was "a bummer." Volunteers for the combat arms declined, and draftees gradually came to represent an increasing proportion of front-line soldiers and casualties. In 1965, draftees represented only 16 percent of the total battle deaths in the war. In 1966, they constituted 21 percent; in 1967, 34 percent; in 1968, 34 percent; in 1969, 40 percent; and in 1970, 43 percent of combat fatalities.[7] The Army,* in particular, came to rely heavily on draftees. By 1969, 62 percent of all Army combat deaths were draftees.[8] For fiscal 1970, according to a study by the Army General Staff, draftees represented 70 percent of all combat soldiers. They comprised 88 percent of infantry riflemen, while first-term volunteers represented only 10 percent and career Army men 2 percent. Less than 5 percent of volunteers were asking to be trained in combat specialties. "We've studied this problem very carefully," one Defense Department official told the *National Journal* in 1970. "People don't seem to enlist in the Army to fight."

"As strange as it sounds," said William K. Brehm, Assistant Secretary of the Army for Manpower and Reserve Affairs, "only 800 young men a month out of 200 million Americans are enlisting for combat. . . . The popular jobs are the ones for which people enlist. They don't enlist for the hard-core combat skills." [9]

The result was that, in the Army, draftees were assuming the heaviest burden of the war and being killed and wounded at nearly double the rate of non-draftee enlisted men. In 1969, according to the report of the Army General Staff, the casualty rate for Army draftees was 234 per 1,000. For non-draftees, on the other hand, it was 137 per 1,000. The fatality rate for draftees was 31 per 1,000; for volunteers, 17 per 1,000. Or, to look at it another way, an Army draftee in 1969 had a 23.4 percent chance of becoming a casualty and a 3.1 percent chance of getting killed. A volunteer in 1969 had a 13.7 chance of becoming a casualty and a 1.7 chance of getting killed. Few Americans understood how serious the risks were and especially how high they were for draftees.

The Army assumed a remarkable shape in Vietnam. In most organizations it is the permanent, long-standing members who usually take on the most critical tasks; the more transient and less skilled members are relegated to support roles. But not so in the Army during the Vietnam War. There the "regulars" did less of the fighting than the amateurs who had been pressed into the enterprise against their will.

Such, however, were the choices the government had made. Unable to attract enough volunteers to fight, it had to rely heavily

---

* Capitalized, "Army" refers to one branch of the armed forces. In lower case, it refers to the military as a whole.

CASUALTY RISKS (Army)

	1969		1965–(March) 1970	
	Draftee	Volunteer	Draftee	Volunteer
Chance of being killed..........	3.1%	1.7%	2.44	1.58
Chance of being wounded*......	20.3	12.0	10.54	6.84
Total........................	23.4	13.7	12.98	8.42

* Seriously enough to require treatment at a medical facility.

Source: Study by the Army General Staff, reported in the *National Journal,* August 15, 1970.

on conscription. Unable to win the allegiance of the better educated, and anxious not to stir up even more opposition on the nation's campuses, it placed a disproportionate burden on the politically unorganized working class. Unable to generate strong support for the aims of the war even there, it had to appeal to recruits on the basis of personal interests and offer them a greater chance of avoiding combat than draftees had. Each of these was a reasonable decision given the initial framework. Only the results were disastrous. Having fielded an army of the reluctant and unconvinced, the nation had no right to be surprised by the rebellion, racial unrest, and drug addiction that would bring the army to the edge of disorder in Vietnam.

There were exceptions to this pattern. Not all the services would experience the same problems to the same degree. The Marines filled their ranks almost entirely with volunteers and suffered a third of the fatalities in Southeast Asia, though they represent only a twelfth of the armed forces. And there were men, as there are in every war, who found combat attractive. Much of the routine and protocol of the military vanished under combat conditions. There was more freedom in the war zone for some, more freedom from responsibility for others. There was also more fellowship. And in the intensity of combat, one might come closer to heroism than one could ever come back home. But this was only part of the picture.

★ *Surviving*

To show that Vietnam was hell would be nothing special. All wars are hell, and men always suffer in them. But there are times when hell can be crossed and the burden of pain and sacrifice absorbed. That, however, requires a sense of purpose. "What makes people rebel against suffering is not really suffering itself," Nietzsche wrote, "but the senselessness of suffering. . . . Man, the most courageous animal, and the most inured to trouble, does not deny suffering *per se;* he wants it, he seeks it out, provided that it can be given a meaning." [10] What the war in Vietnam lacked for the American soldier was that meaning. If the soldiers who fought in Southeast Asia had fought defending their homeland from a threat they perceived as real, as many and more might have died or been wounded, but that hell could have been crossed, that sacrifice could have been sustained and accepted without remorse and without a loss of respect for human life. Those are the conditions under which Americans have fought in the past. But they were not the conditions in Vietnam.

The war that was fought in a moral vacuum was also fought in a technological blizzard. The American forces had air, naval, and electronic capabilities that dwarfed the small arms of the Viet Cong and North Vietnamese. This technical sophistication of the American army had a variety of consequences. The conflict was not merely between those having different political intentions. It was a war between societies standing at vastly different levels of economic development. And it was a war between peoples different in race and culture. These too would be important elements in the war experience.

One consequence of the technical organization of the American army lay in the distribution of personnel. Like other industries, the military has become more automated, and personnel on the operational level have been displaced to more specialized support functions. Since World War II, the proportion of soldiers in ground combat roles has declined substantially: 39.3 percent in 1945, 34.4 percent in 1953, 28.8 percent in 1963, and apparently 14 percent in 1967. (An equal proportion in 1967 were in close combat-support units and also continually exposed to enemy fire.[11]) As we shall see, the changing technical nature of the military has not only led to a decline in the number of combat troops. It has also altered the military function of the infantry and the subjective experience of the average ground combat soldier.

The technical capability of the United States presented Americans with a bewildering set of anomalies. Having assembled a massive array of weapons and equipment, the American forces were unable to apply them decisively. All the conventional wisdom about military might, strategic bargaining, threats, and deterrents said that the Americans should have won. But victory was eluding them. Technological might and heavily concentrated firepower were often devastatingly effective in the narrow sense, but ultimately they were

insufficient and even counterproductive. Villages bombed by accident created, at once, new recruits for the VC and new refugees to
be supported by the Saigon regime. Supplying superior weapons to
the South Vietnamese Army (ARVN) often meant that future Viet
Cong would be better armed. Defoliating the countryside along
roads could improve the view of enemy snipers. In a hostile climate
the advantages of technology translated poorly into victory. The
sociologist Morris Janowitz has suggested that modern military
history can be seen as a struggle between "heroic leaders"
embodying courage and glory and "military managers" intent on
pursuing war by scientific and rational means.[12] Vietnam marked
the absolute triumph of the managerial perspective in the military
and its utter checkmate in war.

For the individual soldier, the technical capability of the U.S.
eased somewhat the physical exigencies of the war zone, but it
created further anomalies as well. The transmission of radio and
television broadcasts directly from home, for example, at times lent
an air of unreality to the whole experience and accentuated the
sense of relative deprivation.

No matter how well trained, soldiers could not come adequately
prepared for the paradoxes of the American presence in Vietnam.
Perhaps the best trained were the worst prepared.

*"I landed down there in the Danang airport and there were these
Braniff planes and these stewardesses walking around, and there
was a Shell truck out there. In Okinawa, we [had] put on utilities,
and I made sure I had my knife, and I had a green T-shirt in case we
landed at night. I didn't want a white T-shirt to show me off. And I
thought they were going to bring weapons on the airplane before we
got off. I didn't want to get off without a fucking rifle. But I got there
and it's like Atlanta airport . . . a real gentleman's war. . . . And
somebody said—this is as we were pressed together in the back of
the truck—'A bunch of sachel charges were dumped on the end of
the field last night and blew up two Phantoms. And they got one of
the guys that did it. He drives a Shell truck for the base.' And I said,
'Did they shoot him?' and he said, 'Naw, they fired him.' And I said,
'Jesus, this is the war?'*

*"And then we got in a GV which was going to fly us down to Chu
Lai, but first it had to go up to Phu Bai, and then it had to go up to
Dong Ha. And when it was between Phu Bai and Dong Ha coming
in and landing, the guy that was sitting . . . in the row opposite me,
about ten people up, fell over dead because a sniper round got him.*

And that sort of freaked me out a little bit. And when we came in, everybody filed off, stepping over him, and then they put him in a body bag, and the body bag came off after everyone came off."

For many observers, the critical strategic aspect of the war was simply that it had no front. It was a war, as Frances Fitzgerald writes, "fought at points rather than along lines." [13] Equally important, if not more so, was a fundamental disparity in intelligence between the two sides. The North Vietnamese and Viet Cong almost invariably knew more about the location and movements of American units than we did about theirs. This gave them the initiative in deciding when and under what conditions most engagements would take place. A May 1967 memorandum by Alain C. Enthoven, Assistant Secretary of Defense for Systems Analysis, indicates that about 80 percent of the engagements were initiated by NVA or VC troops:

TYPES OF ENGAGEMENTS IN COMBAT NARRATIVES[14]

Category Description	*percent of total*
1. Hot landing zone. Enemy attacks U.S. troops as they deploy on to battlefield...................................	12.5
2. Organized enemy attack against U.S. static defense perimeter..	30.4
3. VC/NVA ambush or encircle a moving U.S. unit, using what is obviously a preconceived battle plan....................	23.2
4. A moving U.S. unit engaged the enemy in a dug-in or fortified position:	
(a) The main engagement comes as a surprise to the American tactical commander because the enemy is well concealed and has been alerted..................................	12.5
(b) The U.S. tactical commander has reasonably accurate knowledge of enemy positions and strength before committing his forces...	5.4
5. U.S. unit ambushes a moving enemy unit.................	8.9
6. Chance engagement, both sides surprised.................	7.1

The American strategy sought to take account of this pattern and make the North Vietnamese and Viet Cong pay whenever they attacked. Writes John Helmer: "If we never knew where or when the enemy would strike, he had to be lured into attacking us—but when we were ready for him. To do this the principal tactic was the search and destroy operation. Since our side never knew the enemy's movements well enough to mount effective ambushes, it became standard practice to entice the enemy to ambush us instead, thereby giving his position away. Once he had been identified, the field commander was then in a position to call in the artillery, helicopter gunships and close air support planes (napalm, bombs, strafing) to destroy him. . . . The infantryman does not do too much damage by comparison—but then in Vietnam that is not his job. In the search and destroy tactic he is, strictly speaking, the bait to catch the enemy. According to plan, he is intended to be a target, a sitting duck for the other side to attack at their ultimate cost. But the cost of the action from the American perspective is inevitable casualties among GIs. In no other war which the army has fought has the infantry role come down to this point of expendability." [15]

The same pattern is described by former intelligence specialist John Paul Kent: "The usual mission of an infantry company is to act as a forward and mobile sensor unit. Primarily they are to seek out concentrations of enemy soldiers, but once contact is established they are to disengage and allow superior fire power to actually defeat the enemy. A sense of futility is engendered by the hard facts of experience—that left to their own devices, an American ground unit would come off second best against an NVA unit." [16]

The sense of futility was heightened by other factors as well. Much of the fighting was at night, and even at other times American soldiers rarely saw whom they were fighting. Death seemed to strike out of nowhere. More than half the casualties in some regions were caused by booby traps and mines. And the American forces never seemed to be making any discernible progress. It was an endless process of going over the same ground.

"You just sit on this little hill and in about six or seven weeks you leave it and you go take this other little hill and then you come off that and you come back here and then you take this hill and then you come off that and in another four or five weeks you're back on this hill. It just didn't make any sense. Completely useless. Unbelievable."

"Monday morning we'd hit Barrier Island, we'd clean up the whole island and kill any gooks and take everybody off the island. Then on Friday we'd just leave. Then maybe two weeks later we'd have to come back and do the same thing again. . . . None of the operations we made made any sense. It's like taking land for a week and letting it go. And like we'd lose maybe—just in my unit we lost maybe six or seven guys each time we went on the island."

"What happened was the company the day before got wiped. They were just patrolling and they got hit up there [on a hill] and they left some bodies up there. And I don't know if it's true, but they say the Marines never leave their men up there. So the Captain got reprimanded and everything, and the next day we sent up the rest of that company and our company to get the three bodies. And we ended up leaving thirteen anyways up there. So we had to go up the next day to get them, you know. . . . This corpsman, he was my best friend, you know, like we used to have a few weeds together, but he was really a close friend. And I don't even know his name now. And I think of him cause like, when we were going up the hill there, before we approached the hill we had nothing better to do, so we were bullshitting, and I bet him five bucks that he'd get killed, and he bet me five bucks that I'd get killed. Well, it ended up he got killed, you know, and I walked back, I carried him back to the helicopter, talking to him, telling him, you know, 'You don't . . . fuck the five dollars.' "

There is an eeriness to the stories Vietnam veterans tell, a sense not just of frustration but of complete absurdity. Nothing about the war made any sense to them. It might be said that individual soldiers never see the full picture of a war and can never make sense of their particular actions. But in a way, these men saw exactly what was happening. The American forces were covering the same ground, losing lives to save the dead.

What made it all even more surreal was the juxtaposition of the agony of death with the euphoria of drugs, the desperation of uprooted villagers next to the cosmopolitan wealth of Saigon profiteers, and the privations of the average American "grunt" next to the unruffled privileges of officers.

"And it's just . . . one morning, you're flying medevac, and you'll see these guys who haven't had a hot meal for four days. And you land at noon, 'cause you're going to fly the general around, he's going inspecting, and the general brings you in to eat in an air-conditioned room with a tablecloth and sterling silver and two crystal wine glasses, and you eat pheasant with a really good cherry sauce."

The fantasy-like quality of the war was also maintained by the nature of the opposition. The Viet Cong and the NVA were nothing like what they had expected. Except for occasional contact with Red Chinese advisors who were over six feet in height,[17] most enemy soldiers were under five feet five inches tall. They were often quite young as well; in the late stages of the war, as the manpower available in villages was depleted, the VC were forced to accept recruits as young as fourteen years old. Booby traps were set by children who were even younger, and even four-year-olds might be given live grenades by adults to carry into the ranks of Americans.

"We had a case where a kid who couldn't have been any more than four years of age blew himself and four Marines up with a frag, while his mother watched. This apparently happened quite often in other areas. What can you do? Shoot the kid?"

Sometimes they did.

Soldiers had anticipated fighting honorably "out in the open, like men, with men." Instead, they found themselves at war with a people who resembled, and often were, children. What was worse, the foe was sometimes female. The courage and strength that women demonstrated in combat clashed sharply with American stereotypes of femininity.

"I was carrying this woman to the dustoff. She was carrying three M-16 rounds right down her middle. She was still alive, even though they had probably shattered her spine. She looked up at me and spat beetlenut juice all over me. Tough, really tough."

"I had met this girl in the village where we were staying, and she helped me with my Vietnamese. We used to spend a lot of time together, but only during the day. I grew quite attached to her, she was really pretty and gentle. We never discussed the war. Then one night my unit got ambushed by VC, and the next morning we found her body among the other Viet Cong. We were making love in the day, and she was trying like hell to kill me at night. I may have even killed her myself when we returned fire, I don't know. Anyway, she was dead."

The effect of fighting an invisible and unconventional foe was strengthened by the fact that nominal allies and the general population could not be trusted. If the Viet Cong were certain about whom it was they were fighting, the Americans were not. Many of the civilians they met were openly antagonistic. Unable to distinguish the enemy army from civilians, they had to be suspicious of all Vietnamese.

*"When you're over there, you don't know who the hell's who.
That's the problem. I mean, I could be talking to you like tonight,
say you were Vietnamese. Tomorrow morning I might walk outside,
and you might shoot me in the goddamn head. 'Cause you don't
know. They're farmers, and we've seen 'em, but we've seen 'em with
their tools out there hoeing down their rice paddies, and then you're
walking back, and all of a sudden they drop their hoe and pull out
their rifle. You know, so who the hell you gonna trust? So if you're
walking down, and you don't care if he is sixteen or two years old,
you think he's gonna kill you, you're gonna kill him anyways. I
mean, let's face it, life is, you know, important to most people."*

To suggest that American soldiers were suspicious and distrustful
of the Vietnamese merely because they were prejudiced against
Orientals would be unfair. The men were placed in a situation
where to survive they had to become suspicious because the
Vietnamese could not, in fact, be trusted. "The enemy remained
invisible," Frances Fitzgerald writes, "not only in the jungle but
among the people of the villages—an almost metaphysical enemy
who inflicted upon them heat, boredom, terror, and death and gave
them nothing to show for it—no territory taken, no visible sign of
progress except the bodies of small yellow men." [18]
Inevitably there were continual outbursts of hostility against
them.

*"They were like animals, really, because like, well, during the day
they're your friends, because they want you for everything you can
get. And then at night, you know, you don't know who's a VC. You
don't, because they all dress alike. It's a weird feeling. You don't like
them 'cause they're screwing you. After a while you literally spit on
them, kick them, like we used to be on convoy, we'd take apples, see
who could hit them, knock them over. You know, I guess everybody
does that. I did. Stand on the trucks, lean over the side, piss on them.
Because you knew in a minute they'd screw you."*

*"That's one thing that shocked me, when I first went over there,
because I saw several incidents of just general brutality toward
them. . . . And then after I'd been there about six or seven months,
I developed the same kind of feeling, I couldn't care less about them.
I really didn't. I couldn't trust them.
"A lot of kids are really cute and everything, but then they're
always asking for food, and it gets on your nerves. . . . You get
increasingly hardened to it. For example, there was a guy named*

*Toffy in Delta company. Every time we'd go by this one area there'd
be this kid out there who'd ask him if he had any food left, when he
was going back to the rear. And if he did, he'd give him whatever
C-rations he had left. Well, one day he didn't have any food left.
And the kid got behind him and hit him in the head [with a rock]. So
Toffy, at that point, well, it was about one hundred twenty degrees
that day, and at that point Toffy turned around and with a 16 blew
a hole in the kid's head, and killed him. I could understand it. I
realized that there is a definite breaking point. It's a combination of
the heat, the fact that you've been walking three or four miles, with
fifty or sixty pounds, thinking about booby traps and everything
else, and going back to the rear, where at least you're going to get a
shower and a Coke and something else. And then some little kid hits
you in the head with a rock, somebody you've been kind to, you
know, before. I can see him break like that. And by the way, he was
cleared of charges."*

The hostility that Americans acquired for Vietnamese civilians
was in part a consequence of the American presence itself. Children
nagged them for food because they had nothing to eat, and they had
nothing to eat because their families had been swept off their land
and left without any means of gaining a livelihood. The hostility and
fear evinced by the Vietnamese served, in turn, to rationalize the
abuse directed against them in the normal course of operations.

*"Most of the hooches [huts] would have haystacks behind them.
First you stick your bayonet in there to see if there's any people
hiding in there. And if there's people hiding in there on you, they
can't be friendly, right? So if you stick your bayonet in there and
you kill them, what can you say, right? They shouldn't have been
hiding on you in the first place. (What if they were just afraid of
Americans?) That's too bad. Like we're supposed to be helping them.
Why should they be scared of us?"*

General distrust and violent treatment of the Vietnamese were
also encouraged by the incompetence and divided loyalties of the
South Vietnamese Army. Almost without exception, the veterans
that we interviewed expressed more hatred for the ARVN soldiers
than they did for the Viet Cong or the NVA. Often, these feelings
resulted from direct encounters with ARVN troops.

*"We got into a steady firefight with those bastards. (The VC?) No,
man, the ARVNs. They opened fire on us, maybe a mistake, we*

didn't wait to see. Just let 'em have it, 'cause one dead gook was the same as another when they're shooting at you. We even tried to get a body count. But somebody higher up said no."

The inability to make any human contact with the Vietnamese encouraged American soldiers to see them more as a single people than the Vietnamese saw themselves. For the average GI, the most striking fact about them was their poverty. Like other Westerners before him, he tended to judge their low standard of living as evidence of laziness and a lack of drive. The Vietnamese were almost as bad as welfare recipients.

"They got nothing. They got no form of communication what-soever. No automobiles and stuff like that. They were people, I guess, but they lived like animals. I don't think I seen one of them taking a bath. Like every one of them I was near stunk. I mean, stunk like a pig or something. They're not civilized. They got no baths, no wash houses, no nothing. They don't seem to want to better themselves in any way. They don't want to help themselves."

Paradoxically, while the feeling of superiority led earlier Western visitors to sense a natural right of dominion, it led most of the GIs to question why they were there. After all, if the Vietnamese were not going to help themselves, why should Americans risk their necks for them?

There were many exceptions to the pattern of contempt and hostility, particularly among soldiers from middle-class backgrounds who were not directly engaged in combat and who had an opportunity to see the Vietnamese under less trying circumstances. But they were very consciously in the minority.

"The whole time I was there I was the only person they had ever met who spoke Vietnamese. Out of all the Marines, Army, Air Force, everyone. So I was a very popular figure there. I was approached by Vietnamese people for just about everything, when they felt they had to deal with Americans. I liked them a lot, they were a very interesting people, they had an entirely different outlook. I was trying to understand them, to learn their ways. I earned the name 'gook lover' in my unit because I liked the Vietnamese people."

Some working-class combat veterans also felt great sympathy for the Vietnamese, especially for their habits of close friendship and affection.

"The ones I saw, you know, they're just like people here. They were a little more ignorant. They didn't even know what the hell was going on. Like we were the first infantry division up there, and they had never seen Americans before. They're scared of you, as much as you are of them. I felt sorry for them at times, but other times I felt they deserved it. . . . I thought they were cute, myself. The first thing is, some of them are so friendly though, that you think the guy is queer, because they hug you and kiss you, you know, I mean on the cheeks, and stuff like this, it's sort of a weird feeling at first. But after a while you just learn that it's their custom. A lot of guys, they have their set ways, they won't bend at all. They won't go near them. 'These guys are faggots, and only a fag would do that,' they say."

In spite of a fairly widespread belief that the Vietnamese were lazy, deceitful, and untrustworthy, many veterans express considerable respect for the courage and persistence of their foe.

"They have a lot of balls, let me tell you. If I was in a tree line, and Phantoms were dropping napalm on me, I wouldn't stick around. I'd either run out and surrender or run the other way. Those little nuts stand right up and shoot at the Phantoms flying by."

"I just can't imagine how they pulled it off. We landed on a hill once, in the hill-hopping exercises, and ran a routine patrol down the side. This hill, just before we got there, had been bombed because it was a suspected position—B-52s, nothing but huge craters. Ran a routine patrol down the side and found a couple tunnel rats and a whole hospital complex and tons of rice. [They] hadn't even been fazed. It's said you could go from the base of the Ho Chi Minh trail up by Khe Sanh and down to Saigon and never see daylight. It's awesome. I just can't imagine how it's done. The ARVN—uh, we're the ARVN's mentors and we're teaching them to fight our kind of war—we just figured we were better off without them. Anything was to get done, well, let's not bring in home town participation. Let's go out and do it right. . . . I really don't see how anybody couldn't have had more respect for the NVA than the ARVN. I mean, the ARVN were followers, and the NVA were doers."

The contempt the American GI developed for the ARVN and the respect he had for the Viet Cong and the North Vietnamese introduced a further note of confusion. Soldiers didn't take the enemy's side, but they didn't see much reason for taking the side of their nominal ally either. Few of the GIs, in fact, saw any reason why they should be in Vietnam at all. In a study of combat soldiers in the "bush," sociologist Charles Moskos asked thirty-seven men why they thought they were there. Nearly all of them answered in terms of personal misfortune—that they had been drafted, or just had bad luck in getting assigned there. Moskos then asked why the United States was in Vietnam. About half the men at this point said "to stop communism"; the rest shrugged their shoulders. Asked to describe what it was about communism that was so important to stop, the first group referred most frequently to its authoritarian aspects. "Communism is something like the army," one of the soldiers observed.[19]

But indifference, doubt, even cynicism about the purposes of the war did not ordinarily turn the men into advocates of peace and de-escalation. While they were in Vietnam fighting, any proposal to curb the war effort—particularly the bombing—only seemed to endanger their lives further. Especially in the earlier years of the war, they reacted angrily and indignantly to antiwar demonstrations at home, in much the same way as Willie reacts to Joe in one of Bill Mauldin's World War II cartoons: "What do y'mean this ain't the most important hole in the world? I'm in it!" There was no chance to deliberate peaceful solutions in the heat of battle; besides, that wasn't their job.

"While the shit was happening, you had to be violent, you had to fight and kill and all that. I didn't have any time to think about love and peace. . . . You can't afford to think like that. You die if you think like that."

From their perspective, especially before the withdrawals began in 1969, the course that seemed to make the most sense was pursuit of victory by the most effective means available. They were, however, hawks more by condition than by belief.

"I said we ought to bomb the Ho Chi Minh trail and so forth 'cause all the stuff coming down the trail was getting shot at us. But as far as really thinking that these guys had no business to do that, well, I didn't think that. I respected them for a lot of things."

"When you was younger, and you'd get involved in a fight, you was taught to win, not lose. How were your feelings then? You win, you win. Right? You was a winner. That's the way I felt there."

"I hadn't been persuaded that the war was right. I was never persuaded that the war was right. But when I say I was a hawk, I was saying, OK, here we are, we're faced with it, and whether it's right or wrong is of no consequence to the men who's fighting it. And so how best to get on with it. Well, you attack, you don't sit there and take it. And I still think that is right."

The paradox, then, is that many of the same men who advocated stepping up the bombing readily concede that it never really mattered to them who won the war. Their preferences are not inconsistent. "It's a war. If you're gonna fight it, fight to win." But basically, "I don't really give a damn."

The one survey that we have of Vietnam veterans' attitudes toward the war—taken in 1971 among 244 soldiers, all below the rank of E-6, as they shipped out of San Francisco—indicates that 47 percent thought the war was a mistake, while 40 percent thought it wasn't a mistake but was fought incorrectly.[20] Attempts at classifying attitudes, however, seem, by and large, pointless and irrelevant. The same men were often both "hawks" and "doves," and yet there was nothing contradictory about their position. It was a consistent ambivalence. In the early years of the war, when more of the soldiers were professionals and volunteers, and the Green Berets enjoyed considerable popularity at home, the atmosphere seems to have been different. But by 1969, whatever enthusiasm had existed at the beginning was gone, and acid rock, drugs and peace emblems were as easy to find in I Corps as they were in California (probably easier in the case of drugs). The men fought, but they fought only to live.

"I went over with the idea of helping somebody. After two months I just cared about surviving. If guys didn't get that attitude, something was wrong. . . . Some of the South Vietnamese are just making a mint off the war."

"All anybody ever did was really look forward to their twelve [months] and twenty [days] when they got to go home. Count off your days, figure out when your R and R was gonna be, there was no real motivated attitude toward it. . . . It was just my own survival; it was the survival of the people around me also. I was in a position of responsibility and I figured it was best to . . . well, I had other people to look out for. I realized that if the Communists take over the country that they're not gonna kill everybody—sort of realized that when I got over there. They're not going to come down

*and wipe out every Vietnamese person; they were all Vietnamese. I
began to understand the nationalistic side of it."*

*"I didn't have to believe in it. Like the typical GI, I fought for my
ass. I fought to get out of there. And I did everything I knew how,
everything they taught me to get out of there, and I came out of
there, you know, that was the main issue. Survival. And that's what
I did."*

As gravity pulls a river to the sea, so the will to survive pulled the
men through the war. The universal objective was not victory but
DEROS (Date Expected to Return from Overseas); nothing was at
stake so much as time. Every GI had exactly 365 days of duty in
Vietnam (except for Marines, who had an extra twenty). The
preoccupation with time was intense. Time "in country" was almost
as important a basis of status as military rank. Men who had spent
more time there stood above the "cherries" who had just arrived.
Time governed the psychology of the individual soldier. According
to psychiatrists and other observers, men generally seemed to pass
through three phases: at first, great anxiety and uncertainty, then
increasing confidence as they grew more accustomed to the
situation, and finally a period of rising tension and insecurity as they
"got short" (approached the end of the year) and feared that
something might go wrong at the last minute.[21]

Combat training socialized young men into military life and
taught them to function as a team; the rotation system privatized
the war experience and encouraged them to function as separate
individuals. Men felt no continuity, writes one military psychiatrist,
with those who preceded or followed them. The staggered arrivals
and departures eroded the traditional solidarity of the small unit. To
a lesser extent, so did regular mail and occasional telephone calls
and vacations, which made it possible to maintain contacts with
family and friends at home.[22] Few veterans report lasting friend-
ships with men they knew during the war.

*"Most of the people rotated in and out or got killed, or got
wounded, got reassigned, you know, and then, like you're out in the
field, you know, you'd ask the cat what are you gonna do when you
go back home, and you talk about that all the time, but, uh, the
thought never came to you, man, to take down an address and put it
in your address book, because you felt like you had time enough to
do that. But before it happened they got bopped off or got rotated,*

and by the time you thought to do that you'd be waving goodbye to the cat. . . ."

Although the rotation system vitiated the solidarity of the small unit in Vietnam, it did succeed in keeping down psychiatric casualties, which were much lower than in World War II or Korea. In wars where soldiers fought "for the duration," there were no legitimate exits from combat except death, injury, or mental breakdown. The rotation system, together with periods of "rest and relaxation" (R&R), provided a schedule of hope. But another reason why psychiatric evacuations may have been lower was the general availability of drugs, including one very powerful tranquilizer—heroin.

As the bonds of association were somewhat weakened by the rotation system, so the bonds of traditional values were weakened by the social psychology of the war zone. Vietnam was not unusual in this regard. Near death men feel they have an absolute right to pleasure, and so the war zone paradoxically breeds hedonism as much as it breeds destruction. The absence of restraint on aggressive behavior encourages unrestraint in every sphere. Authorization to violate some sacred values easily expands into a general license to violate others. Men who would never steal a nickel at home buy and sell on the black market. Men from small towns who would never drink at home suddenly begin taking drugs. Traditional values come apart in the war zone, the forbidden loses its terror because of the proximity of greater terrors, the leash of society unravels, and inevitably some men become unstuck. The stress was accentuated by the distinctive aspects of the Vietnam War. Facing death is hard enough; facing it under conditions of ambiguity and doubt is still more difficult. Men deal with such situations in a variety of ways. One way is to think about it as little as possible, to "get on with it" and "get it over." In Vietnam, if you couldn't do that on your own, there were always plenty of drugs around to help. Where the stress became intolerable, they provided a way of drawing a curtain over reality. And the men thought they had every right to whatever relief drugs might bring.

"Maybe you've talked to infantry guys and Marine guys who brag about the morale . . . but most of the infantry guys I knew just hated it. . . . And our place [an office near Long Binh] was no different. People would do things—people would drink, get stoned every night, just to escape, just to forget what they were doing."

"Even if we were getting hit . . . you'd light up a 'J' [marijuana]. You know, it was easier to get them than cigarettes. It was easier than getting beer. You know, it was something to do. It was something to pacify yourself. It was a free ticket home. Just siddown, have a J, think about it for a while, everything was fine, sit around, get to know the guys. You could remove yourself from the war zone . . . it was fantastic."

The use of drugs in Vietnam was the embodiment of the wish to be elsewhere, a kind of unilateral withdrawal, a soldier's verdict on the war. For the nation, with the rise of heroin use in 1970 and 1971, it became the symbol of everything that went wrong in Vietnam.

There were other ways of adjusting too—higher forms of avoiding contact with reality, practiced not so much by frontline soldiers as by those more removed from combat. The war could be converted into a series of technical problems, a series of contests, a game. For those that did it well, it could be a source of satisfaction, even if they disapproved of the war.

"A friend of mine killed a thousand men in an afternoon. He was a military analyst, and he figured something out. And not only figured it out but persuaded the General to take action. He said, 'They've got to be here because of this and this,' and they said, 'We'll send a helicopter to check it out.' And he said, 'If you send a helicopter they will see the helicopter and just scatter, and by the time your troops get there there'll be nobody there. What we should do is this and this. . . .' It is an extraordinary situation when an enlisted man has something like that, but an analyst has a great deal of it; he can build a reputation in an afternoon. So he killed 1,000 in an afternoon. (How did he feel?) He was proud. (Did he believe in the war?) No. But he did a good job. Which wasn't very far from what my own feeling was. (Were you proud of your own role?) No, but I found it very interesting."

(How did you feel about the artillery?) "I was proud of its capability. We'd spend a lot more time in peacetime to refine it as an art. And I was very interested. We developed a little computer called FADAC. With FADAC you can scientifically compute your Kentucky windage. It can really work well, quite well. And it was fast. And I was very interested in this. But I was also quite proud of the procedures that we could build up which allowed our part of the artillery to respond accurately and work together as a team. Seeing

an FDC in operation, a good one, is quite impressive, to stand there watching the shit go off. A good battery, to me, is quite a sight. What happens at the other end when the round lands is quite impressive and quite enjoyable, really. It was one of the things that helped me keep my sanity. I brought home a field manual; I still have it. I was very good at it."

The preoccupation with technique, the sense of achievement even where the ultimate goals might be disapproved, the involvement in the mechanics of war perhaps as a relief from its human consequences—these too were common responses, highly adaptive ones from the military point of view. Military speech, with its euphemisms for everyday language, facilitates this kind of depersonalized adjustment. War can become more violent, but less angry. The mechanization of the language and perception of war is the counterpart in the realm of thought to the mechanization of the army itself.

Withdrawal (through drugs) was one way to deal with a deeply troubling situation, immersion in technique was another, and resistance a third. The most frequently mentioned form resistance took in Vietnam was "fragging," the killing of officers and senior NCOs by enlisted men. Many fraggings were probably the result of nothing more than personal vendettas; others were seen by the men as acts of self-defense. There is a direct connection between such murders and the nature of the American presence. For if soldiers fight only to survive, then anyone who threatens that survival becomes a reasonable target, even an American. To infantrymen, a green and overly zealous lieutenant just out of West Point could be as much of a threat as the enemy. If he exposed his men to unwarranted dangers in the afternoon, a grenade might find its way into his tent at night. Some officers say they responded to this occupational hazard by becoming more prudent.

"You knew it was a possibility, so you weren't gonna go up and just ride roughshod over people. You knew if you did that you might get fragged."

Accurate estimates of the number of fragging incidents are impossible. Many combat veterans say they personally knew of a fragging. A conspiracy of silence usually ensured that only they would know of it.

For the military, internal resistance became a severe problem during the Vietnam War, but not so much on the front lines. The

obstacles were considerable, the costs for enlisted men too high.
Whatever the national policy on the war, the rotation system
offered each soldier a "date certain" for his withdrawal, and by
weakening the solidarity of the unit it made collective forms of
resistance very difficult. Even for those who detested the war,
refusing orders and deserting were simply not very feasible options
halfway across the globe from home. So they fought, for themselves
and for each other.

*"Strange war. Going for something they didn't believe in or, for
that matter, didn't care about, just to make it three hundred
sixty-five days and be done with it. They'd go though; even freaked
out, they'd go. They'd do whatever he [Sergeant Mayfield] told them.
Three mornings in a row after lying in the mud all night, they got up
and pushed the gooks back so the choppers could get the wounded
out. They charged, every time, just got up and went, right over the
RPGs and the AKs. No flags, no noise, no abuse. They just got up
and blew themselves to shit because it had to be done. The same
with ambushes. They'd do it, and if led right, they'd do it well. But
they always let him know somehow that they would rather be left
alone; it would be OK if they caught the gooks, but if they didn't,
that would be fine too. At first it had been disconcerting—troopers
who didn't care but who'd fight anyway, sloppy soldiers smoking
grass whenever they could, but would do whatever was asked.
Skeptical kids who made no friends outside their own company and
sometimes only in their own squads, who'd go out and tear
themselves apart to help another unit and then leave it when it was
over without asking a name or taking a thanks, if any were offered.
"It had taken Mayfield a while to get used to it, but after a month
in Nam he began to realize and then to understand that his troops
weren't acting strangely at all, that, if anything, they were
amazingly professional. They did what they were supposed to do,
and it was enough. They had no illusions why they were here. There
was no need for propaganda, for flag waving. Even if there were,
these kids wouldn't have bought it. Killing toughens you, and these
kids were there to kill, and they knew it. They took their cues from
the top, and all that mattered from USARV to the Battalion
Commanders was body counts."* [23]

The war was an extremely complicated event in the lives of the
soldiers who fought it. Some of them say, "It was a waste," and
leave it at that; many others think they learned a great deal and

matured. Even in men who hated the war, who lost close friends, there is a strange ambivalence.

"I don't know if this will explain it, but when I was in California for training I lived with [a friend]. He went overseas about a month before I did, and then I went over, and we happened to get in the same battalion together. And we even slept in the same tent, so we were even closer. And like three months later—the war didn't mean much to me, you know, no feelings—but he got killed. He got hit with a 127 recoilless rifle. The round is probably five feet long, and he was only five-two and it hit, and when it hit his belt buckle it point detonated. He blew up, and the biggest piece of him was a chunk of flesh on his wallet. And after that I figured that the war was a waste. . . .

"I figured I wasted four years of my life, and it's just gone. Like I could have really been better off now if I didn't go. But then again, I think that if I had it to do again, I'd probably do the same thing. I don't know why. It makes no sense at all. I know that even if I went to work for the four years or to school for the four years, I would be much better off. But then again, inside, I would feel that I had missed something."

These are retrospective thoughts. As the men "got short" in Vietnam, there weren't too many who wanted to do it over again. There is a verse from a short poem by a Vietnam veteran that probably captures how they felt far better than anything else:[24]

> *If you have a farm in Vietnam*
> *and a house in hell*
> *Sell the farm*
> *and go home*

★ Going Home

Heady anticipation beforehand, shock from the suddenness of the change, then a slowing down of time, a loss of fatefulness in events, a sense of anticlimax, depression, a feeling of isolation, and gradually attempts to put back the pieces and begin again—this is how many veterans (with plenty of variations) describe the road back from Vietnam.

"I spent an awful lot of time dreaming about what I would do—you know, you're sitting in the middle of the night, you wake

up, and you've got three hundred days left to go. And I spent a lot of time thinking about how it tastes and how it feels, and the sense of prosperity—not the prosperity of the city, but the sense of personal emotional prosperity which I thought I was going to get. . . . I left on the fourteenth of December and arrived here on the fourteenth of December across the dateline. And I flew more than halfway around the world without stopping. We island-hopped, went to Guam, then to Hawaii, and we were grounded in most places for an hour, and it was tropical in most cases. We landed at Travis, we hopped on a bus, drove down to Oakland, and in a period of about four hours they gave us green uniforms, we'd come back in khakis, which were not too good for cold weather. And after four hours in Oakland I was on a plane to Boston, which was more than one hundred eighty degrees around the world. And the temperature change I went through was more than one hundred degrees. . . . I could not take a walk, I could not go out in a Boston December, I couldn't do it. . . .

"I didn't do anything, I didn't have anything to do. I had nothing that I was doing yesterday that I had to continue today. . . . Then the next day to discover all these incredible changes. . . . I hadn't really understood that you can't go back, that everything goes on without you, and coming back to America is not a coming back at all, it is a starting again. I wasn't ready to start again, I had to get used to it. . . . I was pretty lost for a couple of months."

After other wars, soldiers had come back overland, trudging through towns that had been ravaged earlier, long columns of tired, dirty, stubborn men; or they came back in ships, weeks across the sea, then halfway across a continent by train to small towns where banners across Main Street and headlines in the local newspapers announced their return. Their wars had been hard on them, every bit as hard as Vietnam has been on its veterans. But when Vietnam veterans have come home, there has been a difference. They have flown home alone, not in units, and so the experience has been private in two senses: It is not shared with their brothers and it does not ordinarily command any public notice. Everyone has remarked that there have been no victory parades, but this suggests it is the absence of a triumphant return, of honor and celebration, that matters. But it goes even deeper: it is the absence of any awareness, of any attention, of any visible concern at all.

"Well, first you think there's going to be a big band coming back for you, you know. There's nothing there. People walk by you like you're not even there. . . . There was nothing to do, you know."

"They didn't give a shit. They didn't have to. Everybody had enough sugar, and there wasn't any rationing on tires. . . . It's just another TV show. And they don't have to watch it if they don't want to. And then, 'Yeah, it's too bad about those kids, but I gotta go to work and earn a buck.' "

The Vietnam veteran confronts a people who never really went to war, a society that has perhaps been immobilized in its opposition but certainly never mobilized in support of the war effort. The conflict has been waged without any privation at home, and the result has been an enormous disproportion of sacrifice. A few have been asked to die; virtually nothing has been asked of everyone else. So the veteran who has seen the deepest terror in death comes back to a people who have made no sacrifices at all, who have gone on with life as usual, who have no direct experience associated with the war, and who may even fear him, question his character, suspect him of harboring an addiction to heroin or a streak of violence. And these suspicions strike him as the final, unspeakable injustice. For it is not simply indifference that he faces; it is indifference coupled with a certain wariness. People are afraid, and they hold back.

"When you first come home it's really bad because everybody's quiet to you. It gives you a weird feeling like they're checking you out. See, everybody's scared. They figure you've been through a lot, but they treat you like a baby."

Occasionally the apprehensions come out into the open. In Washington, D.C., the manager of a night club tried to stop a group of wounded veterans from coming to see a revue. Their presence, he was quoted as saying, would "depress the paying customers." [25]

This is not to suggest that Americans have lost all feelings of generosity and good will toward veterans. Those feelings are there, but there is an ambivalence as well, and it is much more accentuated than after past wars because of the nature of the Vietnam conflict. In the imagery of public sentiment, there are two pictures of the Vietnam veteran. One picture is displayed on public occasions: the veteran as hero. The other pervades the stories on the six o'clock news and dominates informal conversation: the veteran as misfit. Neither picture has much credible appeal. The heroic version is too forced; there is a certain patronizing tone in the voice of some admirers.

"Well, you've done an admirable job," replied Representative Conte. *"You ought to be patted on the back."*

The tense black veteran exploded. *"We don't want to be patted on the back,"* he shouted as the room rang with approving applause. *"You pat little boys on the back."* [26]

The image of the veteran as misfit has even less appeal, but it too is hard to shake off. Although there are millions of Vietnam veterans, let one hijack an airliner and while he may have a dozen other salient characteristics, it is his status as veteran that appears in the headlines. There is a spill-over effect too from the unfortunately accurate reports of widespread drug addiction in Vietnam. More contagious than the use of drugs themselves is the stigma associated with them. The attitudes of employers have been particularly affected. "With the spread of drug abuse in schools and among members of the armed forces in Vietnam," the New York State Chamber of Commerce warned members in 1971 in a pamphlet on drug abuse as a business problem, "it would be unrealistic for business to assume it could recruit from these markets and not risk bringing abuse, narcotics addicts, and pushers into companies, despite all sophisticated screening available." [27] Such sensible, pragmatic advice, and yet it inadvertently says of veterans: "A bad lot, one must be careful with them."

In a report called *Wasted Men*, ex-servicemen at Southern Illinois University called attention to the danger of discussing veterans "in terms of *pathology*, what is or might be wrong with them . . . violence, drugs, mental illness, 'anti-social attitudes,' reluctance to use the GI Bill, unemployment, and unemployability." This popular attitude, they wrote, "is not justified by the facts, is viciously unfair to veterans and will be a national disaster in denying the positive potential and heightening the bitterness and sense of isolation of millions of valuable human beings." Their report does go on to discuss many of the problems veterans face, but the image they convey is not of a group of misfits, but of a lost generation, men wasted by their own country. "This is probably the most capable and highly educated generation of veterans in history, with powerful latent motivation to contribute to the rebuilding of America, and their own society thinks of them as dregs and dropouts, dehumanized killers and drug addicts or pitiful victims of a hated war to be avoided and shunned." [28]

But just as exaggeration suggests pathology, so the pretense that all is well suggests insensitivity. There is a need for understanding without overstatement, respect without illusions, help without condescension.

"For the individual to adjust most comfortably and easily on his return," writes the former military psychiatrist Peter Bourne, "it is not so important that he be treated as a hero, but that some recognition be given to the experiences and suffering he has endured. Without question, for most young veterans their combat experiences are the most significant events in their lives and are seared into their memories so that they are repeatedly and sometimes compulsively thought about and relived. By their very significance . . . they serve to make him feel set apart. . . . Many returning GIs, when they first arrive back in the United States, are so preoccupied with working through those experiences in their own minds and perceive the civilian society as so incapable of understanding their feelings that they just wall themselves off, refusing to discuss the war. . . . This in turn only aggravates their sense of alienation." [29]

A great many veterans do try to forget about what happened and "wall off" that part of their life. "I acted like I was dead two years and just come back," says one veteran from West Virginia. And another describes his experience going to college afterward: "I came here into an atmosphere and a society where nobody really gave a damn anyway, so you'd say you were a veteran and people would say, well, that's interesting, which was fine with me, because there was nothing that I really wanted to talk about. My whole attitude had been to go get it, do it, and get it over with, and I'd done that . . . and now I was in my next stage and as far as I was concerned, I'd just as soon forget what happened."

But many have trouble forgetting. There are things that stick in their minds, and they work through them a thousand times.

"I made a mistake once, which was a pure . . . it was negligent, which cost some Vietnamese lives. . . . It was a case where the district chief came around, you know, and he said, 'Look, the government has decided that this area is pacified. So we're going to tell the people that they can go back to their villages.' So I said, all right, and I forgot. And that evening when I was drawing my random crosses on the chart, lining my H and Is [harassment and interdiction], I just . . . I just forgot all about it. I put a couple of random crosses through that and about three o'clock in the morning about thirty-two rounds of four-inch mortars went in there and wiped out eight of them. I was, you know, sick when I discovered it,

but I was also very happy when the Vietnamese were so garbled in their reporting of it that the investigating team went to the wrong village and consequently I didn't go to jail. That was sheer luck. I could have gone to jail for it. . . . That's human error. I was handling . . . I was responsible for an incredible number of rounds in the time that I was there, that's my business. And to make no mistakes for a year is a pretty large order. And I was pretty short, I was . . . let's face it, I slacked off. That's what happened. But it wasn't a conscious act, it was just a goof. Most people made those."

Veterans who turn against the war afterward and begin to question their own role are especially prone to feelings of guilt. Some who are able to repress any doubts in Vietnam because of the imperatives of the situation confront them only later.

"I avoided thinking about it pretty well. It didn't start getting to me when I was in Vietnam too much. . . . But when I got back to the States, I could not sit alone. I had to be reading something, I had to be watching television, or talking to someone. Anything to avoid being alone and thinking about it. Because it was just too much to tolerate.

". . . I have nightmares about [some things], like seeing a guy's neck fall back when you cut through it, and giving a guy mouth-to-mouth one time who had the top of his head—I think he was peeping up over a wall—and he got hit right at the hairline, and it was cut off like a hard soft-boiled egg. His brains were just sitting there like jelly, like guava jelly. . . . And I gave him mouth-to-mouth. I can still see him. And I can still see one guy who was in the field, who had been shot on patrol, just as he'd been tied by a medic and given a shot of morphine, and just as he was leaving he [the medic] pulled a grenade out of the pouch and threw it in the guy's lap and told him to hold on to it so he could kill himself. Instances like that I wasn't prepared for. But the overall experience, I was expecting it, you know. And I knew things like that would happen. I'd read about them.

"When I'd lie in bed and I knew I was going to have nightmares, I'd say to myself, 'Well, don't forget, there's a thousand people who would probably be dead if you hadn't pulled them out of that bush,' and that gave me enough to go on.

". . . I could go into the villages and see little kids, babies especially, and realize that they were just people, just that there was no difference between him and me. And I started realizing the conflicts here. And that's when I started questioning things and

seeing a lot of hypocrisy. . . . And that's when I began getting really sick and pissed and tied up inside about the hypocrisy, the contemptuousness, with which government agencies and the military primarily treat human beings. I tried to make myself a part of it, you know, and I started really trying to buy into Establishment values. And I couldn't make myself do it, because it was just . . . it made me too uncomfortable. I just couldn't take it.

"I became much more sensitive, but much more callous in my behavior. I mean, inside I was a lot more aware of the ugliness that was going on outside. . . . It was sort of as if there was a secret little me inside that was the real me and just couldn't tell anybody else that he was alive."

Certainly many veterans are ill at ease about their experiences in the war, but it would be wrong to suggest that guilt is a prevalent emotion among them. It is, however, very prevalent among those who write about Vietnam veterans, and this leads to no end of confusion. Our own impression from interviews is that veterans—even those who oppose the war—generally do not feel ashamed of what they did, that they believe they were much more sinned against than sinning, and that they feel overwhelmingly that people who were not in Vietnam have no right to judge them, that such judgments are a luxury of those who stayed at home and have nothing to do with the situations they confronted. Nevertheless, many do feel they were used, sent to fight for no good reason, and then abandoned when it was all over, despised for things most of them never wanted to do in the first place and never did in the second. Not surprisingly, there is a great deal of disorientation, anger and resentment, rage and bewilderment, quiet desperation and violent discontent in these men. Those who have a predilection for names, even when the phenomenon is vague, call it "post-Vietnam syndrome." Its manifestations are varied and mostly subclinical: reticence, edginess, unprovoked outbursts, feelings of hopelessness, and purposelessness. But the consequences can be personal disasters: marriages broken up soon after return, intensified drug use, lost jobs, one-car accidents.

There are no studies to indicate how widespread such problems are, and in any case, studies of subclinical behavioral problems are notoriously unreliable. Those who have come back from Vietnam disoriented and unsettled, it is true, are a minority. But like those other minorities—the 56,000 who were killed and the 300,000 who were wounded—they deserve a measure of concern out of proportion to their numbers.

Concern, however, is no basis for exaggeration. There have been a number of magazine articles purporting to show that Vietnam veterans are especially prone to erratic and violent behavior. "America's Human Time Bombs" one piece actually called them, and in *Time* magazine they were simply "The Violent Veterans." [30] The principal source for this view is a sociologist named Charles Levy, who suggested that on return from Vietnam all veterans be put through special "boot camps in reverse" where, through the counsel of professional psychotherapists, they would learn to be nonviolent. Several things need to be said about this line of thought: (1) There is no significant evidence indicating that violence among veterans is especially widespread. A few widely publicized incidents do not constitute an epidemic. (2) There is no significant evidence that violent behavior is any more frequent among veterans than among other young men from working-class backgrounds. One would need a carefully controlled study to show this. (3) There is no significant evidence that professionals of any kind know how to train people to be nonviolent. (4) The entire argument rests on the dubious hypothesis of "brutalization," i.e., that large numbers of men undergo basic psychological changes in being trained to fight that continue to influence their behavior later on. In our view, this underestimates the potential of ordinary men with normal temperaments to kill in situations where killing is sanctioned and where they face the immediate threat of extinction. The army, it is said, never makes you fight. It just puts you down in the middle of a war and lets you make up your own mind. And in a sense, that is the really tragic aspect of war—not that men become brutalized by the experience, but that we all can kill without being brutalized. (5) Finally, the view that veterans may flare into sudden violence only encourages unjustified wariness and suspicions of the men; it illustrates again the dangers of that propensity for sympathetic exaggeration which only yields an image of the veteran as pathological misfit. [31]

Too often, in our eagerness to show how bad the war has been, we blame it for the sins of peace. But if there is disenchantment among veterans, it has as much to do with dissatisfaction at home as disillusionment with the war. If there is drug addiction among veterans, it has as much to do with America as Southeast Asia. And how much more sobering a thought that is. For, in a way, it would be comforting to think that all problems lay in the past, that all would be right except for Vietnam.

Probably far more important than the psychological residues of the war has been the fact that the largest numbers of Vietnam veterans came home at a time of rising unemployment. As late entrants to the labor force, with little work experience, they suffered the worst of the recession. At its height in early 1971, unemployment among Vietnam veterans reached 11 percent. The worst hit were younger veterans and those from minority groups. Among black veterans age twenty to twenty-four, for example, 22.4 percent were out of work as late as the first quarter of 1972 [32]—a level worthy of the Depression. Unemployment rates have since declined substantially as the economy has picked up steam, but the damage already done has been severe, and veterans are still nowhere near full employment. Moreover, the issue is not only a shortage of jobs, but a shortage of good jobs—jobs that offer decent working conditions, reasonable pay, and opportunities for self-direction and advancement. Much of the unemployment among Vietnam veterans stems not from an absence of any work opportunities—there are almost always "dirt jobs" around in areas of the economy not protected by minimum wage laws—but from the limited nature of available opportunities. As Willy put it, "I've been getting jobs, but there's a difference between jobs and careers."

If the military's promises of valuable work experience were true, veterans should not experience such high levels of unemployment. But a series of studies have convincingly documented the low rate of transferability of military training to civilian life. In 1964 a survey by the National Opinion Research Center found that two in every five Navy and Air Force veterans and two in every seven Army and Marine Corps veterans had expected their military experience would be of value. But only one in twelve (8.9 percent) actually made considerable use of his training. "Once in the real civilian occupational world," comments Charles Moskos in *The American Enlisted Man*, "the anticipated benefits of military training . . . proved to be largely illusory." [33]

This has been the finding of other studies as well. A report by economists at the University of Maryland in 1969 indicated that only 16 percent of Army veterans and 28 percent of Navy veterans found work related to their military training. "Not only was there a relatively low rate of utilization of the skills," the authors concluded, "but we found that the market did not work effectively in aiding those veterans who were interested in using their service experience. For veterans who did look and find jobs related to their military experience, we inquired about benefits received and whether, in fact, these were attributable to the military experience. We found that half of the Army veterans [who found related jobs] received no benefit at all as a result of their military experience.

They said that there were no monetary or job characteristic rewards. . . ." [34]

A study of problems of economically and socially disadvantaged veterans, conducted by the Bureau of the Budget in 1969, disclosed the same pattern. If any group stood in need of benefiting from military training, it would be the disadvantaged. But the study found that only 12 percent of employed veterans had used skills acquired in the military since they had been discharged.[35]

The low transferability of military training, rising unemployment, the stigma of drug addiction, the sense of isolation among veterans coming home alone, an ambivalent public reception—these were some of the things that have complicated the return of men from Vietnam. At the same time, as serious as these problems have been, there were certain favorable circumstances that should have facilitated their assimilation into civilian life. We must note these as well.

The men had not been gone five years, as had many of their fathers during World War II, and so the interruption of their careers was perhaps not as severe. The gradual return of soldiers from Vietnam, moreover, should have made it easier for the economy and the government to cope with veterans' problems. As the Administrator of Veterans Affairs told a Congressional committee in 1968, "Today's war is so different from what we have known in the past. Men go in for a specified time. They come out at a specified time. We are getting them in a very orderly fashion, about 70,000 a month. We are fully equipped. . . ." [36]

The Veterans Administration has had certain other advantages. There has been no need to improvise; a vast administrative and legal structure for dealing with veterans' problems was already in existence long before Americans had ever heard of Pleiku, Hue, or Anloc. The VA had more than two decades of experience in nearly all the programs it was to handle. The agency could hardly argue its efforts were hampered by insufficient time for planning and evaluation.

In addition, virtually all major programs for veterans are federally controlled and operated. Although a few of the VA's functions are decentralized and delegated to the states, there is a minimum of interference from other levels of government. It should, therefore, be easier for the VA to respond to veterans' needs and make changes where necessary. "We do not have to depend upon the support of any other governmental activity, be it local, state or federal," the VA administrator has said. "We can see something that needs to be done and do it." [37]

The VA, furthermore, occupies a favored position in the federal government. Few other agencies are treated as generously by Congress. Veterans belong to that group of select social categories sacrosanct in the eyes of politicians—like grandmothers, gun owners, and small children. It is a rare day when a request for funds from the VA goes unheeded. More commonly, Congressmen have been eager to anticipate VA needs and increase budgetary allocations above administration requests. Although the public may have been ambivalent in its reception of Vietnam veterans, there is no serious question as to the legitimacy of special assistance for them. Social welfare programs raise the suspicions of conservatives, military expenditures the ire of the left, but programs for Vietnam veterans provoke little partisan opposition.

In some ways, then, the VA has operated under optimal conditions: a steady and predictable flow of claimants, a large body of relevant experience, a minimum of interference from other levels of government, a relatively congenial political climate. Yet in spite of these favorable circumstances, there has been much wanting in the VA's performance. Many of the basic services the nation has committed itself, at least rhetorically, to providing Vietnam veterans are simply not reaching them. Our purpose here is to document the dimensions of this situation, inquire into its basic causes, and propose what remedies we can.

2

The Machinery of Government

With a budget of $12.2 billion, the Veterans Administration is now the third largest agency of the federal government, standing beneath only the Departments of Defense and Health, Education, and Welfare.

One might expect that an agency with a budget that large, and with programs as diverse as those of the VA, would be more than adequate to cope with the problems of returning veterans. But that assumes a scale of priorities not objectively apparent in the VA's budget. The greater part of its funds actually go to programs for older veterans for needs unrelated to their earlier military service. And as we shall see in the chapters that follow, the institutions that have been established to meet the needs of returning veterans, particularly the veterans' hospitals, are not at all oriented to dealing with their problems.

Before evaluating veterans' benefits and programs, one has to ask: What should their purposes be? What is the whole enterprise about?

The central paradox of the VA is that there is probably a greater consensus on this question than on many other public issues, and yet that consensus has had no impact on national policy. Back in 1954, a Roper poll surveyed 2,900 veterans, asking them what programs for veterans they favored. Virtually all approved compensation for service-connected disabilities and thought that it deserved the highest priority. The poll found that 86 percent believed medical care for service-connected disabilities was warranted, and 66 percent favored schooling at government expense. But only 22 percent believed veterans ought to receive nonservice-connected medical care and just 13 percent supported nonservice-connected pensions.[1] Interpreting these results in 1956, the President's Commission on Veterans' Pensions, chaired by General Omar Bradley, observed that the average veteran "asks for aid in getting started in civilian life—for readjustment benefits. He approves of the utmost in compensation, medical care, and rehabilitation for the veteran with a service-connected disability. He approves of low-cost home building or housing loans (and exhibits every intent of repaying the contractual debt). And if the draft has interrupted his schooling, the young veteran believes he is entitled to educational aid at the government's expense. At the same time, he places the nonservice-connected veterans' benefits—medical care and pensions—very low on the list." [2]

Over the years, the expectations of veterans have not changed that much. A Harris poll of Vietnam veterans in 1971 indicated a scale of priorities similar to that registered seventeen years before.[3] The consensus among veterans, and probably among the public at large, seems to be that veterans' programs should be aimed primarily at facilitating readjustment after military service and providing compensation and assistance to men who have incurred disabilities. In other words, aid should be concentrated at the time it is needed most—just after discharge when the men are getting resettled—and among those veterans who need it the most. But that, unfortunately, is not the way veterans' programs work. Because of the pressure of a well-organized professional veterans' lobby, programs applying to nonservice-connected needs for men at ages far from military service take up half the VA budget. And since the lobby has insisted that benefits be available across the board, there are virtually no special provisions for the men who need them the most—the combat veterans, those who went in with the least education, were the most likely to be exposed to death, the least likely to acquire the skills transferable to civilian life, and the most likely to go home with injuries or psychological problems. As a result, the larger part of the benefits go to veterans who never saw combat, at ages when their readjustment needs have passed, and for problems unrelated to military service. This is the achievement of a powerful lobby, a compliant Congress, and a supine executive agency.

A glance at the VA budget tells the story. The three largest appropriation items for fiscal year 1974 are disability compensation and nonservice-connected pensions,* $6,506 million; medical pro-

* In the special terminology of the VA, "compensation" refers to payments made to veterans and their families for disabilities and deaths related to military service. "Pensions," on the other hand, refer to payments for disabilities unrelated to military service. All veterans over sixty-five are considered "permanently and totally disabled" because of their age and consequently are eligible for pensions subject to income limitations. Also included in the appropriation for compensation and pensions are the cost of several other minor VA programs such as burial benefits.

grams, $2,762 million; and readjustment benefits, primarily GI Bill aid for education and training, $2,526 million. These three items account for 97 percent of the VA budget, the rest being primarily absorbed by general operating expenses and construction funds.[4] How much of that budget goes for nonservice-connected benefits? In the area of medical care, 85 percent of hospital discharges have been for nonservice-connected conditions.[5] Counting that proportion of the medical budget as nonservice-connected ($2,348 million) and adding to that the cost of nonservice-connected pensions ($2,653 million), one accounts for over 40 percent of the VA budget. Were we to add the proportion of general operating expenses, construction funds, and miscellaneous programs also attributable to nonservice-connected claims, the amount would be more nearly 50 percent of VA appropriations.

Making similarly rough estimates, we can determine the proportion of the budget that goes to Vietnam veterans. Here one must use the data for fiscal year 1972, the last period for which all the necessary breakdowns are available. Out of a total of $6,248 million paid out in 1972 in compensation and pensions, Vietnam era veterans and their dependents and survivors received $551 million, almost entirely in compensation payments.[6] During 1972 Vietnam era veterans accounted for 14.8 percent of VA hospital discharges.[7] With the medical care budget at $2,394 million that year, the cost of care that Vietnam veterans received may be put at $354 million. Readjustment benefits that year amounted to $1,889 million, nearly all of it going toward education and training benefits under the GI Bill.[8] Since about 80 percent of the persons receiving GI Bill funds have been Vietnam era veterans (the rest coming from an earlier period), they seem to have received about $1,511 million in readjustment benefits. In all, looking at the three major budget items, it appears that Vietnam era veterans received about $2,416 million out of a total of $10,531 million, or 23 percent of major expenditures. Since only about half of Vietnam era veterans actually served in Southeast Asia, it seems likely that Vietnam *war* veterans were getting only 12 to 15 percent of the VA budget.[9] We will see, moreover, that in the GI Bill programs, participation has been inverse to need because of the insufficiency of allowances for subsistence and tuition. No one, of course, ever consciously denied combat veterans from poor backgrounds any aid. It just works out that, given the way the programs are set up, they don't get very much.

Curiously enough, in 1972 Vietnam veterans represented about 21 percent of the total number of veterans in the United States.[10] In other words, they were receiving a share of the VA budget just about proportional to their numbers. Some would say this was entirely proper. We would argue, following what we think is a consensus indicated by the Roper poll, the Bradley Commission, and other sources, that veterans' programs should be primarily oriented to young veterans when they have the most immediate readjustment needs.

The Nixon administration has, of course, professed the deepest concern for Vietnam veterans. It has also asked the public to watch what it does, not what it says. In early 1973, just after the President's reelection, the Administration announced it was going to reduce compensation payments to amputees and other disabled veterans of the Vietnam War, while keeping payments to older disabled veterans unchanged. The decision created such an uproar in Congress, however, that it had to be withdrawn only days after it was announced.

To indicate how much nonservice-connected benefits cost annually today is to give no idea of what they will cost in the future. When the millions of veterans of World War II begin passing age sixty-five and become automatically eligible for pensions (under certain income limitations), the budget for veterans' pensions will skyrocket. Even if the rates of payment remain the same, which is highly unlikely, the government will be paying out somewhere near $13 billion annually in VA pensions by 1990, more than the entire VA budget today.[11] This is not to mention military retirement pay, which will easily push the total over $20 billion a year.

Equally staggering amounts have been paid decades after previous wars. On the basis of America's past experience, it has been estimated that veterans' pensions ultimately cost about two to three times as much as the original expenditures for the wars they fought.[12] Because of provisions for dependents and survivors, payments tend to continue long after the last veteran has died. In no case have veterans' pensions lasted less than 113 years. The federal government stopped paying out benefits for the Revolutionary War only in 1911, for the War of 1812 in 1946, and for the Mexican War in 1963.[13] It is still paying out money for the Civil War, the Indian Wars, incidents on the Mexican border, the Boxer Rebellion, the Spanish American War, the Philippine Insurrection, and the intervention in Russia in the 1920s, an affair which may have left its traces on the VA alone and nowhere else in the American memory. Moreover, since pensions have historically been the greatest cost, benefits reach their peak forty to seventy years after the war ends. Assuming no change in current laws, Professor James L. Clayton of the University of Utah estimates that pensions for Vietnam will peak about the year 2020 and that the total cost of Vietnam veterans' pensions will be about $220 billion (a low estimate, since benefit levels will undoubtedly rise).[14] In view of the increasing life expectancy, we can probably count on paying out veterans' pensions for the Vietnam War well into the twenty-second century—if we last that long.

The nonservice-connected pensions that loom into our distant future open up a completely different set of issues from those which concern us in this report. Our interest lies with the programs for soldiers returning from Vietnam which are—and should be—aimed at compensation for the sacrifices of health and personal opportunity they have made. The legitimacy of their immediate claims on our society is unquestionable. However, benefits which are not related to sacrifices made in war but which confer on veterans a separate status for life are another matter entirely. Forty years ago, in October 1933, Franklin Roosevelt went before a convention of the American Legion and declared "that no person, because he wore a uniform, must thereafter be placed in a special class of beneficiaries over and above all other citizens." [15] The principle has too often been forgotten in the intervening years. Not only are permanent benefits dubious as social policy, but there is a real question whether they have not interfered with the programs for returning servicemen that should be the legitimate and preeminent concern of the Veterans Administration.

Why programs for nonservice-connected needs have gained a secure and ample lodging in the VA has primarily to do with the structure of veterans' politics. For a variety of reasons, veterans' organizations tend to be dominated by older veterans, who use the VA as a general social welfare agency.

But to understand the structure and history of the VA, it must be seen as more than a welfare agency. It is a cross between the Pentagon and HEW, serving both military and welfare functions. The VA is that point in the federal government where the demands for guns and butter resonate. For the military, veterans' benefits serve a number of important functions. They facilitate military recruitment, in that potential enlistees may be promised not only "adventure" abroad but also security when they come back home. Benefits also facilitate social control within the army. By threatening soldiers with less than honorable discharges, the military can deny them subsequent advantages. Perhaps most important, an extensive system of veterans' services fosters a continued identification with the military among large segments of the population. This strengthens the military's domestic political position.

On the other hand, veterans' benefits do create one problem

for the armed services: They tend to discourage re-enlistment. Throughout the mid-Sixties, the Pentagon repeatedly objected to restoration of the GI Bill of Rights precisely on those grounds.[16]

As a system of social welfare programs, veterans' services have two different and complex functions. While in all societies veterans are officially the subject of nothing but panegyrics, they are also regarded with a certain unspoken apprehension. As Willard Waller pointed out some years ago, every society exploits its soldiers in the sense that it imposes risks that can never be compensated.[17] It fears the dread possibility that those who fought abroad will strike back in fury on their return home, feeling cheated and bitter at the depth of their sacrifice, the meagerness of their rewards, and the seeming ingratitude of their countrymen. History is replete with examples of riots and rebellions by returning soldiers, most recently by South Vietnamese veterans in Saigon. Veterans' benefits, consequently, have as their function not only the provision of services to a group thought especially deserving, but also the mollification of men regarded as having a great potential for civil disruption. Ultimately, it is not just a nation's enemies but also its heroes that must be pacified. In this respect, the functions of veterans' programs are no different from the functions of social welfare programs generally, which have historically been a means both of providing assistance and of maintaining order.

A number of other uses should also be noted. As veterans' benefits help veterans readjust to civilian life, so they also help the economy adjust to them. In the aftermath of World War II, the effects of sudden demobilization were partially blunted by ample benefits for education that drew millions of veterans off the labor market and helped avoid a reversion to the unemployment levels of the Depression. "On the one hand," says a VA publication rather melodramatically, "were all the ingredients for near national breakdown. On the other, the GI Bill of Rights." [18] Partly because the Vietnam War has not seen the kind of sudden demobilization that took place after World War II, the benefits available for veterans have not been as handsome. Nowhere has there developed any great sense of urgency about the economic impact of the war's termination.

Veterans' benefits have also been a channel for federal funds to specific economic institutions. The GI Bill helped finance the expansion of American universities in the post-World War II era. Similarly, guarantees for home loans encouraged new construction. In 1950 veterans' programs represented 20.4 percent of the federal budget—considerable fuel for the economy. In 1972, primarily because of the growth of federal spending in other areas, veterans' programs represented only 4.7 percent of the budget.[19] As other programs have burgeoned, the importance of veterans' benefits to the private sector has correspondingly diminished. Universities now clamor for aid through research programs. The housing industry is much more concerned about Housing and Urban Development (HUD). Thus, lobbies which were once heard in favor of more substantial readjustment programs for veterans are now off plowing other agencies. Consequently, Vietnam era veterans have lost some potential special interest allies (not that they should depend on them). If politics makes strange bedfellows, it also unmakes them.

Special interests have not, however, abandoned the VA. The airlines have been concerned to see that the VA provides ample benefits for commercial flight training, since pilots come to them in large measure from the military and receive their additional training under the GI Bill.[20] Career and correspondence schools also have a large interest in seeing ample education benefits—and loose regulatory controls by the VA—since a large proportion of their clients enroll with GI Bill money.

To consider only the material uses of veterans' benefits would be to ignore their social and psychological functions. These can be seen most clearly where ordinary government programs, unrelated to military service, are nevertheless defined as veterans' benefits. As already noted, the overwhelming majority of patients receiving care in VA hospitals are there for nonservice-connected medical problems. Even more striking is the separate program of income maintenance for veterans, over and above social security. That men receive such assistance *as veterans* has an enormous impact on the way they are treated and see themselves. Unlike a welfare check, a veteran's pension carries no stigma. There are no demeaning investigations into the recipient's personal life, no sense that he is leeching off the public till. After two consecutive years as a pensioner, a veteran over seventy-two need not even fill out an income questionnaire. Whenever attempts are made to rationalize the nation's social security and welfare system and integrate veterans' pensions with other programs of income maintenance, it is not surprising that veterans vehemently resist such changes. They have an interest not just in the amount of benefits, but in the way they are defined.

Veterans' organizations have an even larger stake than the pensioners in the definition of federal programs as veterans' benefits. It is a common oversimplification to say that the structure of private interests determines the structure of government programs. The process actually goes both ways: The structure of government programs also influences the kinds of private interests that coalesce. If a government program is structured along certain axes, then private organizations will define themselves along those same axes simply because that is the most effective way for the clients of that agency to exercise influence. This is nowhere more true than in the area of veterans' programs. On leaving the army, the average soldier does not join a veterans' association. It is primarily when he wants something from the VA and has trouble getting it that he turns to one of the veterans' organizations for help. Were federal programs defined along other lines, he would turn to some other kind of organization for assistance. In other words, by providing assistance separately to veterans, the government encourages veterans to organize themselves into a separate interest group.

This kind of private replication of government structure obviously sets up enormous obstacles in the path of reform. Any proposal to merge veterans' programs with other federal activities runs up not only against the inertia of government but against the interests of large nongovernmental organizations whose power is premised on the existing definition of services. Even where separate veterans' programs provide inadequate services and where the interests of individual veterans would be served by wider social programs, the veterans' organizations may be expected to fight to preserve their separate status and the separate administrative structure of veterans' benefits.

Currently, all but a few veterans' services are located in the Veterans Administration. The major exceptions are the benefits for retired officers, which are administered by the Defense Department and now amount to $5 billion annually, and employment services, which are the responsibility of the Department of Labor and amount to very little. The veterans' lobby has successfully resisted the proliferation of veterans' programs outside the VA, even at the cost of eliminating them entirely. In 1968, for example, the Office of Education initiated a pilot program called Veterans in Public Service (VIPS) that enabled a small number of Vietnam veterans to supplement their GI Bill education allowance with earnings from part-time work as teacher aides in public schools. When the pilot project ended in August 1970, HEW asked Congress to renew it and extend it into the health fields. The proposal died when the veterans' lobby unanimously objected to it as "diluting" the power of the Veterans Administration.[21]

To those unfamiliar with the VA, the size and range of its programs come as a surprise. Since it is not a cabinet-level department, the VA is assumed to be relatively small, but as we noted earlier, its budget of $12 billion places it third among federal agencies in expenditures. In number of employees, it ranks second to the Pentagon. What makes the VA particularly unusual is the diversity of its programs—it runs the full gamut of social services. Unlike other agencies, whose objectives are functionally specific and whose activities are more sharply circumscribed, the VA takes an active role in providing education, on-the-job training, vocational rehabilitation, home loan guarantees, disability compensation, income maintenance, a great deal of health care, aid to widows and dependents, life insurance, old age care, even management of estates and burial benefits. Although the veterans' organizations would deny it, the VA represents the most highly elaborated form the welfare state has reached in America.

The agency classifies its multifarious programs into four major categories: (1) readjustment benefits; (2) health services; (3) compensation and pensions; and (4) life insurance. As we have seen, the first three of these account for 97 percent of its budget.

The programs vary greatly in structure. For example, education and training benefits are distributed as direct grants to individual veterans, which they may use at approved institutions of their choice. On the other hand, medical benefits are delivered through a separate set of veterans' institutions. The structure could, hypothetically, be the other way around. That is, one might have separate schools and training programs for veterans and individual grants for medical care, which ex-servicemen could use at community hospitals of their choice. The reasons for the structure of each program lie in its history. Those reasons may have long ceased to be compelling, but no matter—as the years go by, programs accumulate vested interests like so many barnacles on the side of a ship.

Of the four major program areas of the VA, we will be concerned with those that most directly affect Vietnam veterans—primarily readjustment benefits and health services, and, to a lesser extent, compensation and pensions. The fourth area unfortunately has much less relevance. The VA's life insurance programs, which make it the fourth largest insurance company in the country and which have provided veterans of earlier wars with the best terms available in the United States, have been effectively eliminated for Vietnam veterans at the behest of the insurance industry. Vietnam veterans no longer have the option of keeping inexpensive government insurance initiated during military service. If they wish to continue coverage, they must convert to a policy from a private insurance firm. Instead of providing veterans with cheaper insurance than private companies would offer, the system now serves to channel them into the private insurance market.

In addition to VA programs, we will also look into the activities of the Defense and Labor Departments that affect Vietnam veterans. Part Two (*Legacies of War*) covers the medical, psychological, and legal injuries of Vietnam. In it we deal with military disability retirement, military drug programs, and military discharges, as well as VA medical services. Part Three (*Trials of Peace*) concerns social and economic problems. There we discuss not only VA readjustment benefits, but also employment programs in the Labor Department and a Pentagon project in which military service was ostensibly used as a form of social rehabilitation.

In all these areas, we try not just to evaluate the impact on Vietnam veterans, but to determine how the programs affect other veterans and other citizens and how they interrelate with other federal programs and other institutions. In discussing veterans' hospitals, we must bring in their relationship to other health services in the nation. In discussing military and VA drug programs, it is necessary to look at the background of the drug addiction problem. In discussing unemployment among veterans, unavoidably one must look at the general economic policies that have given rise to unemployment. In looking at the GI Bill, there is no alternative but to examine its relationship to educational institutions. The diversity of veterans' programs necessarily takes us into a number of widely disparate fields, but certain recurrent themes should underlie them: the failure of veterans' programs to fulfill their legitimate purpose in aiding returning veterans; the lack of congruence between benefits and need; the regulatory failure of the VA, particularly in the area of education; and the problem of coordination between programs in the VA and other parts of the federal government. This last issue poses some of the most important policy questions for the future, because as federal programs covering much the same ground as the VA have grown in other agencies, conflicts and overlaps have multiplied.

Despite the size and scope of the VA's programs and the enormous changes in the role of the federal government since their inception, the agency has been the object of remarkably little critical analysis. Thousands of complaints, of course, have been made about its services, but these have generally been piecemeal; social scientists and policy makers have not given veterans' programs much sustained attention since the Bradley Commission. Indeed, the VA has been an administrator's dream: high in budget, low in visibility. It is hard to think of any other unit of government —or any private organization—that has a budget of $12 billion and is as inconspicuous as the Veterans Administration. Over the years, the VA has carried on its operations like a large, silent gray machine, attended by political appointees who have neither the interest nor the mandate to consider whether its role and structure need to be overhauled.

This low visibility is largely a product of routinization. Veterans' programs have retained roughly the form they took at the end of World War II. With the Vietnam War, all the government needed to do was reactivate the readjustment benefits that had lapsed by the early Sixties. The current conflict has occasioned no serious rethinking of veterans' services, no new departures, no significant evolution.

Another important factor in the low visibility of the VA is the remarkable insulation of all veterans' institutions from outside criticism and control. This insulation is established in part by law: No appeals on rulings by the VA, except where constitutional issues are involved, may be brought into federal courts. All matters are handled within a VA appeal system, the ultimate arbiter being the Administrator of Veterans' Affairs. This arrangement, which its advocates claim protects the veteran, also conveniently protects the agency from any outside meddlers. The system is strengthened by regulations that effectively prevent all but representatives of old-line veterans' organizations from serving as counsel at VA hearings. The regulations limit the fee any professional lawyer can take from a case before the VA to $10, and there are simply not many lawyers willing to work at that rate of pay. The combination of no judicial review, plus no legal counsel at VA hearings, effectively seals off the agency's proceedings.

The field of veterans' affairs is run largely by a limited, interlocking network formed by the leading veterans' organizations, the Veterans Administration and the House Veterans' Affairs Committee. There is a continual exchange of personnel among these three centers of influence. Donald Johnson, currently the Administrator of the VA, was formerly national commander of the American Legion. Herbert Rainwater, now the director of the Veterans' Employment Service in the Department of Labor, was national commander of the Veterans of Foreign Wars. Richard Roudebush also once served as a national commander of the VFW. When he was elected to the House, he joined the Committee on Veterans' Affairs, and when he left the House after his defeat for the Senate, he became a special counselor to Johnson. Roudebush has managed to make all three stops.

This sort of internal cohesiveness no doubt fosters the best of relations among those concerned with setting policy. But it also raises questions about the potential for feedback and adaptation. Perhaps it is time someone outside the family had a look at vererans' benefits.

part two ★ ★ ★ ★ ★
Legacies of War

Orators . . . began to find the presence of Thomas Ordway there in the front row of seats, a ring of vacant ones setting him apart, with that fixed and empty gaze of his, an accusation and an embarrassment. So did the other, unwounded veterans. They had come to think of the day as their annual get-together rather than one to honor their dead comrades-in-arms, and to their reminiscences of youthful highjinks and derring-do they found that broken groping stinking figure a hinderance. They suspected him of subversive reservations as to the truth and beauty of what they had done, even of doubts as to the justice of the cause for which they had fought.

William Humphrey, The Ordways

3

A Trade in Scars

★ *Endurance*

It was Thanksgiving Day 1967, and he was walking point in the darkness somewhere near Quangtri. Almost two years ago, when he was seventeen, Ned had decided he had had it with his mother and with high school and so he dropped out, said good-by, and joined the Marines. It wasn't going to be a career, just a few years before he'd go back and maybe become an FBI or Secret Service agent. He wasn't really sure what he wanted to do. But now he was in the infantry, walking point ahead of a company of 150 men, must be four hours walking point, and it was dark, and no one knew what to expect.

"I'll take over," said the team leader, and just then Ned stepped on it, there was a green flash, and he felt as if he were floating, numb and weightless. Then dirt started coming down in his face and he landed and tried to yell, but the wind was knocked out of him. Nearby the team leader was killed by the mine; so were the squad leader and lieutenant. Finally he managed to call out, "Squid," and the corpsman came and lit a lantern. Ned glimpsed one of his own feet lying in the grass some distance away. Pain welled up all over him.

The corpsman gave him a shot of morphine and began to bandage him up; another shot of morphine, and the pain ebbed. Finally, a chopper came in, and it took no more than fifteen minutes to bring him to the rear. Just as he reached the landing zone, Ned passed out.

The men who make it through "medevac" nearly always make it. One of the grim ironies of the Vietnam War has been that

America's greater capacity to prevent death on the battlefield has yielded a more tortured legacy of survivors. Rapid helicopter evacuation and sophisticated medical science have combined to save thousands of soldiers in Vietnam who would have died in previous wars. In World War II the ratio of wounded to killed was 3.1 to 1, in Korea 4 to 1, but in Vietnam it was 5.6 to 1. The Army, which bore the brunt of the casualties, reports that 81 percent of its wounded survived in Southeast Asia, compared with 74 percent in Korea and 71 percent in World War II.[1] From that data it appears that about 30,000 soldiers wounded in Vietnam would not have made it home were our medical and transportation technology still at the level of World War II. In other words, we would have lost 76,000 men in action in Vietnam—65 percent more than we actually did lose.

But progress in reducing deaths has not been matched by progress in restoring health. More men come home, but more come home with severe and permanent injuries. Among wounded Army men discharged for disability, the proportion of amputees has risen from 18 percent in World War II to 28.3 percent in Vietnam; this, in spite of advances in vascular surgery that enable us to repair arteries and avoid amputations that were previously necessary. Paralysis of the extremities accounted for only 3.1 percent of wounded Army disability separations in World War II; for Vietnam the figure has been 25.2 percent.[2] Other sources corroborate this picture. Data on compensation cases from the Veterans Administration indicate that the rate for leg amputations in Vietnam has been 70 percent higher than in Korea and 300 percent above World War II; for functional loss of the lower extremities (paraplegia), the incidence has been 50 percent higher than in Korea and 1,000 percent over World War II.[3] Aside from the improved survival record, there is the additional factor of heavy use of land mines and booby traps in Vietnam.

Ned woke up.

"It's about time," said a corpsman sitting by his bed. He thought it was the morning after Thanksgiving, but actually it was about a week later, and he was in a hospital north of Danang. Instinctively, he reached for a cigarette, but the corpsman motioned to the oxygen tents. Slowly it dawned on him where he was and what had happened. He was missing his left leg, and the rest of his body was badly mangled.

After an operation, Ned was airlifted to the hospital ship *Repose* off the coast. Skin grafts on his back and arm made it almost impossible for him to move around. One night he screamed again and again for help, and when no one came, he finally gave vent to his bladder over one side of the bed and to his bowels over the other. An aide found the mess later and upbraided him in anger.

A surgeon on the ship told Ned he would have to have another operation. Nothing major, the doctor reassured him. When it was over, he woke and found the surgeon leaning over his bed. "I had to take your right leg off," he said softly and Ned punched him once, and then a second time, as the nurses came in and subdued him with tranquilizers. Ned tried to hit him a third time, but couldn't make it.

He never saw the doctor again. Ned hated him as much as one man can hate another.

"The most striking difference in the amputees from the Vietnam conflict," notes the medical director of the VA, Dr. Marc Musser, *"is the frequency of multiple amputations." In World War II, only 5.7 percent of the amputees had multiple amputations or other major injuries. In Vietnam the proportion has been 18.4 percent. "This poses one of our greatest problems in caring for these amputee veterans."* [4]

In other groups, such as burn victims, the proportion of the severely injured has also risen. With the use of new drugs that curb bacterial infection in burned areas of the body, we are now saving nearly twice as many burn victims as in the past. Among patients with burns over half their bodies, nearly 60 percent formerly died, whereas now fewer than 30 percent are lost.

The new drugs, however, cannot undo mutilation. Plastic surgery helps, but it has limits, as a surgeon who sees war casualties at Chelsea Naval Hospital points out: "I have to tell them that I can't restore their original looks. I say, 'Son, I'm only a surgeon, and when I do scar revisions, I only trade one scar for another.' " [5]

Ned was taken to Japan. On a bus trip from the airport to the hospital, the stumps of his legs burst open and were bleeding. When he reached the hospital, the doctor found his crotch hadn't been properly bathed for days, and the skin grafts were obviously not going to take.

While under treatment, he got hooked on drugs—demerol and morphine. "I'd wake up and I wouldn't have to ask for a shot. There would be a nurse right there. They were trying to do the best by me, but they were hooking me at the same time."

The plane that took him back to the United States in December made a stopover in Alaska, but then went straight on to Philadelphia, where he was placed in a military hospital.

"I was hurting most of the way and yelling for shots every three hours, but they could only give them to me every four. . . . In Philly the doctor took me off drugs, except for Darvon. Then I was really hurting. I hadn't come to the point where I could distinguish between the pain and the need for drugs. He tried to take me off drugs, but I just couldn't hack it, so he put me back on.

"After about a week I was moved to an amputee ward. At least 75 percent of the guys were hooked when I got there. We used to lay there—this was after the pain of the wound had subsided—and we'd bawl, cry for the need of the drugs. But we'd tell the nurses it was pain. They couldn't distinguish, because the two are so much alike. There were a couple of corpsmen who would steal drugs for you. We never gave away their identity to anybody official, because our supply would've been cut.

"After three months, I would go out [in a wheelchair]. If you wanted drugs, you could sit out on the street uptown in Philly and make a contact. I always got a couple of guys who would take me uptown."

Before going to Vietnam, Ned had been dating a girl from back home, and she stuck by him in spite of his injury. At one point he went AWOL from the hospital in Philadelphia to go home to see her. Shortly thereafter, he was given leave, and the couple were married. It didn't work. In two months he asked her for a divorce. The way he tells it, it took a year before she agreed. During that time, he was discharged and transferred to a VA hospital near his home. He would spend most of his time there on the psychiatric ward.

Since the war began, the VA has received about 20,000 men directly from the military, nearly all of them totally disabled. About 30 percent of the cases have been psychiatric, another 30 percent with nervous system injuries, 10 percent amputees, and 8 percent with tuberculosis.[6] These men have entered a hospital system that is overwhelmingly dominated by the aged. In spite of the large number of casualties from the war, Vietnam veterans make up a small proportion of VA hospital patients—9.4 percent on a given day, a third of whom have "service-connected" medical problems.[7] Since about half of these service-connected disabilities are related to combat, Vietnam war casualties represent about 2 percent of the total VA patient population. "Young veterans," the VA itself

*concedes in its 1971 Annual Report, "tend to feel powerless about
their ability to effect change and, compared to older veterans, they
feel isolated in a VA hospital. Such feelings are understandable,
because the young veterans do represent a decided minority group
among all hospitalized veterans."* [8]

And a troublesome minority group they have been. As elsewhere
in America, the new generation has different tastes in music, drugs,
sexual behavior, politics, and personal appearance—tastes which
Legionnaires and others commonly interpret as subversive and
morally decadent. There is a strongly felt age gap not only between
Vietnam veterans and older patients, but between young veterans
and the hospital staff, many of whom came on board in the years
immediately after World War II (the "class of '46" they are called).
The VA is unable to attract recent graduates of American medical
schools and tends to rely on older physicians who have entered
semi-retirement and foreign physicians whose formal qualifications
may be excellent but who often have great language difficulties.

Studies undertaken by the VA indicate that problems of communication and impersonal treatment irritate many of its patients, but the
reports also reveal a higher level of discontent among Vietnam
veterans. [9] This discontent is not a matter of mere grumbling. Several
surveys have indicated that a higher proportion of Vietnam veteran
patients seek discharges "against medical advice" than do veterans
of World War II. [10]

The VA has sought to propitiate the young by placing them on
wards of their own where possible, organizing Vietnam era committees in the hospitals, and setting up public panel discussions where
young veterans have a chance to air their grievances. These
measures have elicited a predictable reaction from older VA staff
and patients. "The over-thirty staff," concluded a study at the
Houston VA, "resent special handling of young patients and react
punitively to [their] unconventional behavior. . . ." A comment
from an older employee was revealing: "As a veteran of two wars, I
strongly protest the discrimination [against] the older veteran. This is
a Veterans' hospital, and the word 'veteran' does not apply only to
Vietnam vets. If it had not been for us older vets they wouldn't even
be here. Too much emphasis is being placed on the Vietnam vets
which comprise only a small fraction of the veteran population." [11]

It is almost a matter of sibling rivalry.

In February 1969, Ned had his right leg operated on again. (It
had been amputated at the knee.) Three weeks later he was told to

put on wooden legs and begin the painful process of learning to walk all over again. The first time he tried them, the stumps split wide open, blood spilled out, and Ned collapsed, sobbing wildly. He was given a tranquilizer.

"Much of this is hazy to me because I was high at the time."

After his stumps healed, the doctors advised him to try to walk again, but he refused until he thought he was ready. Even then there was seepage. One leg that had been made for him in Philadelphia fitted onto his stump by suction. "Six hours on the outside, and the stump would be blood red. You try to wear a leg like that on a job, and it just won't work.

"VA doctors will tell you that when a patient is ready to walk, he'll walk. It's a bunch of bullshit." Ned wanted to walk, but he says he couldn't with the prosthesis that had been given to him. One day he took the suction leg into a bathroom and in a rage beat it against the tub until it splintered, and he was sure they couldn't fix it. In came a chaplain and a bevy of orderlies; they thought he had gone berserk. Ned did nothing to allay that suspicion. He struck the chaplain, and the doctors put him under heavier sedation.

"I almost lived for pill hour. And when you got them, they made you sleepy, and you went in and lay down. The nurses would try to get you up, so you'd go into the TV room and fall asleep."

Short on personnel and shorter still on imagination, VA psychiatric facilities, like many others, tend to rely on drugs to maintain order on the wards. Although the VA has recently instituted drug abuse treatment programs, its hospitals are among the worst offenders in the country. One recent study of VA psychiatric care sponsored by the Administrative Conference, an independent federal agency, concluded that the system encouraged "unnecessary" and "unnecessarily prolonged" institutionalization in part because of the climate in the hospitals and the inadequacy of outpatient and follow-up services. The author described the condition of the patients at one hospital he visited as "stuporous self-containment." [12] Ned's present wife, who worked in the VA hospital where he was treated, describes the other patients on the psychiatric ward as "walking zombies." Many of them were "doped up" in spite of the fact that they showed no signs of violent behavior.

Ned received a better prosthesis and began making progress. One day in May 1969, the psychiatrist announced, "You're discharged today." He had been in the hospital six months and he had no place to go. He couldn't go back to live with his mother and he was getting divorced from his wife. So he telephoned another patient who had left the hospital and was living in a specially adapted home. Michael invited Ned to come live with him, and he did. With his friend's help, he began learning how to make his way in the world. Michael assisted him with such things as getting an allowance from the VA for a car with hand controls that he would be able to drive.

In the next few months, Ned wrecked the car six times. After the fourth accident, he was afraid the insurance company would cancel his policy and so he decided to pay for the damage out of his own pocket. While in the hospital, he had accumulated $6,000 or $7,000 in compensation payments. He used up most of the money to keep his car.

Ned spent the latter half of 1969 running around in his car, getting drunk, getting pills, and moving in and out of the psychiatric ward at the local VA hospital. In November, during one of his stints at the hospital, he met a young nurse's aide. She was pretty, blond, petite, the rootless daughter of an army family, raised at bases all over the country, already divorced herself, though barely twenty. Three weeks after they met, they were married.

"When I met him," Diana says now, "he was bitter. I was afraid to do anything. He'd get sharp with me for touching any of his things. I didn't know he was hooked at the time."

For the first month, there was continual bickering. One night Ned drove Diana home in silence. "I tried to talk to him," Diana says, "but he didn't want to talk." Finally, she went to take a bath. After a while Ned came into the bathroom and announced, "You'll be happy to know I'm going to kill myself and you can have all my money, because that's all you've wanted." She didn't believe him.

A moment later there was a shot in the bedroom. When Diana got there, she found Ned bleeding from the stomach, still alive.

Although reliable statistics are nonexistent, suicide appears to be one of the leading causes of death among Vietnam veterans in general and disabled veterans in particular.[13] One other cause rivaling suicide is drug use, and the two have much in common—an overwhelming desire for surcease from pain.

In most wars a disabled veteran must negotiate a painful transition from wounded war hero to crippled adult in a society that is less and less interested in the source of his injury. But in this war the disabled have even been deprived of that evanescent prestige conferred after more popular conflicts. As Max Cleland, a triple amputee and state senator from Georgia, has said, "To the devastating psychological effect of getting maimed, paralyzed, or in some way unable to reenter American life as you left it, is the added psychological weight that it may not have been worth it; that the war may have been a cruel hoax, an American tragedy, that left a small minority of young American males holding the bag.

"These psychological repercussions do not hit you right away. . . . [They] come months later, like a series of secondary explosions long after the excitement of the battlefield is far behind. . . ." [14]

Ned lay bleeding in the bedroom while his wife called for a doctor. It took an hour for one to come; there are no "medevacs" in the United States. After the operation, the surgeon came out and found Diana. "What that boy needs is faith," he said, "and it's about time someone gave it."

But things did not improve: instead of recovering, Ned went into withdrawal. He begged Diana to ask the nurse for pills, but the nurse said no. One day, believing that he wasn't at the hospital at all, he called Diana and told her he was on his way home. She went to the hospital and found him delirious. His temperature was up to 105°, and for the next two days he was reliving the war all over again.

After his suicide attempt, Ned had been treated at a community hospital, but it was soon decided to transfer him to the psychiatric ward at the VA. He thought it was a plot and that Diana was trying to have him committed. At the VA he managed to acquire pills and began popping them with increasing frequency. "He'd just act like he was on a trip every time I saw him," Diana recalls. Ned suspected her of taking his money and, when she became pregnant, of sleeping with someone else. She insisted the child was his.

"He was fighting me all the way," Diana says. "He didn't want the kid at first, but he's a good father now."

Ned traces the beginning of his recovery to conversations with a psychologist at the VA who kept saying that no one could help him except himself. "It sort of hit me that she didn't have anything to do with the problems I had brought on myself." In February 1971, he left the hospital and began seeing about an education.

The first effort, radio and TV repair, ended after two sessions at a program run by the state rehabilitation commission. Ned switched to business administration and stayed in the state program for the entire year. He began to enjoy the work.

"The way they talked," Diana says, "it was going to count. But he couldn't get a job with it."

"The diploma," Ned adds bitterly, "isn't worth the paper it's written on."

During the year at the state program, however, Ned came into contact with disabled children. "They adjust to it much more easily," he observes. "One kid made me ashamed. He just strapped those legs on and went right up the steps. That's something that really got to me."

It's not something he could have seen at a veterans' hospital. The models there are generally chronic invalids who have had the greatest trouble adjusting to their injuries, or whose families have failed to take responsibility for them.

In the spring Ned looked for a better program in business administration. "It would be pretty stupid not to go to school, when they're paying tuition plus more than two hundred dollars." At a local state college, which has an open admissions policy for veterans, he immediately hit it off with the assistant registrar, who happened to have been a teacher of his back in the ninth grade. The fellow took a special interest in him and saw to it that he received special parking privileges and assistance in getting his books and assignments. "They treated me like a big wheel," Ned says with some surprise, and a smile comes to his face for the first time. He had never before been treated as somebody important.

One evening after a course in introductory psychology, Ned walks out with some fellow students, also veterans. They come to a slope and, with hardly a word, someone offers Ned a shoulder to help him make it down. But it's hard work for him, and he thinks out loud about the coming winter, shaking his head, wondering what he'll do when snow covers the ground.

Most nights Ned and Diana sit at home in the small town where they live. Their community is newly built, clean, flat, too new to have any tall trees or ivy—or slums. They have a well-furnished single-level house with wide doorways and no steps. Although the VA helped them buy it with a grant of $12,500,[15] they resent those who think they are getting it free. But no matter what they receive from the government, there is not much for them to do. Diana wishes there were groups of disabled persons in their area. All other contacts are uncomfortable. People stare at Ned, unconsciously, but with great curiosity, and make it difficult for them to carry on normal activities or make friends. So, to avoid the discomfort of society, they keep to themselves. It is a struggle, a private struggle, just to go on. For Ned, the war will never be over.

★ *An Indelicate Imbalance*

The Vietnam conflict, like other wars before it, has left a myriad of personal tragedies in its wake. To speak of 300,000 Americans wounded, and a few million Vietnamese, gives no idea of the dimensions of suffering. "Statistics don't bleed," Arthur Koestler once wrote, "it is the detail which counts. We are unable to embrace the total process with our awareness; we can only focus on little lumps of reality." [16]

Against all odds, through their own strength of will, and with the assistance of others, many of the victims overcome their injuries and make new lives for themselves. The role of government is to facilitate and encourage that process by making available necessary resources. To that end, the nation has long provided compensation for service-connected injuries. It would be unrealistic to expect such benefits to restore irreparable losses, but it is entirely reasonable to expect that they be equitable, that they be efficiently administered, and that they provide an adequate level of support without vitiating incentives to work and reenter community life. Unfortunately, the current system has not always lived up to those expectations. There are problems in each of the three areas: equity, efficiency, and incentives for positive readjustment.

Perhaps the most serious of these is the issue of equity. Consider the case of John Lavelle.[17]

General Lavelle, who was retired in April 1972 for "personal and health" reasons after he carried out unauthorized bombings of North Vietnam, was ruled 70 percent disabled by the Air Force on the basis of emphysema, a coronary condition, and a slipped disk. Prior to bombing the North, the general had been rated in excellent health and, in fact, was considered fit enough to remain on active flying status up to the day of his retirement.

Lavelle's apparently sudden case of emphysema puzzled associates and must have puzzled even more the doctors who performed his retirement physical at Andrews Air Force Base, just outside of Washington. A pulmonary function study, conducted by doctors at Andrews on April 3, four days before General Lavelle retired, showed the vital capacity of his lungs to have been 101 percent of normal. A second test measured the amount of air he could expel in one second. On this test General Lavelle obtained a rating of seventy-two; a score of sixty-nine is considered normal for a man of his age, and the Air Force requires a score of seventy for its pilots.

The heart condition was equally dubious. On the following day, April 4, a cardiologist examined General Lavelle and concluded that he had "1. calcitic aortic stenosis, probably not hemodynamically significant, and 2. probable angina pectoris."

The aortic stenosis (constriction of the major artery from the heart) had been known to exist for three years and had been waived to allow General Lavelle to continue on flight status and to collect his extra flight pay. The cardiologist found it was "probably not hemodynamically significant," which means it apparently did not interfere with the blood flow and therefore was not serious. Yet at retirement it was used as a basis for his 70 percent disability.

The consultant's diagnosis of "probable angina pectoris" was not supported by any objective evidence. His records show that the Masters Test, the EKG, and all the clinical evidence were negative. The only indication of "probable angina pectoris" was General Lavelle's subjective statement that he had an occasional pain in his chest.

Subjective evidence appears also to have been the basis for the determination by the Air Force's examination board that General Lavelle had a bad back. Although veterans frequently go to the VA complaining of back injuries, often difficult to verify, they are not awarded disability payments unless they can produce objective evidence of the disability. For General Lavelle, however, the demands of objective proof seem to have been less rigorously applied.

Moreover, even if the three conditions were confirmed, and even if Lavelle had not violated his rules of engagement, there is the further question of why the government should be providing compensation for disabilities of advancing age that had no clear relationship to the performance of military duties.

Despite his breach of authority, Lavelle was awarded a handsome retirement income of $27,000 a year. Because of his disability rating, 70 percent of that income is tax free. In addition, General Lavelle receives a further tax exemption of $5,200 under a "sick pay" proviso. The annual tax on the remaining $2,900, for a married couple filing a joint return, would be $16.

General Lavelle is not alone in his good fortune. In 1965, when Curtis Lemay retired as Air Force Chief of Staff, he received a 60 percent disability rating on the basis of deafness, poor eyesight, prostate troubles, and partial facial paralysis stemming from a slight stroke he had suffered in the 1940s. In spite of these problems, General Lemay had been piloting jet planes up to the time he retired. Within ten days after his retirement, he received a private pilot's license from the Federal Aviation Agency at a special ceremony in the office of Administrator Najeeb Halaby.[18] As of

August 1972, General Lemay still retained that license. In 1968 he was well enough to run for Vice President under George Wallace and, presumably, well enough to serve.

Because of his 60 percent disability rating, Lemay need not pay federal income taxes on about $10,000 of his retirement pay.

Are these isolated cases? Data from three separate sources suggest they are not.

1. In the wake of the Lavelle disclosures, Senator William Proxmire asked the General Accounting Office to determine how many Air Force generals retired for disability had been receiving flight pay. GAO found that during the last five years, 327 generals had retired from the Air Force and that of these men, 130 (or 40 percent) retired on 30 percent or more disability. Of these disabled generals, 97 (or 75 percent) had been receiving flight pay during the year immediately preceding their retirement.[19]

2. Nor does it appear that such practices are just of recent origin. In 1956 the Bradley Commission studied 1,000 disability cases that had been evaluated both by the armed services and the Veterans Administration. Although the military uses the VA's schedule for rating disabilities, the results diverged enormously. The correlation between ratings by the two agencies was only .38, where 1 represents perfect agreement and 0 no correlation at all. (Psychologists and educators generally consider tests unacceptable if the correlation between equivalent forms is less than .90.) Even more interesting than the overall divergence—the military gave higher ratings than the VA both to officers and enlisted men—was the difference according to rank. While the military gave only slightly higher ratings to enlisted men than the VA, it gave much higher ratings to officers. For enlisted men, the mean disability rating by the military was 54 percent and by the VA 43 percent. For officers, the mean rating by the military was 48 percent and by the VA 15 percent.[20] The results suggest that if the power to make disability ratings were removed from the military, ratings for officers would decline dramatically.

3. In November 1972, *Armed Forces Journal* obtained data, previously unavailable to Congress, on the percentage of retirements that were for disability, by rank and branch of service, as of June 30, 1971. The data disclosed several interesting patterns. In every branch of the services, two to three times as many generals had been retired for disability (31 percent on the average) as had colonels and majors (14 percent), although the generals are only slightly older at retirement. Colonels and majors, moreover, had

higher rates of disability retirement than senior noncommissioned officers (12.5 percent), who retire at about the same age. The highest rates appropriately went to those who had the most exposure to combat: junior officers (60 percent) and lower-ranked enlisted men (41 percent). Curiously, more Air Force generals were retired for disability (45 percent) than lower-ranked enlisted men. And unsurprisingly, two of every five Air Force generals had been on flying status in the six months prior to retirement.[21]

The number on flight status is a particularly graphic indicator of the degree of misrepresentation in disability ratings. All Air Force officers must be classified as fit for "world-wide service" to collect flight pay, worth an extra $200 a month. Upon retirement, however, they have an incentive to appear in poor health to escape paying taxes on retirement income. Even officers found to have minor disabilities are able to write off $5,200 in taxes annually until age sixty-five as "sick pay" exclusion. As a result, conditions that should have been apparent for years suddenly turn up at retirement physicals. The Air Force insists there is no contradiction since it is possible for an officer to qualify for flying status and yet have "ratable" disabilities—ratable apparently up to 60 and 70 percent.

There is a remarkable symmetry in all this, particularly in the case of Lavelle. The same general who is not punished for real crimes is rewarded for imaginary injuries. Some men suffer grievously for the rest of their lives from the wounds of Vietnam, while others profit for the rest of their lives from the pretense of suffering. At one extreme, there are men like Ned, with injuries for which there can be no real compensation. At the other extreme are men like Lavelle, with compensation and no real injuries.

That, in a nutshell, is the problem of equity.

★ *Patchwork*

Equity and efficiency are directly related. Unjustifiably high ratings for officers absorb funds that might better be spent on services for the genuinely disabled or returned to the public in the form of reduced taxes. Considering the very large expense that military retirement pay already represents ($4.9 billion in 1973), this is an area where an economy-minded administration might well focus its attention.

The potential for waste has been built into the system. All military retirement physicals are performed within the services by military doctors who are often subordinates of the officers they examine. To take an extreme case, in July 1972, Air Force Surgeon General Alonso Towner was processed for retirement at Andrews Air Force Base, where he was examined by his direct subordinates in the Air Force chain of command and ruled 100 percent disabled. Even where conflicts of interest are less apparent, doctors who expect to remain in the military have a strong career interest in evaluating retiring officers favorably. With no outside review or supervision, abuses naturally flourish. So long as disability evaluations are not made by professionals independent of the military, disability pay will probably continue to be regarded as another retirement bonus rather than as compensation for legitimate injuries.

There is a further question as to why there should even be a system of disability benefits administered by the Defense Department, when there is already a parallel system run by the Veterans Administration. Virtually all enlisted men and officers are covered under both programs. This is a prime example of the administrative duplication that pervades the area of veterans' affairs.

The military disability retirement system, initiated during the Civil War, was originally designed only to cover officers and career enlisted men. Unlike veterans' benefits, which are provided without regard to rank, disability retirement pay depends directly on rank and length of service. After World War II, Congress became concerned that short-term enlisted men were not receiving comparable compensation for comparable injuries. In 1949 it passed the Career Compensation Act, throwing open the disability retirement system to short-term enlistees, who previously were required to seek disability compensation through the VA. Although the law stipulated that only one benefit was payable at a time, it left two parallel systems in operation, with each agency conducting its own separate disability evaluations. Given the extremely low correlation between the ratings of the VA and the military, there is naturally a great deal of shopping around by disabled, and nondisabled, servicemen in search of the most sympathetic evaluators. "This double system," stated the Bradley Commission in 1956, "has developed a tremendous duplicate load for the armed services departments and the Veterans Administration." [22]

In practice, officers and senior NCOs generally do better to collect disability retirement pay, whereas lower-grade enlisted men do better under the VA's uniform compensation rates. Officers and enlisted men considered fit by the services, however, can still try their luck at the VA. Although disability evaluations have already been performed by the military, they are repeated all over again when VA claims are submitted. If a retiree submits a claim to the VA and is awarded compensation, his retirement pay is reduced by the amount of compensation he receives. But that can still be to his advantage, for VA disability compensation is 100 percent tax exempt, while the lost retirement pay is not. The existence of the two uncoordinated systems, therefore, provides a ready way to increase tax exemptions, and this encourages some of the unnecessary duplication in physical examinations and administrative effort.

Yet a third agency has entered the picture—the Department of Health, Education, and Welfare. Vietnam veterans with total disabilities can also qualify for benefits under its program of disability insurance. If under twenty-four, they need have made eighteen months of social security payments; if under thirty-one, they must have worked at least half the time after age twenty-one.[23] Since military service (including time spent in hospital care) counts for social security, most are covered. Disability evaluations are performed by state agencies under contract with the Social Security Administration. The judgments of military and VA evaluators are not accepted because of the use of different standards. In the original legislation inaugurating disability insurance there was a provision prohibiting duplicate payment by HEW when another federal agency was already providing benefits. But this provision was soon eliminated after strenuous protests by veterans' organizations.

The result now is that each of the three largest federal agencies has a program covering service-connected injuries: the Department of Defense, through disability retirement; the Veterans Administration, through disability compensation; and HEW, through disability insurance.

The issue is not whether the American people wish to recompense veterans for service-connected injuries. Surely they do. Disability benefits are provided by virtually every nation in the world, and they were the first benefits that the U.S. enacted for veterans. The issue is rather whether we need three different programs in three different agencies to do the same thing. Generosity, we would hope, does not require the multiplication of bureaucracies. A generous compensation program could be administered by a single agency without requiring beneficiaries to fill out several different forms to satisfy slightly different procedures, without duplicating physical examinations, without wasting the time of doctors, evaluation boards, and veterans themselves in endless and redundant proceedings.

The third area that deserves attention is the problem of incentives for positive readjustment, particularly for veterans receiving compensation payments for behavioral and psychiatric problems. As the system currently works, it neatly reverses the usual scheme of rewards and punishments that behavioral psychologists and others use in therapy. Whenever a veteran's condition improves, he is punished by the withdrawal of compensation payments, but so long as his condition persists, he is rewarded with continued benefits. Since hospitalization often serves as proof of ongoing psychiatric problems, the payment system encourages prolonged institutionalization. As Professor Robert Burt of the University of Michigan Law School concludes in a report to the Administrative Conference, "The VA payments eligibility scheme operates in a myriad of ways to reward illness. Whatever its impact regarding physical disabilities, such a scheme must necessarily complicate the treatment of psychiatric disabilities. It creates a stubborn 'defensive reality" which inflicts loss on a veteran and his family on the termination of illness and, even more pointedly, on the termination of inpatient hospitalization." [24]

A veteran who is hospitalized for a service-connected psychiatric illness—and deciding whether such conditions are indeed service-connected represents a problem of Byzantine complexity—is automatically ruled 100 percent disabled after twenty-one days in the hospital. He then receives compensation payments computed, so to speak, from day of deposit to day of withdrawal. Under certain circumstances, he may receive up to six months of payments at the 100 percent rate after he leaves the hospital. Following that period of grace, however, how much he receives is an open question. Writes Professor Burt: "It is possible, of course, that following periodic reexaminations after hospitalization, the 100 percent rating will never be reduced. But neither the hospitalized veteran nor his family can be certain of this. Their only certainty is that continued hospitalization assures continued income at the highest possible rate." [25]

A veteran who is hospitalized for a nonservice-connected psychiatric problem has even more incentive to remain institutionalized. He becomes eligible for a pension only if in need and permanently and totally disabled. No pensions are awarded for partial disability. "A doctor must certify that the nonservice-connected veteran is incurably, i.e., 'permanently,' ill in order to establish eligibility for pension payments while in the hospital. . . . This . . . encourages doctors to give unfavorable prognoses, when in doubt, in order to do a good turn by the nonservice-connected patient and meet his pressing financial needs." [26] However, the moment a nonservice-connected veteran makes steps toward improvement and returning to the community, he endangers his pension payments, for that immediately indicates he is not incurably ill and hence not permanently disabled. It is hard to imagine a system that more effectively undermines the goals of therapy.

A century ago, the U.S. Sanitary Commission established a set of guiding principles for the care of disabled Civil War veterans. They read as follows:[27]

1. As little outside interference with natural laws and self-respect as possible.
2. As much moral and other encouragement and strengthening of the natural reliances as possible.
3. The utmost endeavor to promote the healthy absorption of the invalid class into the homes and into the ordinary industry of the country.

The VA would do well to consider those principles today.

In conclusion, we offer three proposals to deal with some of the problems adumbrated in the preceding pages:

1. That an Independent Medical Board be established to conduct all disability evaluations for federal programs under a uniform set of standards and that its decision be final subject to judicial appeal, now lacking. Such a board, organized on a regional basis, might also be made responsible for conducting physical examinations for military induction, workmen's compensation, civil service retirement, and other programs. Its records would be confidential in the same sense that personal income tax records are kept confidential by the Internal Revenue Service. Such a board would be free of the conflicts of interest apparent in the military retirement system. It would eliminate the costly duplication of examinations among federal agencies. Its judgments on service-connected disabilities would be forwarded to the agency responsible for making payments. This might be the Defense Department, the VA, or HEW—which one is not particularly important.

2. That a critical review be made of military disability retirements and that ratings be reduced wherever evidence for service-connected injuries is lacking.

3. That the practice of awarding disability payments for behavioral and psychiatric problems be reviewed, with an eye to

eliminating the conflict between the compensation system and the goals of treatment, perhaps by shifting funds from monetary payments to the provision of community services aimed at facilitating "the healthy absorption" of the disoriented "into the homes and into the ordinary industry of the country."

This, as we shall see in the next chapter, is only one way in which the amount of institutional care by the VA might be sensibly reduced.

4
Veteran's Hospitals: New Injuries and Old

Among all the programs offered to the nation's veterans, only one involves the maintenance of separate veterans' institutions. Education programs have never entailed the formation of separate veterans' schools or training institutes. In fact, the law requires that every school where veterans enroll with government aid attract a certain proportion of nonveterans as well. Employment programs have not entailed the creation of separate veterans' businesses; rather they have sought to increase veterans' employment within existing businesses and government agencies. Housing programs provide loan guarantees; they do not provide separate veterans' housing.

The sole exception to this policy is the veterans' hospital system, and its unique structure has created a variety of profound and disturbing problems. That these problems should be reviewed at the end of the Vietnam War is entirely proper. It was after World War I that the system was established and after World War II that it grew to its present size. As the victims of war are so easily forgotten during most stretches of peace, so are the institutions where they are treated. Yet the VA system represents the largest in the United States: 170 hospitals, with nearly 100,000 beds and 1 million patients treated annually.

In recent years the veterans' hospitals have had a singularly bad press. Television documentaries and magazine articles have created a picture of misery, inefficiency, filth, and indifference. In some ways these exposés have been both too harsh and too generous. Too harsh, because many community hospitals, in the inner city and rural areas, provide a much lower quality of care than the VA. Too generous, because the exposés have tended to focus on conditions that were scandalous but limited in scope, rather than on the deep-seated structural problems that pervade the VA system.

Also lacking in the public debate on the VA hospitals has been any consideration of their future under a program of national health insurance. Congressional hearings and statements by the Nixon administration on proposed legislation in that area have ignored its possible impact on the VA. The oversight has not been entirely accidental. Knowing that, in the long run, national health insurance probably dooms the VA system, legislators and executive planners have been anxious to avoid stirring up opposition from the powerful veterans' lobby.

The problems that beset the VA hospitals are roughly of three kinds. Some arise from limited resources, others from conflicting functions, and still a third group from the constraints of institutional structure.

Limited resources primarily involve personnel shortages and deteriorating physical facilities. For those who see only a problem of resources in the VA, the object of fiercest criticism is usually the Office of Management and Budget (OMB), which has the unhappy duty of implementing Presidential priorities. But the origin of resource problems is only in part budgetary. Behind a personnel shortage in the VA, for example, stands a general shortage of medical manpower in the nation as a whole and a long history of resistance to the use of paramedical personnel. Behind a shortage of funds in the VA stand rapidly escalating costs throughout the health industry. To blame OMB for these maladies is perhaps convenient, but definitely shortsighted.

The second set of problems involves conflicting functions. The less serious of these we shall discuss rather briefly: the tension between patient care and medical education in the approximately one hundred VA facilities that serve as teaching hospitals. A more critical problem—and one which bears more directly on our general themes—is the conflict created by the arrival of young, recently injured Vietnam veterans in what is essentially a system of health facilities for treatment of the chronically ill.

We take as our basic premise that the preeminent function of the VA system, its whole *raison d'être*, is to treat war casualties and to provide them with superior care that would otherwise be unavailable. But in fact, treating war casualties is a small part of what the VA does; only 15 percent of its cases are service-connected. More important, it does not discharge that function with any marked distinction. The reason is not simply a lack of funds.

As the system has evolved, it has become heavily oriented toward long institutionalization and the care of chronic illness, primarily for the elderly. There is no question that we need facilities for chronic disease, but one may doubt whether we need to treat young veterans in them and whether such institutions afford an optimal climate for their therapy and rehabilitation. That this arrangement is highly unsatisfactory to the men themselves is evident not only from the views they have registered in attitude surveys, but much more graphically in the data on how many hospital discharges they take "against medical advice." One study conducted at the VA hospital in Downey, Illinois, for example, showed that Vietnam veterans treated for psychiatric problems had a significantly higher rate of discharges against medical advice than did older veterans— 23.71 percent versus 14.86 percent.[1] A much larger study of about 2,000 patients admitted to the psychiatric service of the Hines, Illinois, VA hospital, covering the four years between January 1968 and December 1971, showed that 33.8 percent of Vietnam era veterans, but only 13.74 percent of older veterans, sought discharge against medical advice.[2] When a hospital system is losing a quarter to a third of a group of patients against professional judgment, there is surely good cause for inquiry.

The problem of conflicting functions will come up again, even more strongly, in the next chapter when we discuss the VA's programs in the area of drug abuse. Here again a major issue is whether an institution which has become primarily oriented toward institutionalized treatment of the chronic diseases of the aged is the appropriate agency to deal with the very different emotional problems of young veterans. This is a question that arises specifically because the federal government maintains a separate institutional system for delivering health services to veterans, rather than financing programs within general health institutions.

Structurally, the VA system is characterized by two features that distinguish it from other health care facilities. First, it serves a limited but geographically dispersed segment of the nation's population, a segment that is almost entirely male. Nonveterans, including members of a veteran's own family, cannot receive any treatment at the VA. We shall call this the *exclusivity constraint.* Second, by law, the medical services that the VA can provide to its patients are severely circumscribed according to criteria unrelated to medical need. We shall call this the *constraint on service*, and it should be emphasized that this is a legal constraint on medical decisions, not just a limitation in the extent of coverage.

The service constraint requires some elucidation. Some people believe that veterans are eligible only for care of war injuries at the VA; others think they may receive complete medical services there. The truth lies in between, and it is precisely this halfway and ambiguous eligibility that creates a wall of paper between doctor and patient and disturbs continuity of care from one medical problem to the next. As the law now stands, veterans may obtain treatment for all illnesses and injuries certified as "service-connected." But they may receive treatment for "nonservice-connected" medical problems only if they might warrant hospitalization and only if they cannot pay for treatment on their own.

Alone, either of these two structural features—a limited but geographically dispersed patient population and limited authority to care for that population—would be an impediment to good health services. Together, they constitute an obstacle of major proportions. The VA can address itself neither to a whole community nor to a whole family, nor even to a whole patient. The consequences will be elaborated at length below. Briefly we may indicate a few of them:

—VA facilities tend to be relatively inaccessible (compared with other health facilities) and are therefore heavily oriented toward chronic rather than acute care.

—The system is unable to provide comprehensive family medicine, and its patients cannot be treated by their family doctors.

—It does little in the way of preventive care.

—Resources are wasted in determining whether or not medical problems originated in military service instead of simply treating them regardless of their origins.

—The VA system has hospitalized many patients who would be treated better, and more cheaply, on an outpatient basis.

—Because of variations in eligibility, individual veterans cannot be guaranteed continuity of care.

—Admission procedures are highly bureaucratic.

—There tends to be a certain amount of unnecessary duplication of services and equipment by VA and community hospitals, and, especially in smaller communities, nonveterans are sometimes excluded from specialized services available only at the VA.

If someone had planned the VA medical program with deliberation, one would be driven to question the planner's judgment. But the VA system was never planned; it grew incrementally and haphazardly through the push-and-pull of political forces. The push for growth has come principally from veterans' organizations and Congressmen interested in acquiring VA facilities for their home districts regardless of the size of the local veteran population. The resistance to growth has come from powerful medical societies fundamentally hostile to the public provision of health care. Both the limitation of the VA to a specific population and the limitation on services derive essentially from the opposition of organized medicine to the extension of government medical programs. This opposition has been stated explicitly by the American Medical Association on numerous occasions. In 1945, for example, when pressure developed to expand the services of the VA, the AMA quickly registered its displeasure. One resolution before the AMA House of Delegates, indicative of the group's sentiment, reaffirmed the organization's "long-established opposition to any attempt at the socialization of medicine in America by extending medical benefits under the Veterans Administration to encompass disabilities that obviously are not service-connected or to general medical care of the dependents of veterans." [3] Seeking to preserve its clientele and the fee-for-service payment system in ambulatory care, organized medicine used the same political leverage that it used to block comprehensive health insurance to establish the limits—and ultimately the limitations—of VA medicine. The structure of the VA system is more a product of its external political environment than its internal professional judgment.

As the power of the AMA has declined, so the opportunity for reform of the VA has risen. Many of the professionals within the system are well aware of its structural deficiencies. In recent years they have obtained several legislative changes and proposed others to loosen both the exclusivity and service constraints. While these changes have met some problems, they have aggravated others by expanding entitlement to outpatient services without similarly expanding the system's resources. As testimony from individual hospitals indicates, new benefits have been added while personnel and facilities have not grown in proportion, creating a situation where the system has been overtaxed and the quality of care may have deteriorated. In practice, therefore, the problems of limited resources and institutional structure have become inextricably interwoven. Attempts to alleviate the system's structural deficiencies have been hampered by its lack of adequate resources. And the shortage of resources has, in turn, been exacerbated by attempts to reshape the system.

Before discussing these problems, however, it would be wise to examine some basic aspects of the VA system: its origins, the extent of its facilities, its relationship to other medical institutions, and the character of its patients.

★ An Overview

Origins and Organization

The veterans' hospital system was created in the aftermath of World War I, when in 1922 President Warren G. Harding transferred fifty-seven hospitals then being operated for veterans by the U.S. Public Health Service to the Veterans Bureau, predecessor to the VA. The system made an inauspicious public debut. Within two years it was rocked by a scandal that involved the private sale of medical supplies, extravagant land deals, and misuse of public funds and that ended in the suicide of the General Counsel of the bureau and the conviction and imprisonment of its Director, Colonel Charles Forbes. Soon thereafter the system passed from notoriety into mediocrity and oblivion. Though it expanded during the Depression, the VA was generally considered a backwater of American medicine and had great difficulty attracting competent physicians. It was rescued finally by a surge of public concern at the end of World War II. The system was reinvigorated with new leadership, doctors who had served in the armed forces were induced to transfer into the VA, affiliations with medical schools were established, the number of hospitals jumped from ninety to about 160, and the quality of care seems to have been significantly upgraded.

Since that time, veterans' hospitals have remained essentially stable in number and organization. While new hospitals have been built, old ones have been taken out of service, and the veterans' organizations have had their hands full just trying to keep more from being closed down. With new federal health care programs likely in the near future, the government has been reluctant to make any long-term investments in the VA. While it represents the largest organized system of health services in the country, the VA is an aging system with an uncertain future.

Physically, the system consists of a network of 136 general medical and surgical hospitals and thirty-four neuropsychiatric hospitals. (These numbers are subject to slight variation; the trend is to eliminate separate mental hospitals and convert them to general hospitals with large psychiatric services.) The agency operates about 200 outpatient clinics, thirty-six of them physically autonomous from the hospitals. It also maintains an array of extended care facilities—sixteen domiciles, six restoration centers, and seventy-six nursing bed care units (located within hospitals).[4] Size affords a number of advantages. Complicated conditions such as blindness and spinal cord injury can be handled in specialized treatment centers. The system is large enough to do its own data processing. Drugs and supplies are purchased in quantity and below market prices, though not as cheaply as the military acquires them. Medical research can draw on a uniquely large national reservoir of subjects in highly controlled and standardized settings. There are certain economies of scale in management. In many ways, the VA hospitals, simply because they are part of a system, are less inefficient than most community hospitals, which operate without the benefit of any coordination or system of accountability. This is an aspect of the VA that must be kept in mind before rendering a judgment on it.

While the VA is authorized to maintain 125,000 hospital beds, it has never reached that number; during fiscal year 1972, its operating beds averaged 98,352. Currently the average daily patient census stands at approximately 82,000.[5] Thus the occupancy rate has been around 83 percent, which is generally considered normal.

Since the late Fifties and at an accelerating pace after 1965, the VA has been reducing both the number of its hospital beds and its daily census. In 1958 the system maintained 121,000 beds and a census of 111,000; since then, its capacity has been cut by about 20 percent. The reductions have been offset by an increasing rate of patient turnover, so that the total number of patients treated annually in the VA has not fallen. (Table 4.1)

Most of the reduction in VA capacity has come from psychiatric hospitals, which have lost more than 15,000 beds since 1965. The cutback does not signify any reduction in care. "It reflects the extent to which we are using more outpatient facilities, day care centers, and the like," explains Dr. Marc Musser, VA Medical Director. "This is in line with the effort to keep psychiatric patients in the community and minimize hospitalization."[6] In this respect, the VA has not been unique, since similar shifts have been taking place in psychiatric care throughout the country. The real question, in fact, is not why the VA has reduced its institutionalized psychiatric population, but why it has not reduced it further.

Three additional reasons for the overall drop in capacity have been of lesser magnitude. First, a number of hospital beds were not really lost, but converted to nursing care. Second, about 1,200 were eliminated in 1965 when six outmoded hospitals were closed by Presidential order. Third, shortages of personnel caused by the

TABLE 4.1. TRENDS IN THE VA MEDICAL SYSTEM

	1960	1965	1970
Hospital Inpatients			
Operating beds (average)	120,257	119,118	102,634
General medical & surgical	65,056	62,970	60,934
Psychiatric	55,201	56,148	41,700
Average daily census	111,408	109,183	85,547
Patients treated	637,377	730,511	780,487
Turnover rate	38.3	46.2	65.4
Domiciliary Members			
Operating beds (average)	17,486	16,544	13,220
Average daily census	16,856	14,380	11,998
Nursing Care Patients			
Operating beds (average)	—	208	4,002
Average daily census	—	150	3,760

Sources: *Veterans' Administration Hospital Funding and Personnel Needs*, Hearings Before the Subcommittee on Hospitals of the Committee on Veterans' Affairs, House of Representatives, 91st Cong. 2nd sess., 1970, p. 2877; *1970 Annual Report*, Administrator of Veterans' Affairs. Washington, D.C.: Government Printing Office, 1971.

Revenue and Expenditure Control Act of 1968 forced the VA to deactivate a number of bed sections.[7]

Since 1968, the personnel lost under that act have been restored, but the beds have not. Indeed, further reductions in capacity have taken place. VA Administrator Donald Johnson has defended these additional cutbacks with the argument that they are the only means available for improving the ratio of staff to patients. "Our position," Mr. Johnson told a House Appropriations Subcommittee in 1970, "is that if we are to attack the problem of staffing ratios, with the national problem of scarcity of health personnel, we do have to limit the patient census in our hospitals, in order to bring this staffing ratio up to an acceptable level." [8]

Institutional Linkages

Since private doctors are not allowed to treat patients at VA hospitals, and VA doctors are not supposed to have private practices, the VA system is rather sharply separated from the networks of private medical practice. But it is by no means cut off from the centers of medical education. More than half of the VA hospitals—just over one hundred—are affiliated with medical schools and serve as teaching hospitals.

In earlier days, many VA facilities, particularly those for psychiatric illnesses and tuberculosis, were built in rural areas on the thesis that a pastoral environment was conducive to patient recovery and a satisfied rural Congressman was conducive to higher budgets. Unfortunately, it proved rather difficult to recruit topflight medical personnel to such bucolic spots, and the quality of care in VA hospitals suffered enormously. General Paul Hawley, who became medical director of the VA immediately after World War II, abruptly reversed the agency's construction policy. ("To hell with the scenery," he is reputed to have said. "We want the best doctors." [9]) The decision turned out to be a watershed in the VA's development. Since that time, virtually all new hospitals have been built in urban areas in the vicinity of medical schools. The result today is what Dr. David Rutstein of Harvard, a member of an advisory committee to the VA, calls a "double system." [10] The affiliated hospitals not only enjoy an advantage in recruitment of personnel, but are more modern and more centrally located than the unaffiliated institutions. They have established residency and internship programs and added skilled medical professors and researchers to their staffs. Training programs in affiliated hospitals not only attract more competent personnel; they facilitate the assimilation of new medical knowledge into patient care.

But at the same time, affiliation has introduced new interests and new conflicts into the VA. There is, for example, an unfortunate tendency in most teaching hospitals to pay more attention to "interesting cases" than to people who are very sick in an ordinary way. This arises not out of insensitivity, but from a difference in priorities. While patient care mostly involves routine, professional instruction necessarily aims at preparing students to handle the difficult cases that deviate from routine. Moreover, some "interesting" patients quite reasonably resent being used for someone else's instruction. They just want to go home well.[11]

Another major consequence of medical school affiliation is that the VA has increasingly been drawn into direct support of biomedical research, in terms of both budget and space. Again, as with teaching, the function of research is not incompatible with patient care, but a difference in priorities does exist. Moreover, the activities of the VA in the area of research and training, as James A. Shannon, former director of the National Institutes of Health, has said, "are not subject to central review in the development of overall national objectives for biomedical research, medical education, residency training, and the production of other health manpower. These VA activities are not meaningfully related to broader community planning directed toward the evolution of more rational means of provision of health care. Further, they are not considered in relation to other Federal health programs. . . ." [12]

The medical profession in the United States has traditionally been split between private practitioners with an entrepreneurial outlook and hospital-based academic physicians with a predominantly scientific and technocratic outlook. The private practitioners have never looked with favor on the VA, considering it a fledgling form of socialized medicine. It was natural, therefore, that the VA should have allied itself with the teaching and research institutions. They have generally been a more progressive force, and the association has probably benefited VA patients a great deal. But at the same time, academic physicians too have their distinct interests, and any system of health services that places patient care first must guard jealously against their inroads.

Patterns of Utilization

Much of the character of a health system depends upon the character of its patients. To say without elaboration that the VA hospitals treat veterans would be misleading; they treat a small fraction of them. According to data from the National Center for Health Statistics, only about 14.6 percent of the hospitalizations of veterans take place at the VA.[13] In other words, when a veteran needs hospital care, the odds are about six to one that he will *not* enter a hospital run by the Veterans Administration.

Since care in a VA hospital is free of charge for those that are eligible, this low rate of utilization may seem puzzling. The enigma disappears, however, if one looks at the structure of opportunities and costs facing the individual veteran at the point of decision.

Two of the most important elements in a decision on hospitalization will be the accessibility and expense of care. Since other health facilities are more widely distributed than those of the VA, a community hospital will ordinarily be closer to a veteran's home or workplace. So long as there are more than 7,000 community hospitals and only 170 VA hospitals, this situation will persist. No amount of careful planning can alter the balance of convenience. The relative inaccessibility of the VA system stems directly from the exclusivity constraint mentioned earlier.

As for expense, about 80 percent of the nation's veterans are currently covered by some form of health insurance, usually either a private plan provided through a collective bargaining agreement or a governmental program such as Medicare and Medicaid.[14] Consequently, at the point of decision, utilization of a VA facility will not necessarily entail a financial saving.

A number of other considerations act as a deterrent to using the VA. The regulations on eligibility have both direct and indirect effects. The veteran with a nonservice-oriented condition may be unable to sign the statement that he is too poor to pay the costs of private hospitalization either because he considers the "pauper's oath" an indignity or because it simply would be untrue. He may also be uncertain whether his illness qualifies for VA care. Rather than confront possible bureaucratic difficulties in gaining admission, he may choose another institution where he is sure to be treated. This is likely to be of great importance in acute conditions. Finally, a veteran who wants to be treated by a trusted family physician, or who is unimpressed with the quality of care in VA hospitals, may go elsewhere, even if the expense is greater.

These considerations influencing the veteran's decision—accessibility, expense, eligibility regulations, uncertainty, and reputation—do not act with equal force on all veterans at all times. They tend to select out a patient population that is poorer, older, and more subject to chronic disease than the average. These tendencies can be verified directly from government statistics on hospital utilization.

As a veteran's income rises, according to a study by the National Center for Health Statistics, his use of federal hospitals decreases sharply. (Data for the study were drawn from household surveys around 1960. Though the income levels would be scaled upward today to take account of inflation and some growth in real wages, there is no reason to believe that the basic patterns have changed in the intervening years.) Among veterans with incomes less than $2,000, about four of every ten hospitalizations occurred in federal hospitals. This proportion drops to less than three in ten for those with incomes between $2,000 and $3,999 and falls to less than one in ten for those with incomes over $4,000.[15] The preponderance of the indigent and the medically indigent in VA hospitals is hardly surprising. It is written into the laws on financial eligibility.

This pattern is evident among the relatively small number of Vietnam veteran patients. A survey of 200 Vietnam era veterans at the VA hospital in Dallas in 1971 showed that at the time of admission "over 40 percent were unemployed and over 60 percent were either unemployed, retired, or only temporary or part-time employees."[16]

Utilization of VA hospitals increases steeply with age. According to a report in the *American Journal of Public Health*, among veterans under thirty-five, the annual utilization rate is 1.4 per 1,000. The corresponding figure for veterans aged sixty-five to seventy-four rises to more than twelve, and climbs to nineteen for men seventy-five and older.[17] The average age of VA patients is 51.6 years.[18]

Finally, the higher utilization of VA facilities among veterans with chronic diseases appears clearly from data on hospital discharges broken down according to diagnostic categories. While VA hospitals treat between 2 and 10 percent of all veterans hospitalized for appendicitis, hemorrhoids, upper respiratory conditions, fractures, dislocations, and other current injuries, they treat 33 percent of the cases of arthritis and 35 percent of mental disorders.[19]

The predominance of the chronically ill in the VA has had broad implications for the nature and quality of care it provides. It affects the temper and climate of the hospitals, their manpower requirements and costs, personnel recruitment, and the average length of patient stay (which we take up next). But its major consequence is that it has made the VA a particularly inappropriate agency to deal with the mental and physical problems of recently injured young soldiers.

Average Length of Stay

Despite increases in its rate of patient turnover, the average stay in VA general hospitals continues to run three times as long as in community hospitals—twenty-four days in the VA system, eight days elsewhere.[20] The principal reason for this extraordinary difference is clearly the VA's tendency to receive a higher proportion of the chronically ill. However, as Table 4.2 indicates, this is not the only factor. When specific operations are compared, it is evident that VA hospitals take more time than others to complete the same procedures.

Until recently, this pattern was usually explained on the basis of the VA's budgetary procedures. Since an individual VA hospital's budget was determined by its patient census, hospitals with light loads had an incentive to keep patients longer than necessary. According to VA officials, however, criticism by outside analysts brought a change in this practice, and a more complicated budgetary formula, taking turnover into account, is now used. Whether this has altered the situation is unclear. In any event, several additional factors seem to be involved, among them the socio-economic character of the VA patient population and inefficiencies and shortages in the VA system.

TABLE 4.2. AVERAGE LENGTH OF STAY AND TYPE OF OPERATION
(in days)

Operation	Short-term, non-Federal hospitals	VA hospitals
Appendectomy	6.5	10.4
Tonsillectomy	1.9	6.1
Hemorrhoidectomy	8.6	13.9
Herniotomy (inguinal)	7.7	15.7

Source: Testimony of Mr. Dudley Porter, representing the Health Insurance Association of America, in *Veterans' Administration Hospital Funding and Personnel Needs*, Hearings Before the Subcommittee on Hospitals of the Committee on Veterans' Affairs, House of Representatives, 91st Cong. 2nd sess., 1970, p. 3347. The data appear to be from 1966; in the interim, the VA may have partially closed the gap. No attempt to rebut these figures was made at the hearing.

The class status of VA patients prolongs both the early and later phases of care. Few have personal physicians. Of one hundred consecutive admissions to a Boston VA hospital in November 1971, seventy-six walked in on their own, ten had been referred from other facilities, and fourteen had been referred by private doctors.[21] When self-referred patients enter a hospital, a preliminary work-up and diagnosis (ordinarily the job of a family physician) have yet to be done. Often it turns out that mutliple problems are involved, which also prolongs treatment. And finally, the more conscientious staff physicians will tend to delay discharging poorer patients who cannot count on adequate care, food, and housing once they leave the hospital.

The VA can hardly be faulted for such practices. If its hospitals receive more of the poor and the chronically ill, that is not something the agency can or should change. Nonetheless, the longer length of stay in VA hospitals is not entirely a consequence of phenomena beyond its control. Part of the explanation for prolonged hospitalization in the VA is sheer inefficiency. According to doctors who have served both in veterans' hospitals and elsewhere, treatment is retarded by delays in laboratory work due to personnel shortages. It is difficult, says Dr. S. Richardson Hill, director of the University of Alabama Medical Center, "for our students and house staff to provide proper care for Veterans Administration patients because of delays in obtaining tests, such as GI series, glucose tolerance tests, and other tests which they feel are procedurally necessary to diagnose and treat their patients, [so] that sometimes the patient has to remain in the hospital two or three weeks longer than he would otherwise, just to get a particular test." [22]

Congressional interference in the care of specific patients is also reported to be a factor. Staff members at the VA hospital in Martinsburg, West Virginia, explained that they often put a little "u" next to the names of certain patients on their charts to indicate the men are "untouchable." Even though they are healthy enough to leave the hospital, the staff has been told that they cannot be discharged because a Congressman has intervened on their behalf— or rather on behalf of families that do not want to take care of the men at home. [23]

Still other factors prolonging care have to do with the VA's system of disability compensation, which often penalizes a patient and his family by reducing their income when he leaves a hospital. As mentioned earlier, this puts material incentives at odds with the goals of therapy, particularly for psychiatric patients. There are also more elusive, psychological factors involved. For some men, a veterans' hospital offers the same security and camaraderie the military once did, and just as there are men who prefer the security of the army to civilian life, so there are some who prefer the security of the hospital. In *One Flew Over the Cuckoo's Nest*, a satirical novel set in a VA mental hospital on the West Coast, Ken Kesey has given a sympathetic portrait of these men.

★ *Strains and Constraints*

Limited Resources

We have already mentioned that the VA has tried to increase its low staffing levels in part by reducing its patient census and that personnel shortages appear at least partly responsible for the longer average length of stay in VA hospitals. The dimensions of the staffing problem may be seen in rough outline from aggregate statistical data. Despite increases following a Congressional uproar in 1971, the VA still has an overall ratio of only 146 employees for every 100 patients. Of these 146 employees, ninety-three are involved in direct patient care and fifty-three in general and administrative support. [24] Most VA hospitals stand far from the agency's stated objective of a two-to-one staffing ratio for medical and surgical patients. But even if the VA does reach that level, it will rank far below community and university hospitals. In 1970, community hospitals had 292 employees for each hundred patients. [25] The comparable figure for university hospitals stood between 350 and 400.

Officials of the VA have been quick to point out that such overall statistics are in many ways unfair bases of comparison. VA hospitals have no pediatric or obstetric wards, both of which require high staffing levels. Nor do they deal with as many acutely ill patients, who also require more attention. Finally, there are differences in record keeping between VA and community hospitals that render across-the-board comparisons hazardous. However, a VA survey that seems to have taken account of such irregularities disclosed the same pattern and in greater detail. The survey compared nine VA hospitals, ranging from 188 beds to 1,565, with eight community hospitals, ranging from 130 to 1,063 beds. The VA had an overall ratio of 1.70 employees per operating bed and the community hospitals 3.23. The VA did have more voluntary workers, but not enough to make up the difference. When volunteers were added to employees, the VA ratio rose to 1.81 workers per operating bed and the community hospitals' ratio to 3.31. Thus, no matter how one counts, the community hospitals were apparently almost twice as well staffed. Even more graphic were the figures on nursing employees; the VA came out particularly short on the evening and night shifts. The day tour was about 50 percent better staffed in community hospitals, while evening and night tours were about 100 percent better staffed. The survey specifically excluded from consideration nursery, labor, and delivery rooms because the VA does not provide those services.[26]

Turning to surveys of individual VA hospitals, the picture looks equally bleak. A study conducted for the House Veterans' Affairs Committee in November 1970 and published in February 1971 revealed a rather consistent picture. Asked to name their three most pressing needs, the overwhelming majority of the hospitals cited additional staffing. A typical report came from Salisbury, North Carolina: "Over the last three years, the hospital has suffered a reduction in personnel due to the imposition of personnel ceilings and shortages of funds. . . . On the basis of one-to-one staffing ratio for psychiatric patients and two-to-one staffing ratio for GM&S [general medical and surgical] patients, we are in need of one hundred forty-four additional employees. . . . In addition, the outpatient clinic located approximately forty miles north of the hospital, has minimal staffing with a tremendously expanding workload. . . . There is no question that treatment programs are hampered by the lack of highly skilled and competent physicians." [27]

In an internal report in March 1970, the VA's Department of Medicine and Surgery drew the same picture:

Today there are serious constraints on VA's ability to achieve [its] objectives. There are serious shortages in the number of physicians, nurses, and other categories of scarce health personnel which must be overcome by improving VA's ability to attract and retain such personnel. The Federal Government's tight budget policies in its fight against inflation have imposed serious fiscal constraints on our ability to employ adequate numbers of personnel even when available. Budget limitations also restrict our abilities to provide other necessary resources, particularly facilities and equipment.[28]

Congress responded to the situation in early 1971 by providing additional appropriations to the hospitals over the objections of the Nixon administration. These funds apparently relieved some immediate shortages, but the basic problems persist. Commenting in March 1973 on reductions in the VA's requested personnel budget imposed by OMB, a report by the House Appropriations Committee stated that "VA hospitals are being forced to limit their patient workload or operate with staffing shortages which seriously affect the quality of patient care to the point of possibly endangering the health of patients." [29]

The problem is not simply a matter of a parsimonious administration, but of a hospital system that develops shortages as it seeks to correct its organizational handicaps. One of the most critical of these handicaps has been the limitation on outpatient care for nonservice-connected cases. Over the past decade, this constraint has been eased somewhat as Congress has approved limited outpatient services when needed as preparation or follow-up for hospital care. Reports from the hospitals, however, suggest that these changes have been inadequately underwritten and that the demands on the system have been growing beyond its capacity to meet them. "The most pressing problem facing the hospital today," the director of the VA hospital in Atlanta stated in 1970, "is our inability to meet new or increasing demands created by new legislation, new veterans, and an aging population. It appears that the enactment of new legislation providing additional benefits is not usually funded adequately." [30] The Des Moines, Iowa, VA hospital reported the same problem:

The greatest changes in recent years have been the result of liberalization of outpatient benefits; (e.g. in the past four fiscal years) fee dental costs have risen 760 percent; prosthetic costs have risen 23 percent, and staff medical visit costs have risen 22 percent. Most of these and other changes that could be cited were funded "after the fact." Funding has generally given consideration only to the direct costs involved and slighted, if not ignored, the substantial overhead costs necessary to implement the program. These costs include salaries, space, and equipment. As a result of the rapid and unanticipated growth in outpatient activities, the inpatient part of the hospital operation has had to pay.[31]

These reports and others from hospital administrators suggest that the VA's situation may have deteriorated in recent years. There is at least some prima facie evidence for this view in trend data on hospital expenditures, though comparisons are rather tricky, since the VA does not include the same items as community hospitals in computing expenses. Choosing the proper index of measurement is also difficult. The VA is involved primarily in chronic care, and consequently its average costs *per patient day* tend to be significantly lower than those of community hospitals. In 1970 the average cost per patient day was $38.42 in the VA system and $81.01 in community hospitals.[32] Supporters of the VA inevitably point to this comparison as evidence of its superior efficiency.

However, turning to another index of cost—average cost *per patient treated*—the situation looks rather different. In 1970 the average per patient cost was $1,524 in the VA system and $664 in community hospitals.[33] The explanation for this seeming inversion lies in the higher proportion of chronic patients and the longer average length of stay in VA hospitals.

TABLE 4.3. Average Cost Per Patient Day

	VA	Community	VA/Community
1958	$16.84	$28.27	.60
1960	18.44	32.23	.57
1963	21.56	38.91	.55
1965	23.75	44.48	.53
1966	24.90	48.15	.52
1967	27.91	54.08	.50
1968	30.53	61.38	.50
1969	34.16	70.03	.49
1970	38.42	81.01	.47

Sources: For the VA, *HUD-Space-Science Appropriations for 1972*, Hearings Before a Subcommittee of the Committee on Appropriations, House of Representatives, 92nd Cong. 1st sess., 1971, p. 502; for community hospitals, *Hospitals*, 45:454, August 1971.

The interesting point, however, lies in neither of these deceptive comparisons, but rather in the changing ratio of VA to community costs (see Table 4.3, column 3). Since 1958 VA expenditures have been steadily and appreciably declining relative to other hospitals; this, while its turnover rate has been increasing. The probable cause of the decline is that while staffing ratios in community hospitals have been growing significantly over the years, those in the VA have not. What the VA points to as thrift, its patients may see in another light.

This point, however, should not be taken too far. In many respects, VA hospitals are more efficiently run than community hospitals, which for duplication of expensive but rarely used services, conflicts of interest, uncompetitive bidding, and general fiscal unaccountability are hard for any organized system to match. Under the triple influence of growing third-party payment mechanisms, ineffective cost controls and proliferating marginal technology, community hospitals have allowed their costs to rise at twice the rate of inflation. That the Veterans Administration has avoided some of the problems evident among community hospitals is to its credit. That money has also been saved by chronic understaffing is not.

Low personnel levels are only part of the VA's staffing problem. It is not simply that the agency has too few budgeted positions, but that it has difficulty attracting and retaining people to fill them. The extent to which it is forced to rely on foreign-trained doctors is indicative. As of 1970 they constituted about one in every four of the VA's physicians, as opposed to one in every six in the nation as a whole.[34] In a period when the United States has supposedly shown its largesse in foreign aid, it is rather left-handed of us to import large numbers of doctors from developing countries to treat our own war veterans.

Foreign-trained doctors are by no means necessarily less skilled than Americans, but many of them have serious language problems. Gather a group of VA employees together and one soon hears stories about the Swedish psychiatrist who couldn't understand his patients' colloquial speech, the Austrian ear doctor who couldn't make himself understood, and similar cases. The issue is not xenophobia, but communication.

The recruitment of physicians is particularly difficult in the rural unaffiliated hospitals. The VA mental hospital in Brecksville, Ohio, for example, reports an "inability to recruit and retain well-qualified physicians, especially in psychiatry and in medical specialties. In part, this is due to salary, but probably more important is a lack of affiliation with a medical school with resultant active teaching and research programs." [35] Dr. Amos Johnson, past president of the American Academy of Family Practice, says the medical staff of rural VA hospitals is generally comprised of "physicians who are semi-retired, those who have chronic illness which limits their activities, and those who do not anticipate nor meet the challenge of the competitive practice of medicine." [36] At a meeting of VA employees in the Midwest, one nurse's aide from the Tomah, Wisconsin, hospital said, "When we get a new doctor, we usually ask, 'What's *he* suffering from?' " [37]

In the area of nursing, the VA has a severe problem retaining personnel for any length of time. Rapid rates of turnover in a hospital can hurt the quality of care as much as low staffing levels. In recent years the VA has annually lost a fifth of its registered nurses and a quarter of its licensed practical nurses. According to the VA, "The major reasons for leaving were to seek further education or lack of possibility for advancement or both." [38] Paramedical workers who, if used well, could alleviate shortages of manpower have also found their careers blocked. Before 1970, the VA had no place for physicians' assistants—odd considering the vital role medics have played in military medicine. Although VA officials now express strong interest in introducing physicians' assistants, only one in eight VA hospitals has them, and the numbers involved are small. Many ex-corpsmen and medics now serve as nurses' aides—positions where they are unable to use many of the skills they were taught in the service. They find that there are no programs to upgrade their status in the VA, and consequently many leave when better jobs in other fields open up.

In the long run, however, the VA probably offers one of the best opportunities for the reform of professional roles in medicine. Legislation passed in the 92nd Congress to improve VA training programs emphasized the need for training paramedical workers. Moreover, since all VA hospitals are located in federal enclaves, they are unfettered by outdated state licensing laws. If the VA moves forcefully in this direction, it may be able to overcome not only its staffing problems, but its reputation for stodginess.

Structural Constraints (I): Limited Services

When the veterans' hospital system was originally organized after World War I, it was used solely for the care of illnesses and disabilities stemming from the war. Within a few years, however, the number of service-connected cases declined to the point where they were no longer sufficient to fill available beds. "The existence of an underutilized part of any organization," writes the economist Kenneth Boulding, "is a constant provocation to expansion." [39] So it was with veterans' hospitals. In 1924 the Veterans Bureau was authorized by Congress to open its unused hospital beds for treatment of the nonservice-connected conditions of wartime veterans. Under the initial guidelines, only hospitalization would be available; outpatient care would be restricted to service-connected cases to accommodate partisans of the AMA who feared that the government might compete with private practitioners.

Nonservice-connected cases are no longer just taking up excess space in the VA system. Today 85 percent of the discharges from VA hospitals are for problems unrelated to military service.[40] Nevertheless, it is still true that only service-connected cases are entitled to full medical services. The limitations on treatment have had serious consequences both for the patients and for the VA system itself.

If a veteran's condition has been established as service-connected, a number of things will ordinarily follow. First, he will have priority in hospital admissions; if a bed or service is not immediately available, the VA will contract out to another institution or to a private doctor to secure treatment for him. Second, no questions will be asked about his ability to pay for private care. And third, he will be able to receive treatment either as an inpatient in a VA hospital or as an outpatient at a VA clinic.

If, on the other hand, the veteran's problem is unrelated to his military service, the situation will be somewhat different. He will first see an admitting physician to determine whether hospital care is warranted. If the physician decides it is, the veteran will be admitted, provided that space is available and the patient signs a statement saying that he cannot afford the costs of treatment himself. Under new legislation approved in August 1973, the VA can also provide outpatient care to the medically indigent when it is "reasonably necessary to obviate the need for hospital admission." (Previously it could provide ambulatory services only if they preceded or followed hospitalization.) The nonservice-connected patient is ineligible, however, for other regular medical services and must be referred elsewhere.

"Because it is essential that only those nonservice-connected (NSC) veterans who are in financial difficulty be admitted to VA hospitals," explains a veterans' hospital director, "the VA has been asking the NSC veteran to fill out a financial addendum when he submits his request for hospital care. His fiscal statement is reviewed in the light of prevailing medical costs for treatment of his condition. If the VA review of the financial statement suggests the applicant can afford it, he is advised that he ought to consider treatment elsewhere. If he insists on VA treatment in spite of counseling, he is given the benefit of the doubt, but his financial statement is referred to VA attorneys for possible recovery of costs later." [41]

The existence of two classes of medical problems and two classes of patients creates some bizarre situations. Legally, a VA physician is sometimes authorized to treat only the service-connected part of a patient's body, but ethically and professionally, this is unthinkable. If a nonservice-connected patient has other health problems besides the one that specifically led to his admission, a VA physician is technically forbidden to treat it if the treatment will prolong his hospitalization. Most physicians consider such rules absurd, and in many facilities there is a silent and humane conspiracy to ignore, stretch, thwart, circumvent and where necessary subvert the whole system of regulations.

Legislative restrictions on professional judgment have been relaxed substantially in the past few years. Until recently, patients with nonservice-connected problems were ineligible for any ambulatory care. This often placed VA physicians in a dilemma. Either they turned away patients entirely because their problems were not serious enough to require hospitalization, or they hospitalized them unnecessarily so that they might receive medical attention. Given these alternatives, many doctors naturally chose the second. As a result, VA hospitals have for years been filled with patients unnecessarily occupying expensive hospital rooms.

To minimize this drain on its resources, the VA obtained Congressional authorization in the Sixties for "pre-bed" and "post-hospital" care for the nonservice-connected. These programs enabled the agency to reduce the length of hospitalization, to increase its turnover rate and, consequently, to cut back the number of hospital beds and daily patient census—all of which has saved money. Nonetheless, ambulatory care remained contingent upon hospitalization and the VA continued to be overwhelmingly oriented to institutional care. At the Boston VA hospital in November 1971, doctors on the staff estimated that about 20 percent of the patients were being hospitalized unnecessarily because of the unavailability of outpatient services. They suggested that an additional 5 to 10 percent were unnecessarily hospitalized because of the shortage of extended care facilities. [42] At the spinal cord injury unit at West Roxbury in Boston, the chief of service estimated that of his 125 patients, 40 percent did not require hospitalization. [43]

"We are particularly embarrassed at times," Dr. Benjamin Wells, deputy medical director of the VA, admitted at hearings in 1971, "by reason of not being able to handle, on an outpatient ambulatory basis, the type of patient we think could much more efficiently and much more in the patient's interest be handled in that modality. This has been true in the psychiatric area, as psychiatric treatment in this country has moved to the ambulatory rather than inhospital treatment." [44]

In August 1973, these considerations finally resulted in legislation making outpatient care available when necessary to avoid hospitalization. The new law also authorized home care programs which, as Senator Cranston explained, will use mobile teams to "train families to care for patients so they can be released from the hospital sooner and removed from the debilitation and stagnation of institutional life." [45] It also provides for direct admission to nursing homes. (Under previous rules, a veteran had to be hospitalized first.) And it made 205,000 veterans who are 80 percent or more service-disabled eligible for comprehensive medical services for all nonservice-connected problems, regardless of financial status. All these measures have greatly relaxed the constraint on service.

Nonetheless, important problems remain. The record of previous moves to broaden eligibility indicates that adequate funds to underwrite the cost have not simultaneously been made available. On this occasion too, the VA has not sought additional appropriations or prepared plans to expand its already overburdened outpatient clinics. Some VA hospitals, in fact, have no outpatient department at all. It is difficult to see how they can make a transition to greater ambulatory care without major planning and financial support. The strategy of the agency seems to be to get Congressional authorization first and worry about money later. This may be politically necessary, but the resulting budgetary lag seems likely to slow implementation of the new provisions. Reforms that ultimately conserve resources are nevertheless often expensive to introduce.

Second, the new legislation falls short of answering the fundamental limitations of VA organization. It does not make comprehensive medical services available under one roof for those who rely on the VA. Eligibility for health care is still only partial, and a means test is still in force.

Prior to the new legislation, thirty-eight of every one hundred applicants to VA hospitals were being rejected for admission, primarily because they needed less than hospital care. [46] If these patients are to receive treatment, they represent a substantial additional load. If not, then little has changed. The VA Medical

Director has estimated that of the patients not accepted, about a third were given some kind of treatment (which means that, in many cases, doctors ignored regulations and gave limited outpatient services by prescribing drugs, special diets, and so forth). What happened to the remaining two-thirds? The admitting physicians, Dr. Musser explained, "refer these patients to welfare organizations because, by and large, we are dealing with an indigent population; and sometimes in states where there is a liberal enough Medicaid program, they are referred to welfare or those who administer Medicaid, so that they might be picked up under those programs. Then, of course, some of them are referred to their own private physicians, if indeed they have one." [47]

It is precisely this kind of fragmentation that interferes with the practice of good medicine. Care has been arbitrarily and irregularly divided between VA and non-VA facilities. Relationships between doctor and patient have been disrupted. People then complain about "red tape" and the "run-around" they get from the VA and other agencies. These complaints arise not because facilities are provided publicly, but because they are provided haphazardly, with no single facility serving as an unambiguous "entry point" into a comprehensive health system.

The new legislation is a major step forward—we urged its passage in Senate testimony in March 1973—but it leaves considerable ground to cover. Veterans' hospitals still have no authorization to provide standard preventive medical services. VA officials like to think of their program as a prepaid system in which military service constitutes the prepayment. But the special feature of prepaid health plans is that they have a strong incentive to prevent serious illness and the aggravation of minor illness, since that increases the margin between prepayment and costs.[48] No such incentive is evident in the VA. The system is neither authorized nor set up to deal with medical problems in their earliest stages; moreover, only a few selected cases are followed after hospitalization. Before and between periods of serious ill health veterans have little contact with the VA. Few things are as essential in the maintenance of health as continuity of care, but, in part because of the constraint on service, discontinuity is normal and continuity the exception.

Structural Constraints (II): Exclusivity

The inability of the VA to provide continuity of care and preventive services also stems from the intrinsic nature of the system. So long as it serves only a segment of any particular community, the VA cannot make its facilities available on a neighborhood basis. Each of its hospitals must have a large catchment area, occasionally covering all or half of a large state. For veterans on the outer rims of the catchment area, the hospitals cannot possibly provide primary care. The result again is that health care is fragmented, with the VA used intermittently, generally for chronic rather than acute conditions.

This relative inaccessibility is a source of continual irritation for veterans in nearly all parts of the country. Scarcely a Congressional hearing passes without a plea from some veteran representative or Congressman for a new VA facility in his state. The most severe cases are naturally in the less populated areas. For veterans in Las Vegas the nearest VA hospital is in Reno, 460 miles away. Veterans in south Texas, where 80 percent of the population have Spanish surnames, have to travel 250 miles to reach a VA hospital, 150 miles to reach an outpatient clinic.[49] In other words, one of the consequences of maintaining a system of hospitals exclusively for veterans, rather than financing their care in general health institutions, is an objective bias against veterans in small communities and rural areas, who have less access to VA facilities. Unless their problems are service-connected, veterans cannot get any coverage from the VA for care by local doctors, clinics, and hospitals.

Inaccessibility also tends, as do so many other factors, to lengthen hospitalization. A veteran who needs preoperative tests but lives seventy-five or one hundred miles from a VA hospital cannot be asked to return home between those tests and surgery; in the interim he is usually given a hospital bed. Another consequence— one that causes hardship to many patients—is that, while staying in a VA hospital, veterans are frequently separated from their families by a large distance. Transportation for family visits may be difficult and expensive; as a result, communication may be limited. Since so many VA patients are chronic cases with long hospital stays, this diminished familial support can have a serious effect on patient morale.

The exclusivity of the VA disrupts the family in another sense. Because veterans alone are eligible for VA care, they cannot receive treatment from physicians and in institutions that regularly treat other members of their families. Under new legislation, however, the VA can provide counseling for a veteran's family, or members of his household, when it is likely to have some effect on his health. This is a major step forward.

The exclusivity constraint also typically leads to a number of recurrent difficulties in the general organization and planning of health services.

1. Where *both* the VA system and community hospitals seek to provide complete services, there tends to be a certain amount of unnecessary duplication of expensive, specialized equipment and programs. Such duplication occurs most critically today in radiotherapy, cardiac surgery, and organ transplantation.

2. In some smaller communities, where *only* the VA is available, local residents may lack immediate access to health care while VA beds are empty.

3. Insofar as the VA system is run from Washington, its overall development proceeds without significant reference to other community medical resources. On the local level, this means that the VA may decide to cut a hundred beds from one of its hospitals because of insufficient veteran demand, while the state or county is adding a hundred beds at considerable expense to a nearby institution because of population increases.

To some extent, the first two problems described above—duplication on the one hand and underuse of existing capability on the other—have been alleviated in recent years as the VA has developed sharing arrangements with other hospitals. These arrangements have enabled the VA to accept nonveteran patients in its hospitals when comparable treatment was unavailable elsewhere, and correspondingly, to receive services from community hospitals that it has been unable to provide directly. These interchanges are currently at a rather low level, but VA officials have indicated a desire to extend them. "We think a very meaningful move," Dr. Marc Musser has said, "would be to see if there couldn't be a pooling of all health care delivery resources in a community. By various kinds of sharing arrangements we could make widely available the total array of VA resources in a community." As the VA Medical Director puts it, "Frankly, I think it is foolish that a community should have a mental hygiene clinic and that three blocks away is a VA mental hygiene clinic. If we are going to conserve our resources, we must think more in terms of a collaborative effort." [50]

In recent years there has been increasing recognition of the need for regional medical planning to coordinate the plans of hospitals and other medical institutions. Each of the Comprehensive Health Planning units established under federal legislation passed in 1965 includes one representative from the Veterans Administration. These have little power, however, and cannot prevent a hospital from proceeding with construction or additional services that the regional council deems redundant. For this reason, many of the states have passed laws requiring the issuance of a "certificate of need" by a regional planning agency before substantial projects may be undertaken by an individual hospital. Since the VA hospitals are federally run, however, the states have no jurisdiction over their operation unless the federal government cedes it. And that has yet to happen.

The VA has, however, embarked on a regionalization program of its own, creating thirty-seven districts within its national system. "A facility which has the best cardiology diagnostic service in a particular regional district," explains Dr. Musser, "should be able, and encouraged, to use this service to benefit all the facilities in the region.

"In other words, each facility is encouraged, so far as is possible, to do more of the things it does best and to do fewer of the things it does less well or less economically." [51]

But why should regionalization be restricted to the VA? If a veterans' hospital has a better cardiology diagnostic service than nearby community hospitals, why not use that service for all of them? If regionalization makes sense in the VA, it makes even more sense if it embraces both VA and community hospitals. The issue is not just cost. As we will illustrate below, barriers between VA and community hospitals profoundly affect the quality of care veterans receive.

Conflicting Functions

Beyond the problems of resources and structure lie more elusive and informal facets of organization. These are essentially aspects of organizational culture—things that never appear in budgets or statutes but exercise great influence over the life of an institution and the lives of its people.

Students of medical care have long noted that the health of hospital patients is not just a function of the number, skill, and concern of their doctors and nurses or the efficiency and comprehensiveness of their facilities. As workers in a factory are affected by the plant's environment and by the relations they develop with each other, so patients in a hospital are affected by that institution's climate and by the relations they develop among themselves. This is especially true in a system like the VA, where the average stay is so long.

In psychiatric care, the impact of the institutional environment is

a matter of special concern. The brief time that a patient spends
with a therapist may have less influence on him than the much
longer periods he spends with orderlies and other patients. A
syndrome known as "institutionalism" describes the behavior
produced by long-term inactivity and confinement: apathy, loss of a
sense of time, loss of interest and initiative, deterioration of personal
habits. One of the best known studies of the effects of environmental factors on psychiatric care—Leonard Ullman's *Institution and
Outcome*—was actually conducted in veterans' hospitals. Comparing the large, poorly staffed mental hospitals that dominate the VA
system with small, better staffed psychiatric services within VA
general hospitals, Ullman found that patients in the smaller
programs were released earlier and less likely to be reinstitutional-
ized.[52]

Psychiatric patients represented about 46 percent of the VA's
patient census in 1971, and three quarters of these were housed in
large mental hospitals.[53] To say that they were treated there would
be simply dishonest; the ratio of psychiatrists to patients in those
hospitals was 1 to 535.[54] A census taken on October 14, 1970,
showed that there were 28,563 patients in the VA diagnosed as
having psychoses and that 59.3 percent had been there for over one
year, 38.3 percent for over five years, and 28.5 percent for over ten
years.[55] Generally located in small towns inaccessible to large
population centers by public transportation, the VA mental hospitals are almost inevitably custodial in character. During 1970 they
cost about $319 million to operate, with only $21.5 million
budgeted for outpatient psychiatric care.[56] Given that order of
priorities and the character of the institutions, it is no surprise that
Vietnam veterans shun VA psychiatric services. And, as we have
already seen, when they do enter VA hospitals, they have a marked
tendency to seek discharge against medical advice. Although there
has been much evidence that many Vietnam veterans have suffered
from severe psychological problems on their return home, the VA
has been fundamentally unsuited to their needs and utterly
incapable of delivering services to them. Having taken on certain
custodial functions, the VA has been unable to meet readjustment
problems of young veterans. They would have been better served
had the federal government financed programs in general health
institutions, instead of trying to fit them into a hospital system that
patently does not provide the kind of environment where they
would feel at home or be likely to make progress.

Environmental factors affect more than psychiatric treatment.
Nearly all medical problems have psychosomatic dimensions that

are as real and as critical as the purely physiological aspects. Particularly for the severely injured, psychological adjustment is as much a problem as physical recovery. Consequently, their progress is greatly influenced by the atmosphere of treatment and example set by other patients. And it is here again that the preponderance of chronic patients in VA hospitals becomes so relevant to the treatment of young, recently injured Vietnam veterans. To see how the deeply ingrained custodial functions of the VA affect its mandated function of rehabilitating the war injured, we turn to a case study of one facility that specializes in the treatment of paraplegics.

★ *The Wounded and the Refugees*

The VA hospital at West Roxbury in Boston is almost a world apart. Many of the patients on its 125-bed spinal cord injury service have been there for years, some for decades. The VA is their home; their fellow patients are their society. Into that world periodically come a number of young men, some of them with wounds from Vietnam, others hurt in car or sports accidents at home. For a young veteran it is a strange and depressing world to enter. Rather than providing a therapeutic setting for rehabilitation, it provides a distorted and negative picture of their own future.

Traditionally, the VA has been one of the leading institutions in America for the treatment of paraplegia. While Great Britain and many other countries have long had national spinal injury centers for civilians, the United States has had none and has lagged far behind in research and patient care. The VA, which has an extensive network of spinal cord centers within its hospital system, has partially filled the void. It has trained a large number of the physicians and therapists specializing in the field and developed many of the prosthetic devices used by paraplegics.

Not only the VA but veterans themselves have been the chief activists in changing laws and practices that affect paraplegics. The Paralyzed Veterans Association, formed in 1946, preceded and laid the basis for the National Paraplegia Foundation, which now represents the consumer interests of civilian paraplegics. Other veterans' groups, such as the American Legion, have also had a strong interest in rehabilitation.

Considering the pioneering role that the VA and veterans' organizations have played in this area, one might expect that the level of care in VA hospitals would continue to be high. But the past—or rather, the inability to break with the past—has proved to be one of the VA's problems.

Even with the best medical institutions, the rehabilitation of paraplegics and quadriplegics is beset with difficulties. Injury to the spinal cord results not only in impairment of locomotion, but in a host of complications: decubitus ulcers (bedsores), circulation problems, spasticity, urinary tract infections, incontinence, muscular atrophy. In a culture that emphasizes physical appearance, personal independence, and easy mobility, adjustment is necessarily difficult. All the more so for young men, who are too old to be as adaptable as the very young and too young to be as fatalistic as the very old. For a veteran in his early twenties, the injury often comes just after he has left his parents' family but before he has established his own. Suddenly he finds himself cut off, unable to engage in the activities—both work and relaxation—around which his life has been organized. All plans, all ambitions are suspended. There is the bitter, largely unspoken pain that comes with the sense of lessened masculinity.

All these things are somehow easier to take in a military hospital, where there are only men, only soldiers, only the injured. But going home means facing a girlfriend and a family, old friends and new situations where people will not understand no matter how much sympathy they have. If a soldier is badly enough injured, going home means getting transferred to a veterans' hospital before one year is out. For men from New England with injuries to the spinal cord, that hospital will most likely be the one at West Roxbury in Boston. It is not the kind of institution a young veteran would choose on his own.

"I think what's so very discouraging about this place," explains Alan, a twenty-one-year-old Vietnam veteran, "is that you look around and there are guys that have been here twenty, twenty-five years. Those are the people we see. We don't get a chance to see the guys that are out and carrying on their individual lives successfully, going to school, working. Occasionally some of these people will show up, to see old friends. And that's good, but it's not enough. I mean, you see these old geezers every day, and you're just thinking about spending twenty years here. It's anything but encouraging."

"You adjust to it eventually," says Walt, another young patient. "But at first you come in, and the guy you're put next to—someone who's been here thirteen years—and you say to yourself, 'Oh, God, I'm never going to get out of this place.' It's hard to take at first. I don't think those people should be here. It's nothing against them. I think this is a rehabilitation center—that's what you're here for. . . . Some [young] guys get close to them [the older patients] and figure, 'I'll do what they do.' They have a good time, a lot of them. It makes them forget about the therapy."

Rehabilitation for most of the older patients stopped long ago, and the need for medical attention is only intermittent. Dr. Donald M. Watkin, a urologist who was acting chief of service for three years, estimates that 40 percent of the patients do not need to be in the hospital.[57] Most were hurt as civilians and so cannot get disability compensation; a survey of 500 patients indicated that only 24.9 percent had been wounded in action.[58]

Many of the nonservice-disabled patients simply cannot manage to live on their own with the meager pensions available to them. The hospital provides them, on the other hand, with shelter and "three squares" a day. It does more than that. For many paraplegics, the hospital is a less strained, less demanding environment than any they could find outside. Some older veterans have no immediate families or none willing to care for them. Others have severe family conflicts that drive them back into the emotional safety of the hospital whenever they try to leave. There they have the company of men with the same handicaps; it is one place where it is no shame to be paralyzed. A residue of military honor offsets the stigma of disability. The social pressures of the hospital are relatively minimal. For these reasons, it serves some of the older patients well. It is a refuge, and in a sense they are refugees from a society that cannot or will not take the time to take them back.

But, at the same time, the hospital serves the young men very poorly. The low-pressure atmosphere, the lack of activity, the lack of entertainment, the lack of models for emulation all carry over into rehabilitation and produce a kind of therapeutic *laissez-faire*.

"There's therapy here," Walt explains, "but they don't make you go to it. They're willing to help you—if you want to go you can go. If you don't want to, you can stay by your bed all day long and read. There's guys that have been here for eighteen, twenty years. A lot of guys have been here that long. Someone should come up and say, 'You've got to go here.' Some of them that have been here eighteen years never went because they like to drink. So instead of going to therapy, they drink. It's a bad problem in this place. There's aides that can get booze for you. It's no problem. If you want it, you can get anything—I don't care if it's liquor or drugs. You can get it. Some of the help will get it for you."

Ron, a somewhat older veteran, who served in the early Sixties and was recently injured in an auto accident, describes the same situation: "Everybody here is on what you might call voluntary rehabilitation. You are supposed to be at PT—physical therapy—at a certain time, for an hour or whatever. You are supposed to be at CT—corrective therapy—at a given time. . . . Usually, if you need manual assistance or are just doing a project, you have OT—occupational therapy—the old pottery, basket-weaving jazz, or some very, very practical things. Anyway, you're given times when you're supposed to be at these places, but if you don't feel like it, you don't go. So really it's a voluntary therapy in that if you aren't inclined to go, you don't go, you don't get the therapy, therefore you are not rehabilitated, other than possibly mentally, if you're lucky, and then you do it yourself. You can either make this a home for twenty years or you can get disgusted and haul out and do it on your own.

"For instance, when I miss a day down there, there's nobody who calls up and says, 'Why isn't [Ron] down here?' I've noticed a lot of people who have hit a slump. You go just so far and feel that you're going ahead, going ahead. This is a normal situation. All of a sudden, you hit a peak and it levels off, and then for a couple of weeks nothing happens. Consequently, you get a downer on the whole thing, and a lot of guys at this point quit going 'cause they figure it's not doing any good. Well, the people downstairs just go by it. They don't really get particularly upset if you don't show. Which to me is ridiculous, because if you're on rehab you should be there every damned day. I don't know how you're going to tell a thirty-year-old man that he's been a bad boy, but there should be some sort of regulation. You can't force a man, but still there should be something . . . at least somebody come around and say, 'Look, why weren't you down here?' and try at least to convince the man that he should go down and do something. . . . The therapies are useless unless they're a day-to-day deal. . . . Every day that you lie still or move around and not have the muscles that are not being used stretched, they are atrophying and will to the point where you are incapable of getting dressed if you are a self-care patient."

Essie Morgan, a social worker in the Spinal Cord Injury Service in the VA Central Office, says the climate at the West Roxbury is not unique. A recent survey of spinal cord injury centers disclosed what she calls a "trade-off syndrome," essentially a bargain in which the staff tacitly tells the patients, "If you don't bother us, we'll take care of you for the rest of your life."

"We found this time and time again," Ms. Morgan states.[59]

The result of the "trade-off syndrome" is all too often the permanent institutionalization of the patients. The more adjusted they become to the hospital, the less able they are to manage outside. Instead of rehabilitating paraplegics, the hospital trains them to become lifelong patients. Instead of giving them the courage to live on their own, the institution encourages dependence and reinforces their alienation from the rest of society. "There's a mistrust," one younger paraplegic comments. "Some [older] guys won't even talk to people who can walk. It's that weird."

This "disculturation" is not an unusual pattern for a total institution.[60] Created with the intention of reintegrating the disabled into society, the segregated facility often disables them further by removing them from it. "Not merely prisons or mental hospitals," writes the medical sociologist Eliot Freidson, "but also agencies for the physically handicapped have been observed to organize and stabilize behavior into special roles rather than eradicate it." [61]

Another reason why some veteran paraplegics become lifelong patients is the failure of the hospital to bring their families into the process of therapy in the early stages.

"We turn families off," says Essie Morgan. "Families get in our way. We say, 'Get on home, we'll take care of him.' And then bright one Thursday morning you tell them, 'Take him.' And I don't blame them one bit if they say, 'Oh no, you keep him.' They haven't been prepared."

Families could be involved in rehabilitation directly, Ms. Morgan states, if they were taught basic genitourinary care and turning and positioning procedures necessary to prevent bedsores and atrophy. They would also benefit from counseling. And once the patient has returned to his family, there is a need for continuing medical and personal assistance from the spinal injury center. Currently, however, the VA has no regular post-discharge program even for patients, much less their families; there is no follow-up once the paraplegic leaves the hospital. He can be readmitted for further hospitalization but as the West Roxbury administration itself points out, "There is no provision for the outpatient treatment of spinal cord injury patients." [62] Under such conditions it would be a mystery if overinstitutionalization did not take place.

The VA cannot, of course, guarantee willingness on the part of the veterans' families. But it can do something about their ability to give care, which in turn affects willingness. Counseling programs are not an integral part of the VA's program today. The agency has only recently undertaken a pilot study of hospital-based home care on the West Coast. That the VA is thinking about such programs is good, indeed long overdue, but it faces a fundamental problem, mentioned earlier. VA hospitals are not community institutions; they tend to be located farther from a patient's home than other health facilities. Their responsibility has traditionally and legally been to veterans, not to their families. They do not have family health workers, nor are they in a favorable position to provide noninstitutional services efficiently. Discontinuity between hospital care and home support is, therefore, not so much a result of professional misjudgment as it is of institutional limitations.

The tragedy at West Roxbury, however, is not just the institutionalization of older paraplegics, which in some cases may have been unavoidable. The further tragedy is that this has had a deleterious effect on the medical care given to the newly injured, younger veterans.

"There are people who should not be in this hospital, no way, shape or form," Ron explains. "They are taking up space. For fifteen years they have been living in a home where they should not have a damn bed. There are guys who have waited two or three months to get in this hospital. And arrived in terrible shape. Had their original applications for a bed been approved immediately, [they would not have] ended up coming in here and spending months just being cured of what happened to them in the other [community] hospital—the bedsores, atrophy. Very few hospitals know what to do with the para or the quad."

During the years 1969 and 1970, when the flood of casualties from Vietnam was at its height, the VA was barely able to handle the influx of new spinal injury cases, so committed were its facilities to older patients no longer in need of active treatment. Ironically, the VA, once a pioneer in rehabilitation, could not release itself from its old obligations and proved unable to perform well its primary responsibility to rehabilitate the war injured. As in other areas, it had grown soft in the slack interwar years, accumulating patients who had little need of medical attention, but who could fill beds that would otherwise have been empty. When the time came to provide the kind of care that people had come to expect, the VA was incapacitated, its wards filled with residents more than patients, its staff depleted. In these respects, the situation at West Roxbury exemplifies what has happened to the VA as a whole.

The Logic of Integration

Spinal cord injury offers a graphic illustration of the human and social costs of disorganized health services. The most critical period in a spinal cord injury is the first few hours after trauma. With new techniques, it is becoming increasingly possible to attenuate the paralyzing effects of spinal cord lesions, few of which are actually complete cord transections.[63] Any effective system for dealing with such cases, therefore, must see to it that patients reach skilled specialists in as short a time as possible. In Britain this is accomplished by airlifting accident victims to a Spinal Injury Center at Stoke Mandeville, where they are seen by specialists in traumatology.

In most areas of the United States, on the other hand, there are no paraplegic treatment centers, nor are there even systematic procedures for handling such cases and financing their care within our present institutions. The result is a haphazard process in which patients often do not see a physician familiar with spinal cord injury until weeks, let alone hours, after trauma.

In the New England region, which is probably typical in this regard, slightly over 100 hospitals accept spinal injury victims for treatment. But since 67 percent of these hospitals see fewer than five cases annually, they have little opportunity to accumulate expertise in the field.[64] This is decentralization with a vengeance. More than half of the hospitals offering treatment have no rehabilitation facilities, so that physical therapy, which might begin early, is unnecessarily delayed. The delay may be a matter of weeks, because the hospitals tend to hold onto their patients as long as their insurance lasts. When it runs out, state and federal agencies enter the picture, and the patient may be transferred elsewhere for rehabilitation. If the patient happens to be a veteran, he is shipped to the VA, which places him in one of its spinal injury centers provided a bed is available. But by then it is often too late. All sorts of complications may have set in, and the VA has its hands full trying to undo the damage caused by weeks of uninformed treatment.

"We don't get patients soon enough." That complaint, from West Roxbury's Dr. Watkin, is echoed by nearly everyone concerned with the VA's spinal cord injury centers. It reflects the whole panoply of problems that arise from uncoordinated health services. Within the larger medical system, the VA functions as a secondary referral institution. To a large extent, it inherits problems that others prefer not to handle, or cannot afford to handle. The spinal cord injured do not arrive at a VA center as soon as they can be transported there, but only when the community hospitals where they first land can no longer get reimbursed for their care. So long as the system works that way for all but the very wealthy, it will work that way for veterans injured in civilian accidents. Research may give us new techniques for dealing with traumatic injury, but patients will be stranded far from the point where they can benefit from them.

"This nation's existing capability to provide optimal treatment of spinal cord injury continues to be thwarted by our inability to organize systems of care," says Dr. John Young, director of the Spinal Injury Service at the Good Samaritan Hospital in Phoenix, Arizona. "The primary obstacle to development is the fragmentation of care stemming from bureaucratic and institutional chauvinism, calcified (often prestigious) vested interests, and multiplicity of sources for financial support." In Arizona Dr. Young directs the only coordinated treatment system in the country. He describes it as having five subsystems: 1) evacuation, within two hours; 2) traumatology, up to two weeks; 3) restoration, three to four months; 4) adjustment, lasting anywhere from six to twelve months; and 5) follow-up, covering a lifetime.[65]

"We are actually shooting for one hundred days from the date of injury to get the patient back into his community," Dr. Young states. The purpose here is clearly to avoid the situation illustrated by West Roxbury, where the patient is removed from family and community for an extended period and stands a chance of becoming permanently institutionalized.

Regional systems on the Arizona or British models face a number of hurdles, financial and political. Most of the hospitals which now offer treatment for spinal cord injury have to be convinced to transfer such patients out as soon as they leave intensive care. This would be difficult at any time, but if catastrophic health insurance is introduced, community hospitals will have an incentive to keep such patients even longer than they do now. This can only act as a deterrent to the development of regional systems. Second, financing a comprehensive system will be difficult, because no single hospital or agency can easily underwrite the expense. At the national level, responsibility for spinal cord injury is divided among the VA, the Social Rehabilitation Service of HEW (which has funded the Arizona system in conjunction with two hospitals), and the National Institute of Neurological Diseases and Stroke of NIH. But even with these three agencies, there is not that much combined support.

Given the fact that the VA already has a system of spinal injury centers—a system used in large measure for custodial care that could be accomplished better elsewhere—it could reasonably provide the focal point for the organization of coordinated regional systems for the care of all citizens. But, as with the general question of integrating the VA, both legal and resource constraints make such steps unlikely in the immediate future.

In the long run, advances in the treatment and rehabilitation of the spinal cord injured will depend to a large extent on institutional reorganization. It is not solely a matter of the VA upgrading its hospitals, but more generally a matter of ending antiquated boundaries that separate VA services from others. In the area of spinal cord injury it would be tragic if the VA were to maintain a separate system of care—tragic not only because that would deprive new regional centers of the benefit of the VA's experience and would result in costly duplication, but also because it would work against the interests of veterans themselves, particularly those injured in civilian accidents.

But even for the service-connected, separate VA facilities would be a misfortune. By its nature, the VA receives an irregular flow of severely injured patients, high in time of war, lower in time of peace, and this irregularity leads to overextension of facilities at one point and underuse at another. It was during a period of underutilization that the West Roxbury hospital accumulated the large number of patients now residing there who no longer need regular medical attention. And it was precisely this redirection of the hospital toward custodial care and away from rehabilitation that has made it such an inadequate facility for rehabilitation of the war injured.

★ The Future of Veterans' Hospitals

As long as the Veterans Administration operates on the periphery, responding or adjusting, but remaining aloof from commitment and involvement, the system will always be subject to the vagaries of the moment, and its staff will always be second-class citizens. [From an internal report to the Administrator of Veterans Affairs by the VA Department of Medicine and Surgery, March 1970.]

In terms of the quality of care provided for patients in veterans' hospitals today, the question of integration with community health services may seem somewhat marginal. Such matters as the adequacy of staffing levels and the competence and personal concern of doctors and nurses have far greater meaning for the individual patient. Yet in terms of the future of the VA hospital system (and consequently its future patients), the question of integration is absolutely critical. For the way that question is resolved will determine whether there continues to be a separate veterans' hospital system at all.

In the past few years, veterans' organizations and various Congressmen have charged that forces in the government—unnamed bureaucrats at HEW and OMB—were conspiring to do away with veterans' hospitals. The threat to the VA, however, is more serious than a plot hatched in the dark recesses of other executive agencies. It arises from fundamental changes taking place in the general organization and financing of health services.

On the surface, these changes appear in two forms: a generalized shift toward greater integration of health care services and the introduction, in one form or another, of national health insurance. These two developments, we would argue, have a common source in the progressive erosion of the distinction between the public and private sectors of the health economy, which arises, in turn, from the inability of the private sector to support the huge capital outlays required by technological and demographic change. This is true not only in the field of health care; it applies to higher education as well.

Indeed, throughout the service sector of the American economy, wherever institutions were formerly based on private endowments, they have been forced increasingly in the last quarter century under the pressure of expansion to turn to the government for financial support. In the case of universities, this support has been provided first through tax exemptions, funds for research and development, and the GI Bill, but now seems likely to be supplied in direct institutional grants as well or through an expanded federal scholarship program.

In the case of hospitals, government support has come first through aid for construction and more recently in the form of Medicare and Medicaid, which have paid the bills of many of those who previously defaulted or were taken on as charity patients. But even these subsidies have failed to meet the needs and appetites of our hospitals for more funds. Hospitals have annually been raising their rates at a pace far above the general level of inflation, causing higher premiums for private insurance and increases in Blue Cross rates and stimulating, in turn, the clamor for a federal health insurance program. Simultaneously, as costs climb and government subsidies grow, the cry has quite naturally gone up for greater coordination and integration of health services in order to minimize expenditures and enforce cost controls. In effect, government enters the economic equation as the countervailing force that consumers were unable to provide given the economic structure of medical services (i.e., the absence of effective competition among producers, the inability of consumers to evaluate the product, and so on).

These changes may at first glance seem far removed from the veterans' hospital system, which constitutes the only substantial civilian medical resource already under direct federal control. But as we noted at the outset, the structure of the VA system has always been determined more by its external political and economic environment than by internal professional considerations. New forms of coordination and financing cannot fail to affect the VA.

The shift to greater integration of health care delivery systems began rather tentatively during the past decade with federal legislation creating Regional Medical Programs and Comprehensive Health Planning. In 1967 the National Advisory Commission on Health Manpower declared, "Medical care in the United States is more a collection of bits and pieces—with overlapping, duplication, great gaps, high costs, and wasted effort—than an integrated system in which needs and efforts are closely related." [66] The veterans' hospitals are a prime example of the fragmented state of health services; it is unlikely they will, or should, be overlooked in the process of developing a coordinated system. Moreover, the VA itself has come to recognize the costs of isolation and, through sharing agreements, is moving steadily in the direction of integration with community health facilities. The question arises: At what point in the process of integration does it no longer make sense to have a separate VA hospital system run from Washington?

The process of integration seems likely to develop incrementally over a long period; the same is probably true of national health insurance. However, to the extent that national health insurance gains, it will undermine both the legal and the economic basis of the VA system.

Dr. Musser, VA Medical Director, explains why its legal structure would have to be rebuilt:

"One of the laws governing our operation provides for care of veterans with service-connected disabilities. He is entitled to unlimited care for any service-connected disability.

"The other law deals with the veteran who has a nonservice-connected illness. The law indicates that we can take care of this veteran if he is unable to pay for his care and if we have a bed available.

"Now the minute that everybody can pay for his care—or have a third party who will pay—the second law is negated. In operation of the VA, it will be an entirely new ball game." [67]

The problem is not merely that national health insurance would render three-fourths of VA patients ineligible for VA care. The laws on financial eligibility could probably be adjusted. More critically, national health insurance would eliminate the dependence of medically indigent veterans upon the VA system. It would provide them, as it would all veterans, with an alternative avenue for securing medical care. Instead of seeking treatment from the VA, they could go to a community hospital and have their expenses paid by a third party.

The consequences of eliminating their dependence on the VA would be two-fold. First, their interest in maintaining the VA system as a separate system for veterans would virtually evaporate. This would have immediate political implications. And, in a direct economic sense, the demand for VA care would drop. If the past is any indication of the future, the likely response in the Executive Branch at this point would be to cut the operating capacity of the VA to save money, while the response in Congress would be to compensate for the lost demand by broadening eligibility for VA services to dependents and survivors of veterans. But this would only further weaken the VA by undermining its foundations. The more nonveterans appeared in VA hospitals, the more people would ask why those hospitals should be run by the Veterans Administration.

Another possibility is that, as World War II veterans grow older, their increased need for medical care will make up for whatever demand is lost to community hospitals through national health insurance. The effect would be to cancel out any change and leave the VA as it now is—a chronic care system on the periphery of American medicine. Ironically, though this may preserve the VA, it may also preserve its unsuitability for its primary task: the rehabilitation of men with service-connected injuries.

Veterans' organizations and their friends in Congress view the idea that the VA system might be supplanted by health insurance as a threat to the interests of the nation's 28 million veterans. But it is doubtful that this is the majority view among veterans themselves. In a survey conducted for the House Committee on Veterans' Affairs—and there is no more vigorous defender of the VA—veterans receiving compensation or pensions were asked "if they required hospital care today and knew the care would be paid for by the VA, whether they would prefer to receive it in a nearby VA hospital or in a community hospital." Slightly more than half of the respondents (51 percent) chose the community hospital. The younger the veteran, the more likely he was to do so.[68] If this is the opinion among VA beneficiaries, among veterans as a whole the preference for community hospitals is likely to be even stronger. The results suggest that a substantial majority of veterans would prefer a comprehensive health insurance program to the existing VA hospital system.

The reasons why an insurance system would seem preferable are not difficult to understand. Community hospitals inevitably tend to be more accessible simply because there are so many more of them. A veteran may be seen there by his family physician, which is not possible in the VA. An insurance system maximizes freedom of choice, whereas the maintenance of a separate institutional system for veterans limits available alternatives.

This is of concern to veterans of all ages, but as we have indicated previously, it is especially of concern to Vietnam veterans, many of whom find VA hospitals extremely uncongenial. Had there been an insurance system in effect for Vietnam veterans, they would have been free to go to whatever institutions they thought would best be able to help them with their medical and psychological problems. The odds are very low that many of them would have chosen to go to institutions that specialize in treating the chronic diseases of the elderly.

The principle here is really no different from that of the GI Bill. Instead of saying to veterans, "Here, we have a set of institutions just for you, but you can't get any help from us unless you use them," the principle of the GI Bill says, "We will provide the financing for your education (or medical care). Now you choose whatever institutions you think will help you the most."

Assuming for the moment that national health insurance were introduced on a contributory basis, with payments both by employer and employee, how might veterans fit in? We would suggest that the federal government pay for a certain proportion of veterans' contributions out of general revenues. These credits would vary according to the extent of service-connected disability and time elapsed since discharge from the armed forces. In other words, a veteran with 10 or 20 or 30 percent service-connected disability would contribute a certain percentage less than he ordinarily would to cover health insurance; the credits would increase until, say for a veteran 60 percent disabled, they covered the full cost.

Credits would also depend on time elapsed since discharge from the military. Even veterans without any disability would be granted extensive credits in the few years immediately after leaving the service, gradually decreasing to zero, seven years later. (See Table 4.4 for a rough picture of how this might work out.) The emphasis of such a benefit structure would be on health care as part of a readjustment program, except for those with permanent service-connected disabilities, who would receive credits indefinitely.

In politics it is always more realistic to add than subtract, and this is especially true when it comes to veterans' programs. In fact, it might be said of Congressmen and spokesmen for veterans' organizations that they seem to have mastered quite advanced formulas for addition and multiplication without ever having become the least acquainted with the rudiments of subtraction.

TABLE 4.4. Proportion of Health Insurance Costs to be Covered

Service-connected Disability (in %)	Year After Discharge						
	1st	2nd	3rd	4th	5th	6th	7th on
	Costs to be covered (in %)						
None	100	90	70	50	30	10	0
10	100	100	80	60	40	20	10
20	100	100	90	70	50	30	20
30	100	100	100	90	70	50	40
40	100	100	100	100	90	70	60
50	100	100	100	100	100	90	80
60	100						
70	100						
80	100						
90	100						
100	100						

Proportion in Public Education Institutions[29]

	Veterans in %	General population in %
1947–48	47.8	49.4
1956–57	61.8	56.8
1970–71	77.8	73.8

Veterans' Educational Level[36]

	% with high school completion at time of separation	% attending college under GI Bill
World War II	45.4	28.6
Korea	62.5	50.7
Vietnam era	78.9	60.1

At first, it is likely that any health insurance program will be added on top of existing health programs, not substituted for them. There may well be a period when there exists both a VA hospital system and national health insurance, and it may be years before some maladjusted budget-slicer in OMB decides the time has come to put the VA out of its misery. In the meantime, veterans' organizations, Congress, and the Administration have a choice. They can either continue to support a separate system of hospitals for veterans as new health insurance programs are introduced. In that case, the VA will continue to sit outside the mainstream, with a cumbersome and awkward set of rules governing who can and cannot receive care, with a largely chronic population and with very little capability of dealing with young, newly injured men. Or they can choose to seek to establish provisions for veterans within new health insurance legislation and allow the VA to be opened to nonveterans. The system could usefully serve a variety of important purposes. If retained under federal control, the hospitals could provide on a regional basis certain expensive, but rarely needed, forms of medical care that local communities cannot afford. It might be used, for example, for the treatment of major emergency medical problems, such as spinal cord injury, employing the helicopter technology developed in Vietnam to save lives on American highways. But it would be wrong to make the functions of the hospitals arbitrarily nationwide; they might vary from region to region, according to local health needs.

We do not suggest that the veterans' hospitals be closed tomorrow. Quite the contrary. They are a valuable national resource that should be nourished, not neglected. The patients who are treated there now cannot be sacrificed for the cause of long-range reforms. What we do suggest is that as new programs for health insurance are introduced, and greater coordination of health services develops, that the VA not be forgotten. If left out, it will only become more of a backwater than it is now.

Patients in veterans' hospitals are generally poor people. The last thing we would propose is that medical care be withdrawn from them. It is precisely because we think they too should get the best medical care—comprehensive care from an institution of their choice—that we think the VA hospitals are a bad idea and comprehensive health insurance a much better idea.

The special problems that arise because of the limited nature of the VA medical program are particularly evident in the field of drug addiction. Before looking at its efforts in that area, however, we need to take broad measure of the addiction problem. Few issues have been the object of greater interest or the subject of greater confusion.

5

War on Drugs: The Limits of Intervention

I. ORIGINS

In the spring of 1971, two Congressional investigations confirmed reports that large numbers of American soldiers in Vietnam had been using heroin. One study estimated that as many as 10 percent of the men stationed in Vietnam were taking heroin; the other put the figure at from 10 to 15 percent.[1,2]

The news immediately caused a sensation, not just because of the facts themselves, but because of what they reflected about the war and the nation. So grave a problem could not be shrugged off as a momentary aberration or "isolated incident," the official phrase for the massacre at My Lai. The facts spoke plainly of deep and pervasive alienation among American soldiers, a collapse of discipline and breakdown in morale. Men who had not been permitted to come home had sought a kind of unilateral withdrawal. Forbidden the return voyage across the Pacific, they had chosen a voyage into oblivion.

The facts spoke too of the character of those regimes the United States was defending in Southeast Asia. Not just small-time racketeers, but highly placed Laotians, Thais, and South Vietnamese were heavily implicated in the heroin trade. The ample supply of drugs to American troops was not the plot of the National Liberation Front or North Vietnamese, but a very profitable enterprise among our supposed friends. There were even creditable reports that elements of the U.S. Central Intelligence Agency knew about the trade and provided critical logistical support. Much of the opium grown in Laos was produced by the CIA-equipped and CIA-trained Meo tribesmen, whom the U.S. had counted on as a bulwark against the Pathet Lao. The CIA is also the principal source of funds for Air America, whose pilots were reported to be flying opium and heroin from Laos through to Bangkok and into Saigon. It is difficult to believe that an agency whose business is espionage could not have known of these operations.[3]

But though the facts spoke of alienation among our soldiers and corruption among our mercenaries, what they spoke of most eloquently was the degradation to which the United States had fallen in Indochina. In not rooting out the sources of heroin in Laos and Thailand, the government had simply made a calculation that the continued political and military support of those groups profiting from the drug traffic was worth the risk of hooking U.S. soldiers.

The American public was sickened by the news about heroin, but not entirely surprised. After the scandals of brutality like My Lai, the scandals of failure like Tet, and the scandals of deceit like the Pentagon Papers, it seemed in keeping with an era of corruption. The United States had indiscriminately bombed civilian populations and made the people refugees, defoliated the countryside and left the land barren, destroyed traditional communities and caused the cities of Vietnam to swell with dislocated peasants, their young men drafted, their young women turned to prostitutes for our soldiers. In a real sense, we produced our own undoing in Vietnam, for it was these uprooted, desperately poor people, cut off from their traditional means of subsistence, who sold our men heroin. Ultimately, the destruction that we inflicted on Vietnamese society came back to haunt us.

But the immediate conditions of desperation in Vietnam, grave as they were, cannot fully account for the heroin addiction problem. Conditions at home and certain aspects of our cultural history are also intimately involved. In the following pages, therefore, we try to describe not only how drug use evolved among American soldiers, but also how heroin addiction historically developed into a major problem in the United States. Understanding that history is critical in evaluati ; what should be done now.

A few words of caution. In the public uproar over heroin use among American troops, several things were lost sight of. Estimates of heroin use were confused with estimates of heroin addiction, and little attention was paid to the profound differences between heroin use in Vietnam and in the U.S., leaving people to suppose that all soldiers who took heroin were junkies. "Will you do us a favor?" three sailors in the rehabilitation unit at Nha Be asked a Senate investigating team in 1971. "When you get back to the States, get the word out to the people that we're not needle freaks. Sure we smoked some skag and it showed up in the tests. But we're no freaks." [4]

Serious as the heroin problem was, it was not as bad as many made it out to be. One noted columnist writing in a weekly newsmagazine referred to soldiers using heroin as men "who might as well be dead . . . condemned to a life of crime and an early death." [5] Such statements were not only wrong, but responsible for stirring up unwarranted fears and hostilities toward the men themselves. Most soldiers who had used heroin were not addicts and not "condemned" to anything. It is as dangerous to exaggerate their problems as it is to ignore them. The heroin epidemic in Vietnam merits anger, even outrage, but still more desperately requires understanding.

★ Soldiers and Heroin: The Straight Connection

Widespread use of heroin was a comparatively late phenomenon of the war. Prior to 1970, the drug prevalent among American soldiers, as among American youth in general, was marijuana.

"I started smoking pot in the MPs. . . . All the MPs—all the grunts there—started smoking dope because of the bush, and so I got into it with them, you know. . . . I can't say it was peer pressure. A guy would explain it to me. I was pretty naïve and gullible or I wouldn't have been in the Marine Corps, but I just smoked because of curiosity. And after I smoked a while, I got to really enjoy it. It was relaxing."

Though the soldiers' use of marijuana originally sent shock waves through the military and the public, the men themselves insist it actually helped their adjustment to the war. Some psychiatrists are inclined to believe them. One of those is Dr. Peter Bourne, who served as chief of the neuropsychiatry section of the U.S. Army Medical Research Team—Vietnam at the Walter Reed Army Institute of Research. Dr. Bourne wrote: "Not only has drug use become the norm [in Vietnam] but the use especially of marijuana may not be entirely without redeeming features. As one veteran told me, 'We never smoked grass in combat, but I do not think I could have made it without cracking if I had not used it in between patrols.' The relaxing effects of marijuana are beyond dispute. . . ." [6]

Such views did not win favor in the high command. Convinced that "grass" was undermining combat effectiveness, the military desperately sought to stamp out its use. Helicopters were used to locate and destroy marijuana fields, the Vietnam National Police were paid a bounty for every marijuana plant uprooted and turned in, overblown "educational" campaigns warned soldiers of the dangers of marijuana, dogs were trained to sniff out hidden stashes, personal belongings were searched, stiff penalties were imposed for sale or possession. The military at that time made no distinction between marijuana and hard drugs—encouraging soldiers to make none either. Enlisted men adapted to the pressure by shifting to another drug that could be more easily concealed because it was less bulky and gave off no detectable odor when smoked. It also had virtually no visible physical effects. "You can salute an officer with your right hand and take a hit in your left, and the old man would never know," soldiers claimed. The new drug was sometimes referred to as "cocaine" (a misnomer) and sometimes as "skag." Some of the men who took it seem never to have known it was heroin.

The ready availability of cheap, pure heroin in Vietnam had a great impact, of course, on the extent of its use among American troops. Equally important was its effect on the nature of that use. Two factors here were critical: It was high in quality and low in cost.

The strength of the heroin available in Vietnam—96 percent pure as opposed to 3 to 10 percent in the U.S.—obviated the need for injection and permitted it to be smoked in much the same manner as marijuana. Only 5 to 10 percent of soldiers taking heroin in Vietnam injected it, according to a May 1971 report by Congressmen Robert Steele and Morgan Murphy; the rest either smoked or sniffed.[7] The fact that heroin could be smoked made more men willing to try it, affected their reactions when they did try it, and minimized the impact of repeated use on their health. Smoking was easier psychologically—less decisive and less traumatic than mainlining; many soldiers falsely believed it was also nonaddictive. While initial experiences with injection tend to be unpleasant even for those who later become addicted, initial experiences with smoking heroin are almost always euphoric. This too removed a natural impediment to its use. Finally, soldiers who smoked heroin rarely suffered (immediate) physical harm. Most of the medical complications from opiate use, such as hepatitis, arise from the intravenous mode of administration rather than from the drug itself.

The low cost of heroin enormously reduced the social consequences of addiction in Vietnam. The price for a typical 250-milli-
gram vial was about $2. Even an addicted soldier rarely needed as
much as $10 a day to support his habit.[8] With the army supplying
ordinary needs, heroin users were therefore not forced into heavy
involvement in crime and the daily hustle of American street
junkies. By and large, they continued to carry on their military roles.
Addiction could, of course, seriously impair a soldier's ability to
function if he "got strung out," but in most cases the impairment
was minimal. As General Michael Davison, at one time commander
of Army forces in Vietnam, pointed out, "A guy could be on it
[heroin] with light to moderate addiction, and you'd never tell
because he could still fly an airplane or do a complicated task. It's a
very insidious thing." [9] It was just this "insidiousness" that allowed
the military and heroin addicts to live with each other for some time
without a confrontation. Heroin disrupted neither the army's nor
the users' basic ability to function. It was precisely because of the
low impairment of individual performance that the military would
eventually have to initiate an elaborate system of urinalysis
screening to find out just who was using the drug.

The inexpensiveness of heroin affected the social relations among
users. In the United States, with the cost of heroin high, addicts are
driven day to day to raise the necessary cash, each man fending for
himself. Social relations are highly individualized, distrustful, and
manipulative. In Vietnam, on the other hand, the smoking of heroin
became a group activity, and because the drug was cheap, it was
shared, and the brutal and manipulative aspects of addict behavior
were attenuated.

Vials of 96 percent pure white heroin began appearing in
quantity in Saigon around May 1970 and were available throughout
the country by December.[10] As if on cue, the military simultaneously intensified its war against marijuana. By the spring of 1971,
when the situation finally drew public attention, heroin use had
diffused widely.

Just how widely has been a matter of some controversy. Probably
the most reliable indicator of the extent of the epidemic is a study
commissioned by the Defense Department and conducted by the
Human Relations Research Organization (HumRRO).[11] In an anonymous questionnaire survey of 36,510 soldiers in all services during
the fall of 1971, 11.7 percent indicated they had used narcotics
(primarily heroin) during the past year. The proportion in the Army
was 20.1 percent, and for Army men in Vietnam, 28.5 percent.
According to the survey, on the average only about one of every five

soldiers who had taken heroin in the previous year used it every day (i.e., was addicted). Among all Army men in Vietnam, the rate of addiction was 9.2 percent; for Army men stationed in the United States, 5.4 percent.

Defense Department spokesmen now cite the figure of 7 percent as their "best estimate" of heroin addiction among all Army enlisted men. "If an epidemic were to reach such drastic levels in the population of the United States," notes Richard Wilbur, Assistant Secretary of Defense for Health and Environment, "ten to fifteen million victims would be involved." Dr. Wilbur calls the heroin problem "perhaps the gravest disease epidemic in modern military history." [12]

"But the thing that is really eye-opening about it," says General Davison, "is that these kids, and they were kids—nineteen, twenty years old as a median age—looked like an exact cross section of the young men coming into the Army. This business about ghetto kids and high school dropouts—that's a myth. It's a bunch of bunk. These kids are a cross section of what the Selective Service was picking up throughout America. And this is what really shatters you." [13]

In truth, heroin users were not an exact cross section of the Army, though close to it. According to the HumRRO study, there were substantially higher rates of heroin addiction among soldiers from minority groups. However, most Vietnam heroin users—68 percent according to Defense Department data—were white. [14]

A number of observers have suggested that soldiers who used heroin in Vietnam were mostly unstable personalities from broken homes. One of those who disagrees is Dr. Norman Zinberg, a psychiatrist at Harvard Medical School who traveled to Southeast Asia in August and September 1971 under the auspices of the Department of Defense and the Drug Abuse Council. "In Vietnam," he reported, "heroin use is not the habit of a deviant 'loner' from an extremely deprived urban background, but is a social activity occurring mostly in small groups of friends. In this setting there is little of the basic taboo against heroin use that predominates in most social groups in the United States. The typical Vietnam user would fit many people's idea of the healthy, all-around American boy. He is often from a small town in the Midwest or South, is in good physical condition, has used virtually no drugs before joining the Army, and shows no evidence of character disorder." [15]

Here was a remarkable phenomenon: "normal" soldiers taking heroin in a group setting. The conventional wisdom today holds that use of heroin is only a symptom of deeper psychological problems, but in Vietnam at least, it appears to have been minimally related to personality problems and character disorders. The cause lay more in the environment than in the individuals. Pentagon statistics indicate that only 11 percent of the men first used heroin as a civilian. On the other hand, 35 percent began using it within one month of reaching Vietnam.[16] External factors, therefore, seem to have been critical.

Indeed, rather than being an expression of emotional disturbance, heroin use in Vietnam may have been an attempt at self-medication in an oppressive setting. This is not to argue that it was a good idea, only that it may have met an authentic need of normal people. Faced with a hostile population, unable to distinguish enemy from friend, left inactive for long periods, lacking any sense of purpose or conviction in the war, some soldiers turned to heroin for relief from both boredom and anxiety. "The use of drugs in the combat zone," says Dr. Bourne, "has a particular appeal, because the psychological anesthesia provides a ready antidote to the environmental stress. Also there is often a reactive flight into hedonism after times of stress when the GI frequently feels that no pleasure should be out of his reach. He knows how near he has come to dying and what the possibility of death is in the future, and he feels, therefore, no compunction about immersing himself in immediate gratification." [17]

A combat veteran recalls how he began taking heroin:

"How long after you got to Vietnam did you start on drugs?"
"A couple of weeks."
"Who got you started on that?"
"Well, everybody smoked, and you started smoking."
"Opium?"
"Yeah, and grass, everything. You know, some cats are smoking this, and some doing that, and some snorting it [heroin], and you know, that's the way they kept their heads together, to deal with the problem, to keep from going nuts you had to stay high, man, because it's a pretty scary thing, you know, I mean, uh, it's nice to sit down and talk about it but to do it is a heavy thing."
"Did many guys not go on drugs?"
"Not too many. Most everybody smoked."
"Marijuana?"
"Yeah, opium, everything."
"What kind of guys didn't go on? Did you know any?"
"No."
"Did you think it would hurt you after you got out?"

"I didn't know. I didn't have time to think about it."

"Did it all of a sudden hit you that you had a habit?"

"It was when I come back in the states, I fucked around and found out I got a habit."

"You were taking it frequently in Nam, and didn't find out about it till you got back?"

"Well, you see, I didn't know anything about it, and I was just snorting it, once in a while getting off. You know, like I always had it and the thought of getting a habit didn't occur to me. I didn't know what the fuck it was. I had never even heard of it before I went there."

This veteran had been raised in a strict Seventh Day Adventist family, where both tobacco and alcohol had been forbidden. The war made men like him susceptible to heroin use not just because it increased stress, but also because it severely weakened inhibitions. "In the war zone," Dr. Bourne notes, "there is often the feeling that all usual social mores have been suspended, and individuals feel free to engage in behavior both in and out of combat that they would find reprehensible in civilian life." [18] Traditional moral restraints are loosened; anything is possible. Under such conditions, inhibitions that might be counted on in civilian life lose their influence, and radical departures in personal behavior occur—drug use among them.

The environment of war alters the soldiers' perceptions of risk and time. It is almost hopeless to tell a man who is risking his life in a war not to take drugs because they're dangerous. Men who live with dangers that are clear and immediate are unlikely to show much concern over others that are distant and uncertain. The war zone encourages a short-term perspective; the present necessarily becomes a total preoccupation. For the ordinary soldier, the mere passage of time with life intact is a victory. This fixation on time was especially strong in Vietnam, where as a consequence of the rotation system, each soldier spent exactly one year and no more in the war zone. All attention was focused on getting through those 365 days as fast as possible. According to Dr. Zinberg, heroin was functional in dealing with that problem. "New users," he wrote, "discover that while marijuana slows up time, heroin speeds it up. ('It makes time go away. The days go bip, bip, bip.') . . . Heroin's remarkable effect on the time sense provides them an ingenious and effective (in one sense) solution to their problem of getting through their year's tour of duty." [19]

But heroin was not only a drug of adjustment, it was also a drug of defiance. It was a way of handling not only tension and ennui, but also resentment. If heroin quieted fears and made time pass, it also symbolized rebellion. But this was just symbolism, nothing more. Men who became heavily involved with drugs were rarely political. Indeed, black militants and soldiers with strong antiwar feelings considered heroin a threat to their movements, a means of diverting dissatisfaction away from dissent.[20] They instinctively appreciated a point that Seymour Halleck makes in a recent book: "Any drug that makes a person feel better can lessen his motivation to confront an oppressive situation." [21]

In defending itself against criticism, the military has often insisted, with some justification, that it has a drug problem "because the country has a drug problem" and that an army, especially one including draftees, can only reflect civilian society. But the drug problem in Vietnam was radically different from the problem that exists at home. "What struck me about Vietnam," Dr. Zinberg says, "was not that heroin was available, or that reports about extensive addiction in Vietnam were true . . . or that the smokers were doing great harm to themselves, but that heroin use was completely accepted. For in Vietnam . . . a social taboo of no mean power has been smashed, and we need to understand how this occurred and what its implications are." [22]

It would be wrong to attribute elaborate motivation to every soldier who tried heroin. Because it was socially acceptable, some soldiers smoked heroin merely as a "social gesture," an act no more indicative of mental illness, alienation, rebellion, or moral turpitude than taking a casual drink at a cocktail party.

Americans found the disclosures about heroin use in Vietnam hard to understand, in part because we could not grasp how unremarkable it was to the men themselves. We imagined heroin was incapacitating to the user and disruptive to the army, while in fact, its impact on both was rather limited. In many respects, the situation in Vietnam bears a resemblance to the situation in the United States seventy years ago. At both times, opiate addiction itself was widespread before the drug addiction *problem* appeared in the virulent form it takes in America now.

★ The Long Arm of History

Heroin addiction today, more than any other form of drug abuse, is associated with street crime. It is concentrated among men, among the young, among the black, and among the poor. We tend to assume these things have always been true about drug addiction when, in fact, they have been true only in the recent past.

At the turn of the century, heroin, morphine, and other derivatives of opium could be bought at any drugstore in the United States without a prescription. They cost as little as aspirin costs today and were widely recommended by physicians for every imaginable discomfort. Patent medicines containing opiates were also generally available and heavily advertised in the press. Many cough syrups and asthma preparations, in particular, contained heroin, often without label. As a result, the number of people addicted was considerable. Annual opiate consumption in America averaged 38 grains per capita—twelve times as great as in France and eighteen times as great as in Germany. The National Commission on Marijuana and Drug Abuse suggests a "conservative" estimate of the number of addicts in 1900 would be at least 1 percent of the population. Other sources estimate the proportion at 2 to 4 percent. Hypodermics were widely available to the public, and many persons administered drugs intravenously.[23,24,25]

This practice had begun only during the last half of the nineteenth century. Previously, opium had always been taken orally, either eaten or smoked. However, with the introduction of the hypodermic needle in the United States in 1856, it began to be injected into the blood in the form of morphine, and its use as an analgesic became common. During the Civil War, soldiers were given morphine to alleviate pain and illness, and many of them developed physical dependency on the drug. So common was this that withdrawal pains, poorly understood at the time, came to be called "soldier's disease." When the war was over, veterans spread the use of morphine and morphine addiction throughout the nation. So Vietnam may not be totally without precedent.

By the end of the nineteenth century, concern over morphine addiction was growing among physicians. The medical world was, therefore, encouraged when a German pharmaceutical laboratory developed a new substance in 1898 which, it was said, would eliminate the craving for morphine. And indeed it could: The new chemical, diacetylmorphine, was three times as strong. Bayer, which marketed the product in America under the brand name "heroin," advertised it side by side with its other new medication, aspirin: Bayer aspirin for headaches and Bayer heroin, "the sedative for coughs." [26]

Medical journals initially extended heroin an enthusiastic reception as a cough medicine and cure for "morphinism," but within a few years reports began appearing that it too was addictive. By then it was too late: The drug had already become an accepted household remedy. That heroin began as a legitimate form of medication and only gradually came to be used as an intoxicant is intimately related to changes in the way society has dealt with addiction. The original status of opiates as medicine affected what kind of people became addicts, why they became addicted, what they subjectively experienced from the drugs, how others responded to their addiction, and the extent to which their dependency interfered with their lives.

Addicts today are primarily drawn from the lower and working classes and from ethnic minorities. They are overwhelmingly young, and males outnumber females by a large margin. In 1900 virtually all of these patterns were reversed. Contemporary surveys and reports indicate that addiction predominated among the middle-aged rather than the young, among women rather than men, and among the white population rather than the black. Addicts came from all grades of society, though the evidence suggests that a disproportionate number belonged to the middle and upper classes.[27]

Probably very few of these addicts experienced euphoria from the use of drugs, in part because morphine was more commonly used than heroin. But even with heroin, the medical definition of usage may have colored individual reactions. Experiments have since shown that when naïve subjects in a medical setting are administered heroin, few report a pleasurable sensation.[28] To a large extent, the way individuals interpret the objective physiological effects of an opiate depends upon the set of expectations with which they approach the experience. When the use of opiates was socially defined as proper medication and was common in all social strata, expectations were radically different from what they became in a later period, when opiate use was defined as illicit and as a means of sensual gratification and was associated with the underworld. Heroin, of course, was always potentially a euphoriant, but that potential had to be discovered and its initial therapeutic definition overcome.

As the social location and cultural meaning of heroin use in 1900 differed from what they are today, so did attitudes toward the drug addict. Opiate addiction was generally seen as a private misfortune, not a public problem, and accordingly it was handled individually, not socially. Addicts themselves were not condemned or excluded from society for having been addicted by their physicians or druggists.[29] Though people regarded drug dependency as undesirable, they did not initially extend that judgment to the addict himself and view him as immoral, antisocial, or psychologically inadequate. Furthermore, drug addiction did not constitute a *total identity* as it does today. Whereas becoming an addict now means entering an entire way of life, it did not mean that in 1900. For example, a physician who treated drug addicts from 1911 to 1915 in Jacksonville, Florida, reported some years later:

> One of the most important discoveries we made at that time was that a very large proportion of the users of opiate drugs—not cocaine—were respectable, *hard-working* individuals in all walks of life, and that the smaller part only, according to my figures about 18 percent, could in any way be considered as belonging to the underworld.[30]

The inability of addicts to function normally in society today is commonly attributed to the effects of the drugs they take. But in 1900, when addicts had only to cope with the drugs' physical effects, the vast majority appear to have been gainfully employed. Since drugs then cost only a few pennies a day, those addicted to morphine or heroin were not driven to steal in order to raise enough money to support their habits. Nor did they bear the weight of social ostracism that addicts bear today or encounter continual harassment by the police and prosecution under the law. Partly because the society of 1900 had yet to place a moral and legal judgment on drug addiction, it had a less severe social problem than we do today, even though the prevalence of addiction was much greater than it is now.

Reform and Reformation

But America in 1900 did have a drug problem. The indiscriminate use of morphine and heroin by physicians and the presence of opiates in unlabeled patent medicines had addicted thousands of the unsuspecting. Responsible doctors and other reformers, therefore, began to agitate in favor of tighter controls on opiates in order to reduce this accidental therapeutic addiction.

In the effort to limit the availability of narcotics, medical reformers in the Progressive tradition were quickly joined by moral reformers in the Puritan tradition. Though heroin had been introduced as medication, more people were discovering its potential as a euphoriant. And with respect to this kind of drug use, the society of 1900 was almost uniformly unsympathetic. The abstentionist temper was then in high fever. Forces were mobilized not primarily against narcotics, but against tobacco and alcohol. In 1885, for example, *The New York Times* had editorialized: "The decadence of Spain began when the Spaniards adopted cigarettes, and if this pernicious habit obtains among adult Americans, the ruin of the Republic is close at hand." [31] Between 1895 and 1921, fourteen states banned the sale of cigarettes. The battle against alcohol was, of course, more advanced. Even before nationwide Prohibition went into effect in 1919, local and state governments had banned the sale of liquor in half the country. Such a society was not about to condone indulgence in narcotics. Tobacco and alcohol were at least indigenous vices, but opium was associated with the Chinese, the object of intense racial hatred and suspicion. Thus the use of opiates as intoxicants called forth not just the passions of the Puritan spirit, but those of nativism and isolationism as well. The opening salvo in the war against narcotics was, therefore, quite logically the prohibition of opium smoking, the most alien form opiate use took at that time.

Another factor leading to antinarcotics legislation involved reports from the South that cocaine, which at the time was widely used in stimulants, tonics, and even soft drinks, had stirred up mobs of "crazed" Negroes and led them to perpetuate violent sexual crimes against white women. The basis of these reports is dubious, but that they had a public impact is not.

In short, the movement to regulate narcotics use had several distinct sources: the desire on the part of physicians to curb therapeutic addiction, the opposition on the part of moral reformers to the use of any drug as an intoxicant, and the nativist and racist suspicion of outcast minorities such as the Chinese and the blacks, who were associated (falsely in both instances) with opium and cocaine.

Of these three forces, the first was probably the strongest in getting legislation enacted. The antinarcotics movement in the early 1900s never took on the full moral dimensions of the Temperance movement. The issue was carried largely by medical men whose intentions were to prevent the widespread distribution of opiates to a public that was unaware of their addictive properties. Thus an early step in reform was the Pure Food and Drug Act of 1906, which required the identification of all ingredients in commercial medications. There followed international conferences in Shanghai in 1909 and at The Hague in 1912 aimed at limiting trade in opium. Finally, on December 17, 1914, Congress passed the Harrison Narcotics Act, which laid the basis of federal drug control.

Ostensibly a revenue measure, the Harrison Act had three major provisions: 1. Anyone engaged in the production or distribution of narcotics would have to register with the federal government; 2. All such parties would have to pay a tax; and 3. Unregistered persons could purchase drugs only when prescribed by a physician for "legitimate" medical purposes. What constituted a "legitimate" medical purpose was never defined in the act; this turned out to be the focus of judicial and medical controversy for years to come.

In none of its provisions did the Harrison Act make any mention of addicts or addiction. It merely stipulated that all public access to narcotics would henceforth be through authorized medical channels. Ironically, however, precisely the opposite resulted. Within a few years, access to drugs through the medical profession was cut off for addicts, and new, unauthorized channels appeared.

That the Harrison Act was drawn up as tax legislation turned out to have important unanticipated consequences. It placed enforcement of narcotics laws in the Department of the Treasury, where it would remain for decades. As it happened, the enforcement of Prohibition was also lodged in the Treasury, and the same office became responsible for both. The limited purposes of the medical reformers consequently became submerged in the larger moral purposes of Prohibition. Furthermore, as Alfred Lindesmith has pointed out:

> The theory that the narcotics laws are tax measures has obscured and confused issues and prevented such questions as "Who is the criminal?" "Who is the victim?" "What is the crime?" from being asked and rationally considered in shaping the statutes. The inclusion of the use of certain drugs within the scope of the criminal law may well be a mistake, an unwarranted extension of legal controls into the medical field and into the sphere of essentially personal behavior with which the criminal law ought not be concerned, and which it cannot in any case control.[32]

At the time the Harrison Act was passed, a large number of physicians did consider it an unwarranted extension of governmental power into their profession. Those doctors who supported the bill came largely from the liberal faction in medicine, which at that point dominated the American Medical Association. The legislation was opposed by conservative doctors who denounced it as invasion of personal and professional rights.

On the treatment of addiction, medical opinion in this period was also divided. The dominant professional view in this country was that the craving for narcotics could be scientifically eliminated through a process known as the Towns-Lambert treatment and that addicts ought not to be maintained on drugs. Others felt that not all addicts could be treated successfully and that those who could not be cured of their addiction should be kept "comfortable" with drugs provided by a physician or clinic.

This medical dispute was ultimately resolved not by the medical profession, but by the government—in particular, by the Department of the Treasury, in conjunction with the courts. In significant respects, the conservative physicians' fears of state intervention were eventually fulfilled.

The Impact of the Harrison Act

Upon enactment of the Harrison Act, doctors suddenly found themselves faced with thousands of law-abiding addicts desperately in need of prescriptions. Not enough physicians were available to "cure" addicts, had a cure been known—and none was. Consequently, many doctors simply began dispensing drugs freely. It was not long before the Treasury began bringing indictments against physicians for violating the provision in the Harrison Act that narcotics could be prescribed only for "legitimate" medical purposes. The question was whether morphine and heroin maintenance constituted a legitimate medical purpose.

Initially, the courts sided with the physicians and threw out the Treasury indictments. For the first four years of the Harrison Act, therefore, addicts were able to receive drugs through legal channels. Then in 1919, two months after Prohibition became part of the Constitution, the Supreme Court reversed an earlier decision and ruled that a prescription for morphine for an addict "to keep him comfortable by maintaining customary use" was not a prescription within the meaning of the law. The Treasury had won. The prohibition of narcotics had come in on the coattails of Prohibition. "The addict," writes Troy Duster, "found himself being cut off gradually but surely from all legal sources, and he began to turn gradually but surely to the welcome arms of the black market-eers." [33]

Concomitant with the blocking off of legitimate access to drugs was a steep rise in the price of narcotics and a dramatic increase in addict crime. The warden of the Federal prison at Leavenworth, Kansas, for example, reported that from July 1914 to December 31, 1922, 7 percent of the prisoners committed were drug addicts. During 1921, 15½ percent were addicts. From July 1 to December 31, 1922, 24 percent were addicts.[34] A new pattern of crime was emerging.

For a brief period around 1921, the Treasury Department had second thoughts about its categorical opposition to maintenance. It decided that an interim period during which addicts might be supplied with drugs was necessary and opened forty-four maintenance clinics in major cities. The experiment proved short-lived and in any case never involved more than a fraction of the nation's addicts. A number of scandals erupted over the operation of the clinics, particularly in New York, and by 1924 the Treasury had closed them all. The evidence on the narcotics clinics is sparse; some seem to have been badly managed, while others—for example, in Los Angeles and Shreveport, Louisiana—appear to have been successful in weaning addicts away from their habits and in preventing the development of a black market. In each area, when the clinics closed the peddlers returned.[35]

Throughout this period, the composition of the addict population was changing. Many of the middle- and upper-class addicts probably did end their dependency. Addiction had never become a total identity for them, and hence the psychosocial problems of readjustment were minimized. Also, those who were unable to abstain probably were able to secure narcotics from discreet private physicians. Lower- and working-class addicts were not so fortunate; they had to patronize the black market. Within a few years, addiction had gravitated to the unrespectable parts of society. The medical definition of personal opiate use had been suppressed, and only the "street" definition remained. Correspondingly, the epidemiology of addiction began to shift, reversing the patterns of previous years. By the early Twenties, male addicts outnumbered females, young addicts outnumbered the middle-aged, and poor addicts outnumbered the well-off. Public sympathy for the addict was disappearing. By the mid-Twenties, the moral judgment of the addict had been radically transformed. What was once a private misfortune of limited magnitude was now a crime and a cause of crime.[36]

Britain's Alternate History

Great Britain provides an interesting contrast to this history, because the course of events there paralleled what happened in this country until about 1920 and then diverged. In the early 1900s, opiates were widely marketed in Britain, creating the same kind of problem as in America. Parliament responded in 1920 with legislation virtually identical to the Harrison Narcotics Acts. Soon afterward, the question arose, as it did in the U.S., as to whether the maintenance of an addiction constituted a legitimate medical purpose. Instead of resolving this issue in the courts, however, the

British set up a commission primarily of medical experts, which in 1926 ruled that maintenance was acceptable in certain cases. For the next several decades, British doctors were able to dispense morphine and heroin to their addicted patients, most of whom had acquired their dependency during medical treatment. The number of patients maintained on drugs was low, only a few hundred at any given time. Because doctors were permitted to supply drugs to addicts, there never appeared any significant black market traffic; nor did any causal relationship develop between addiction and crime.

During the 1960s, however, with the drug culture flourishing in Britain, some of the interest in marijuana and LSD spilled over to heroin. A new kind of addict appeared—young, defiant, interested in drugs as a way of life.[37] The number of persons maintained by physicians began to climb over 1,000, then past 2,000. In the United States this was taken as evidence that the "British system" had failed. The British, however, saw it as a sign that reform and reorganization were needed to tighten the distribution of opiates. (A few physicians had taken advantage of the new demand for drugs by aggressively peddling heroin for profit.) To deal with the problem, the British restricted distribution to a small number of clinics, where closer supervision would be possible. Some limited social services—not nearly enough according to many critics—were added to meet the needs of the new nontherapeutic addicts. An effort was made to switch as many addicts as possible off heroin and on to methadone, intravenously administered. By 1970, the number of addicts had leveled off. Those maintained on heroin numbered 914, with about 2,000 more on methadone.[38,39] Despite this record, the impression continued to exist in the United States that the British system had failed. We would be lucky to suffer such failures.

★ Social Policy and Addiction

We have recounted at some length the evolution of the addiction problem, not out of antiquarian interest, but because it suggests that the social problem America faces today has more to do with the way our society has reacted than with the drug itself. Undesirable as opiate use may be, it has been far worse under the conditions we have created by making narcotics accessible to addicts only through the black market. The same Puritan strain in our culture which gave us Prohibition also gave us the ban on the medical supervision of addiction—and in the same decade. The irony of such categorical measures has been that they have only exacerbated the original problems, not cured them. Prohibition, Richard Hofstadter once remarked, was "a memento of the strange power of crusades for absolute morality to intensify the evils they mean to destroy." [40] His words apply well to the history of our approach toward narcotic drugs.

But Prohibition had a relatively short career—only fifteen years. Ultimately the Puritan temper was outdistanced by that other great figure in our cultural history, the pragmatic spirit. And it is the latter which, in the past few years, has begun to show its force in the area of addiction.

For decades, social policy toward addiction was dominated by the Treasury's Bureau of Narcotics, the fiefdom of Harry Anslinger, in much the same way as the FBI was the fiefdom of J. Edgar Hoover during the same period. The bureau played two hopeless games, one with numbers and the other with economics. When its statistics showed that addiction was increasing, the bureau explained to the public that stiffer penalties and higher budgets were needed. When the statistics showed addiction wasn't increasing, they proved stiff penalties worked, and the bureau was doing a fine job. It was a game the bureau could not lose.

The other game was one the bureau could not win: attacking the supplies of narcotics, while effectively doing nothing to reduce the demand. The more successfully the bureau attacked the supply, the higher went the prices on the black market and the more attractive it became to new suppliers. In the language of industrial economics, the bureau made possible excess profits by creating artificial barriers to entry through its enforcement strategy.

Before the last decade, medical assistance for drug addicts was virtually nil. Most hospitals turned away addicts requesting help in withdrawal because they could not afford to pay for treatment and because they were deemed responsible for whatever pain they suffered. Using the latter argument, the hospitals could have also excluded sky divers and mountain climbers who broke their legs taking unnecessary risks.

Psychiatric hospitals that did accept an occasional addict for treatment compiled an unimpressive record. As a recent review of treatment practices notes, "Traditional psychiatric approaches used with the general run of mental patients do not seem to have succeeded with drug addicts. When addicts have been placed on the regular psychiatric wards of hospitals, it has usually been to the disservice of themselves, the psychiatric patients, and the staff." [41]

Between 1924—when the last of the narcotics clinics closed and the AMA ruled ambulatory programs for addicts unacceptable—

and the late Fifties, the only major rehabilitation programs specifically for drug addiction were operated by the federal government at Lexington, Kentucky, and Fort Worth, Texas. Both had a psychiatric emphasis. Of the voluntary patients, more than two thirds left "against medical advice." There was no provision for follow-up care after the patients returned to their communities, and a substantial majority relapsed. The two hospitals had some success with middle-class addicts, virtually none with poor blacks and others from ghetto communities.

As the addiction problem deepened in the late Fifties and Sixties, alternatives to narrow punitive measures and psychiatric hospitalization began to get consideration. Ultimately two new approaches gained prominence: drug-free, residential programs, generally called "therapeutic communities," and methadone maintenance. Together with detoxification, these constitute the three principal forms of treatment available today. Their purposes are quite different; so are their results.

Detoxification has the most limited aims. Addicts are administered tranquilizers or diminishing doses of methadone to alleviate the pains of abrupt withdrawal. Usually it is a stopgap measure, relieving the addict's immediate distress, but not producing any long-term change in his behavior. Methadone maintenance has a larger objective: stabilizing the addict's drug dependency so that he can assume a productive role in his community (essentially the British approach). The therapeutic communities have the largest objective: a total reorientation of the addict's personality and complete termination of all drug dependency.

The therapeutic communities, beginning with Synanon in the late Fifties and Daytop Village in the early Sixties, have developed largely out of the efforts of nonprofessional ex-addicts. While varying in style, they share a fairly coherent philosophy of treatment. They view drug abuse not as an illness, but as a symptom of underlying emotional problems brought on by arrested personal development. The programs seek to recreate that development by reducing the addict to the status of a child at the beginning and then allowing him to advance and win privileges by behaving in ways that the community approves. Group sanctions and direct, open emotional confrontations supplant professional psychotherapy. Rather than developing insight through prolonged exploration of the past, the programs seek to develop behavior through conditioning techniques. In the language of psychologist Perry London, they provide "action therapy" rather than "insight therapy." [42] This is what distinguishes their approach from traditional psychiatry.

The principal problem of therapeutic communities has been retention. More than three quarters of those who enter drop out against advice, most in the first month. "No therapeutic community," notes a study of drug abuse treatment, "has yet managed to graduate more than a tiny fraction of those who entered. Add to this the considerable evidence that therapeutic communities mainly attract young people of middle-class background, frequently white, and it becomes evident that their success thus far involves a very small part of the drug abusing population." [43] The most successful programs have had strong religious or political underpinnings, which have enabled them to provide addicts with forms of emotional involvements as intense as their prior immersion in drugs.

From a social standpoint, the significant innovation of the past decade was methadone maintenance. Methadone is a synthetic narcotic that has been used in detoxifying heroin addicts for about twenty-five years. Like heroin, it is an addictive and potent analgesic and can produce a "rush" if injected. Methadone, however, can also be given orally, causes less drowsiness, and has a longer active life (twenty-four to thirty-six hours compared with four to eight hours for heroin). Addicts who have built up tolerance to heroin are also tolerant to methadone.[44]

In the mid-Sixties, two medical researchers in New York, Drs. Marie Nyswander and Vincent Dole, began experimenting with methadone as a maintenance drug for heroin addicts. On the basis of their research, they contended that a stable dosage of methadone could eliminate the craving for drugs and blockade the euphoriant effects of heroin. The FDA assigned the status of "investigational new drug" to methadone as a maintenance agent, and within a few years, hundreds of programs across the country operating under IND licenses were offering methadone to addicts in conjunction with other services. After forty years of resistance, maintenance had reappeared in the United States, entering by the back door in the guise of experimental research.

The reintroduction of maintenance could not, however, erase fifty years of history. The virtue of the British system was not simply that it prevented the development of a lucrative black market by providing medical access to narcotics for the addicted. Its real genius was that it prevented narcotics from becoming associated with illicit pleasure. By labeling heroin the supreme evil and creating a criminal subculture around it, we have paradoxically lent it an enormous fascination. By putting it inside a clinic, the British have turned heroin addiction into something utterly banal and uninteresting. Methadone maintenance arrived late on the American scene, too late to change the cultural meanings that had been established over decades.

The results of methadone programs have been the subject of considerable dispute. On the one hand, they have enabled addicts to escape their dependence on heroin pushers, reduce their involvement in crime, and assume a degree of personal responsibility through taking a job and reestablishing their families. Critics argue, in response, that giving out methadone does nothing to alleviate the basic social and psychological problems causing addiction, that the long-term physiological effects of methadone are unknown, and that large amounts of the drug are now being diverted to the black market and taken in lieu of heroin—all of which are in some degree true, but inconclusive. The social maladies of our time are beyond the ability of any form of drug abuse treatment to eliminate. There may be long-term consequences to methadone maintenance, but none has yet been demonstrated that outweighs its advantages.[45]

In recent years, policy makers have been inclined not to take sides in the internecine warfare between the advocates of methadone programs and therapeutic communities, opting for a "multimodality" approach in which various alternatives coexist, with the addicts choosing among them. As addicts have gravitated toward methadone clinics, they have expanded more rapidly than programs that are drug-free. Even so, methadone maintenance is still not available to most addicts in the country.

While the shift of the past fifteen years from a criminal to a therapeutic model in the management of drug addiction has been a progressive development, it shows no signs of eliminating the general problem of drug abuse. To suggest that it might do so is to confuse drug-taking with addiction, two closely related but different phenomena. Addiction is, in large part, a physical condition that medicine can control in the same sense that it can control diabetes. Drug-taking is a kind of behavior, often compulsive behavior, and there is no convincing evidence that medicine has anything special to contribute to the control of compulsions.

There is an analogy to be made between the history of our war against addiction and the war in Vietnam. In each case, we have been driven, by our own overreactions, into the position of trying to save people by destroying them. In both cases we needed to learn that intervention, however forceful, had limits, however hard to accept.

II. REFLEX AND RESPONSE

In the course of the Vietnam War, the military faced severe problems in the management of its own troops. Racial tensions, antiwar sentiment, and hostility between enlisted men and "lifers" caused the army to recast many of its traditional practices. In the area of drug use, the military shifted from a punitive approach to a policy that mixes rehabilitation with criminal penalties. That evolution, replicating a change that has taken place in civilian society over a much longer period, came about in roughly three stages:

1) an initial hard-line phase, lasting approximately until late 1969, when the policy toward drug users was essentially to prosecute and remove them;

2) a transitional phase lasting from 1969 to June 1971, characterized by the introduction of a limited "amnesty" and scattered treatment and counseling programs amid continuing attempts at repression; and

3) the most recent phase, beginning with the mobilization of June 1971, which has seen a comprehensive system of identification and treatment (and punishment) established.

★ *The Failure of Intimidation:*
  The Army Looks for a Few Bad Men

Drug use in the military has always been a crime, but until recently it was nothing else. All programs, all directives, all actions taken by military authorities were predicated on that fact. Having defined the drug user as a criminal, the military traditionally felt no responsibility toward him. Its only concern was that he represented a threat, and its only response was to discipline and remove him from his unit, either by imprisonment or discharge. Comments by a sergeant major of the 173rd Airborne Brigade before 1971 Congressional hearings capture the "old guard" perspective:

"I have over eleven hundred men and out of eleven hundred I have very few on drugs or marijuana. However, the ones I do have are imported—they come from the States. . . . The thing we really need . . . is a way to get rid of these people as soon as we discover them. Be able to eliminate them." [1]

And try to eliminate them they did. The number of soldiers discharged for drug abuse climbed steadily each year of the war, but somehow the number of new users climbed faster. Drug-related criminal investigations, mostly for marijuana, rose 80 percent from 1968 to 1969 and 38 percent from 1969 to 1970 [2]—large increases but probably not as large as the increases in drug use itself. On all sides, soldiers cooperated in thwarting the efforts of military authorities to suppress drug use.

"The one big thing about dope, if you got busted, as long as you were busted locally you were OK. As long as it stayed within the company, there'd be no sweat. But if the CIDs [Criminal Investigation Division] ever got a hold of you, boy, they could really screw you. They did screw people. Fortunately we had a buddy [on the inside]. . . . What they used to do is bring a sniffing dog through our hootch all the time—like maybe once every couple months. And he'd always tell us when they were coming in advance. What we'd always do is we'd paint the hootch so the dog couldn't smell shit."

Confronted by a wall of quiet resistance, the strategy of intimidation and suppression broke down. In 1970, after touring the Pacific theater, a Defense Department study group reported that officers felt punitive measures were having no deterrent effect on soldiers using drugs.

"The attitude of the EM [enlisted man] is that you can throw all the various types of discharges in the air and take your pick. None of the discharges has any deterrent effect. They do not know or appear to care what a less than honorable discharge means. The troops laugh at Article 15s. Senior NCOs felt that there was nothing they could do to a man that would be effective to discipline him. They felt that their hands were tied. No longer can they grab a man and shake him up to bring him back into line." [3]

The limits of intimidation were also apparent in the Pentagon's "drug education" program. The military made the incomparable error of issuing statements about drugs that large numbers of men knew to be false from their own experience. One film warned that smoking marijuana led to insanity. "It is a drug which has no known beneficial use," intoned a DOD directive from as late as October 1970. Its effects were listed as "psychotic reactions . . . hallucinations . . . anxiety . . . muscular incoordination . . . irritability, confusion, impairment of judgment. . . . All the effects of marijuana use on the human body, mind, personality, and genetic system are not yet known." [4] No one was persuaded. "These kids," one officer bluntly told a Congressional committee, "are going to sit down and roll joints with some of the notebooks they are handing out." [5]

As drug use spread, unchecked by punishment and scare tactics, the military was forced to reevaluate its position. In early 1969, the Army began to experiment with an "amnesty" program (later called "exemption"), which it extended to all commands in October. The other services, where the drug problem was less acute, were reluctant to budge. It would be more than a year before the Air Force and Navy followed the Army's lead.

Under the new program, soldiers involved in drug use but not under prosecution or investigation could ostensibly seek rehabilitation without exposing themselves to punitive action. The purpose was partly humane—to provide an opportunity for drug users to seek help—and partly tactical—to get drug users to identify themselves. The Navy accepted amnesty primarily as a means of generating informers against other soldiers taking drugs.[6]

As the men soon found out, amnesty was not really amnesty at all. "Punitive action" was defined narrowly to mean only punishments meted out through court-martial, and the exemption applied only when possession was the sole offense. A soldier who turned himself in could still be prosecuted for a variety of drug-related offenses, such as sale, or on other charges if, during treatment, he accidentally gave information regarding crimes he committed in the course of drug use. (In the military there is no guarantee of confidentiality between doctor and patient.) He could still receive an undesirable discharge solely on the basis of his drug use—that was an "administrative" not a "punitive" action—or a dishonorable discharge *partly* on the basis of his drug use. He could still lose his security clearance, job classification, and flying status—all of them "administrative" actions. He would definitely lose all time spent in inpatient treatment, since that would be added to the length of his tour of duty. His pay would be docked, his medical records might subsequently be made available to other government agencies such as the FBI, and beyond all that, he would probably be harassed by superiors and assigned to menial tasks when his rehabilitation was over, or even while it was continuing.[7]

Under those circumstances, most soldiers did not think treatment was a good deal. If they sought rehabilitation through the exemption program, it was usually to avoid something worse—like the stockade. Hence the men who entered treatment usually were voluntary patients only in a very limited sense.

Perhaps the greatest danger for the drug user was that the amnesty program left him totally exposed after one attempt at shaking his habit. A soldier could seek exemption only once. From that point on, not only would he be subject to the full range of "punitive" actions, but the authorities would know exactly who he was. Cases in which soldiers were subsequently court-martialed for drug use after turning themselves in have been documented in Congressional hearings. One soldier at Fort Eustis, for example, sought amnesty, received five days of hospitalization for heroin addiction, and was then released. Not surprisingly, the soldier relapsed and was immediately picked up by the Criminal Investigation Division, court-martialed, and given a three-and-a-half-year sentence with a dishonorable discharge.[8]

The amnesty program evoked suspicion, and with good reason. It was, as a Senate staff report described it, "laced with punitive booby traps." [9] Soldiers were guaranteed nothing except that they would not be court-martialed solely on the grounds that they had previously used drugs. That left the army free to punish the men in a variety of other ways.

Of course, the booby traps in amnesty were not the only reason drug-using soldiers refused to turn themselves in. Most simply did not want to be rehabilitated, regardless of legal protection. No matter how much others disapproved, they liked drugs. As the military edged tentatively from a criminal to a quasi-medical approach toward drug use, that resistance to rehabilitation became critical.

★ Crisis and Mobilization

Even as heroin use took on epidemic proportions in 1970, the military publicly denied it had much of a drug problem. But after the press reports and Congressional investigations of spring 1971, the disclaimers ended, and the public clamor for action became impossible to ignore. For society, the military's traditional policy of prosecuting and punitively discharging drug users had been acceptable when the numbers involved were small. But the prospect of legions of heroin addicts returning untreated from Vietnam caused general alarm. Soon there were demands on all sides that the military take responsibility for its drug problem and embark on a serious program of rehabilitation. Significantly, the first time President Nixon acknowledged the existence of drug abuse in the military—at a press conference on June 1, 1971—he promised that the army would treat every drug user, even if it had to hold men past their discharge dates.[10]

Later that month, the President responded to public pressure by creating a new executive office to coordinate federal drug programs and appointing Dr. Jerome Jaffe as its director. At the same time, Secretary of Defense Laird promulgated a four-point program against drug use in the military.

1. All servicemen leaving Vietnam would be tested for drug use through urinalysis.

2. Soldiers identified as users would undergo five to seven days of detoxification prior to returning home.

3. Men whose terms were ending and who needed and desired treatment would be provided an opportunity for thirty days of treatment either in military or VA facilities.

4. Soldiers remaining in the services would be treated there "insofar as possible." [11]

Symbolizing a shift in attitude, the Defense Department transferred drug programs out of Manpower and Reserve Affairs into Health and Environment. The Pentagon also announced that neither urinalysis results nor requests for treatment under the exemption program could be used as grounds for a court-martial or less than honorable administrative discharge. These new rules, plus the threat of detection through urinalysis, led to an upsurge in the number of soldiers seeking amnesty. In the first six months of 1971, the Defense Department granted 15,176 requests for exemption; in the later half of the year, 22,838. About 43 percent of these (16,101) were granted in Vietnam.[12]

★ Operation Golden Flow: Trial by Urine

The critical innovation turned out to be the new urinalysis screening system, a two-stage process involving an initial test by Free Radical Assay Technique (FRAT) with verification by gas-liquid chromatography (GLC). At first, it was applied only to soldiers leaving Southeast Asia. Since the men had advance notice of when they would be tested, those whose use of heroin was discretionary could escape the net. The results, therefore, reflected rates of heroin dependence rather than rates of heroin use. Of the first 22,000 tested 1,000 were positive, a rate of 4.5 percent that Dr. Jaffe and others then cited as evidence that press reports on heroin use had been exaggerated.[13]

But, as Dr. Wilbur, Assistant Secretary of Defense for Health and Environment, later wrote, the 4.5 percent who were caught on their way home represented only "the tip of the iceberg," since the majority of users were able to abstain temporarily and escape detection.[14] The figures also did not include the more than 12,000 soldiers who had been apprehended for drug use or sought amnesty in the first six months of 1971.[15] Finally, the screening system was incredibly porous when it was first set up. Soldiers finessed their way through by substituting urine specimens of obliging friends. With inexperienced personnel there was also a high rate of technical error, mostly false negatives. "I think we must admit we were missing a fair number of people," Dr. Wilbur subsequently conceded.[16]

Even as the screening system improved, problems with reliability continued. Defense Department monitoring of the urinalysis tests subsequently indicated that they pick up only about half of the urine specimens containing drugs. The first omen that the screening was unreliable came when the Pentagon released "quality control" data on three civilian contractors performing the tests in the continental United States. Although their contracts required a 90 percent rate of accuracy, the laboratories were able to identify correctly only 61 percent of urine samples with known contents. No action was ever taken against them for violating the terms of the contracts.[17]

At the time this information was disclosed, the Pentagon insisted that its own laboratories were operating with crack efficiency. But in June 1972 a member of the House Armed Services Committee, Les Aspin (D.-Wis.), obtained data evaluating the accuracy of military laboratories over the previous three months. They had correctly identified only 45 percent of the test samples containing morphine (the form in which heroin is excreted in the urine) and only 52 percent of those containing barbiturates and amphetamines, as well as morphine. The overall accuracy of the tests, for both negative and positive specimens, was 62 percent—almost the same as the civilian contractors.[18]

These results concerned only military laboratories in the United States, but if the laboratories in Vietnam had been any more accurate, the Defense Department would doubtless have released data on them as well.

Virtually all of the technical mistakes have been "false negatives." When "false positives" occur, it is primarily because of defects inherent in the screening system and not because of laboratory error. Specifically, the tests for morphine also register positive for certain prescription drugs like Darvon. In addition, some soldiers who never consciously used narcotics were picked up after unwittingly smoking marijuana laced with heroin.

Although false positives were less common than false negatives, their consequences were more serious. Staff Sergeant Donald L. Fryer, for example, was mistakenly identified as a heroin user by a urinalysis machine in late September 1971 at Long Binh, Vietnam. Despite his protestations of innocence, negative results from subsequent urine tests, a long list of decorations (including an Army commendation medal for his work against drug abuse and for Vietnamese orphans), and the fact that he showed no signs of going into withdrawal, it took Sergeant Fryer ten days before the intervention of his commanding officer could get him released. "An administrative error," everyone agreed, but the affair did not end there. In the meantime, the record of his detention as a drug abuser had spread. Several months later, after he had returned home, the Red Cross denied a request of his to adopt a Vietnamese war orphan on the grounds that he had been an addict. Again it took Sergeant Fryer weeks to clear up the matter, but meanwhile the erroneous report had spread further, and applications for a Vietnamese exit permit and passport for the orphan had been delayed. Several more weeks passed before those matters were resolved. Even now there is no guarantee that the mistake will not come up again from the depths of some uncorrected computer.[19]

Sergeant Fryer was lucky. He had an impeccable Army record and commanding officers who repeatedly intervened on his behalf. Men with less brilliant reputations or with records of nonconformity or political dissent were more vulnerable.

Perhaps the major problem with the screening system, however, was that no one really knew what to do with the men once they were spotted as heroin users. The President had promised, at a minimum, five to seven days of detoxification, but that turned out to mean little more than a week or so of surveillance. "It was more like a detention [center] than a detoxification center," Sergeant Fryer recalled of Long Bihn. "I can tell you that there are seventeen hundred feet of barbed wire and chain link fence and twenty-five hundred feet of cement sidewalk, because I walked every inch of it for ten days. That is about all the men had to do. . . . Also, unfortunately, there were cases of people getting heroin into the center and selling it to the men." [20]

"The mood of this installation is ugly," Dr. Zinberg wrote in a description of a large detoxification center holding 180 to 250 inmates at any one time. "Most of the patients are picked up on routine urine testing prior to DEROS [Date Eligible for Return from Overseas] and are held until they can pass a FRAT test and a GLC test. . . . The average patient stay is 4.2 days. . . . This installation seems to be far more a jail than a hospital. . . . The patients spend much of their time planning either to get drugs or to thwart the authorities. . . . Personnel constantly ask for transfers. Without exception, they feel that all that keeps the place from exploding is 'the ticket,' the ticket home." [21]

Soldiers who were caught in urinalysis claim they were treated "like animals." They were relieved of all personal belongings and possessions, referred to as "junkies," harassed, and never told exactly what would happen to them. Conex boxes, about six feet high, five feet wide and eight feet long, were used for confinement and punishment. Conditions in the detoxification center at Cam Ranh Bay were such that in the fall of 1971, a major riot erupted, and two barracks were set afire. One particularly galling indignity came when the men were flown back to the United States . . . strapped down on litters as if they were berserk.[22]

On their return, the identified soldiers were offered additional treatment either in the military or at veterans' hospitals, which almost all refused. (Later the treatment became involuntary.) "Nobody is going home as a confirmed drug user," Dr. Jaffe told reporters soon after the urinalysis testing began. Pressed by *Medical World News* for an explanation, he amended the statement to: "Practically nobody is going home while still physiologically dependent on heroin." [23]

Concerned that they were reaching heroin users too late or missing them altogether, the military began making random checks on entire units, sometimes descending on them at four in the morning. The idea was to catch "the experimenters, the young men who were just getting started on the drug . . . when they could be cured, not after it was too late." [24] Surprise urinalysis testing, Dr. Jaffe argued, would help the user by moving him into treatment before he left Vietnam and would protect other soldiers by reducing the level of "contagion." [25] Ostensibly, it would have a deterrent effect on the curious, and the rate of heroin use and experimentation would decline.

The results of the surprise screening do show some decline, but not very much. In the first testing period, November 16–30, 1971, the proportion "clinically confirmed positive" was 4.9 percent; in December, 4.4 percent; in January 1972, 5.1 percent; and by June 1972, 4.0 percent.[26] This small drop could be the result of any number of extraneous factors, such as the higher proportion of career men left in Vietnam as troop withdrawals took place. It need not be related to the efficacy of the military's drug program. Furthermore, if monitoring elsewhere was representative, the urinalysis results understated the real extent of heroin use by one half. That the tests missed so many users was probably one reason why they were so weak a deterrent.

To some extent, screening did enable military authorities to locate units with high rates of drug use, to place soldiers using heroin in treatment, and to discharge them if they were found to be recidivist. But the record does not indicate that the identification system brought about a significant reduction in the level of narcotics use among soldiers in Vietnam.

Although the surprise tests probably missed half the men using heroin, many who were picked up were only marginal users. These men, paradoxically, may have been damaged more by the premature intervention of the military drug program than by their very casual involvement with drugs. This could happen in two ways. They might become prematurely stigmatized as addicts by old-line military men, and their contacts with drug users might be reinforced rather than eliminated through involuntary therapy.

A screening system not only identifies, it also labels. And the label "heroin addict" has effects as bad as the drug itself. Hence it is not entirely clear whether it is a good idea to catch people "early" since many of them, especially in the case of soldiers in Vietnam, may not go on to heavy drug use later. In physical illness, early detection often helps cure the disease. But for heroin use, the medical model is deceptive: Early detection may be premature labeling.

"Many of our patients," a sergeant in charge of a detoxification center wrote, "are only occasional users, some have used heroin only once in their lives, and others present convincing stories to indicate the strong possibility of mistaken identity as a user. Relatively few show any demonstrable symptoms of heroin withdrawal while confined. All, however, have a permanent hospital record established. It is reasonable to expect this information to be readily made available to other agencies.

"The issue is whether the individual so identified will be free of the stigma of drug 'use' in his post-military life. It now appears that the identified user will not be free of this label, regardless of the accuracy of the identification." [27]

Among higher echelon officers in charge of the drug program, there seems to be a sharp awareness of this problem and a genuine interest in not labeling young soldiers unfairly. They note that if a soldier returns to duty without further incident, only his medical records will contain any reference to drug involvement and, allegedly, these are unavailable to nonmedical personnel. Whether such views have been translated into practice at a lower level of authority is another matter. According to a Senate staff report, traditional attitudes toward drug use still predominate in the middle and lower officer ranks.[28]

Furthermore, soldiers who are discharged early because of involvement with drugs have a number stamped on their separation papers indicating drug abuse as the reason for discharge. The meaning of that number is now widely known among civilian employers.

Just as screening systems not only identify but also label, so rehabilitation programs provide not just treatment but also new social relations. A casual experimenter placed in a program with hard-core addicts may learn more from his fellow patients than from the staff. As prisons serve as places where young convicts learn from the more experienced, so drug programs provide an informal education of their own. It is a commonplace of modern sociology that the specialized institutions society establishes to suppress deviant behavior are often precisely the institutions through which that behavior is transmitted and reinforced. To be sure, treatment in the military was generally short in duration and not all of it residential, and these aspects probably reduced the extent of inadvertent reinforcement.

We offer these reflections not as decisive arguments against random testing, but as qualifications to the claims that have been made for it. On the one hand, the statistical results of surprise tests do not indicate that there was a significant decline in heroin use in Vietnam. On the other hand, the second-order consequences of both identification and treatment may weaken or even nullify the intended results.

★ Rehabilitation and Secondary Gain

One advantage of the military is that the combination of a rigid command structure and vast resources enables it to carry out decisions much faster than most other institutions. Once the decision was made to attempt to rehabilitate drug users, an extensive network of programs was rapidly established. While the Navy and Air Force chose to set up centralized treatment facilities, the Army followed a decentralized approach, organizing dozens of base rehabilitation programs. Decentralization has permitted much flexibility and experimentation, and the Army's programs have taken a variety of forms—"rap centers," halfway houses, individual counseling, psychiatric hospitalization, residential therapeutic communities.

In spite of this diversity, military rehabilitation programs share certain common problems because of similarities in the kinds of patients they receive, the reasons the patients are there, and the fact that they are all operating within the context of the army. These external constraints impose great limitations on what they are able to do.

One of the basic problems is the disjunction between the major aim of rehabilitation, which is to return men to duty, and the desires of the patients, which are usually the reverse.

A second problem is the resistance of the patients to the very notion they are sick.

A third is the contradiction between the ethics of therapy, which require confidentiality between doctor and patient, and the imperatives of a mission-oriented institution, which require that every commander know the physical and psychological condition of his men.

A fourth problem is the ambiguity of the military's approach to drug abuse. If brought to light through the urinalysis or amnesty programs, it is treated first as a medical problem, but if one attempt at rehabilitation fails, it becomes a disciplinary matter.

These are not problems of inadequate talent, inadequate time, or inadequate command support for drug abuse treatment—though each of those has represented a weakness at one base or another. They are matters that cut across local programs and affect military attempts at rehabilitation generally.

Perhaps the most basic obstacle is the patients' refusal to accept the aims and premises of treatment. Most of the men are under twenty, have used drugs for a relatively short time, and have not yet confronted any severe personal problems as a result of drug use. Their experience has not persuaded them that taking drugs is harmful. While some soldiers who voluntarily enter treatment are genuinely worried about their drug use, many more seek amnesty under duress and have no intention of giving up drugs.

"The guys who use drugs in the military," says an Army psychiatrist, "don't separate their use from the Army. They don't see any purpose in being rehabilitated to go back to the Army. That just doesn't make any sense to them. Using drugs is the way they cope with the Army.

"Now [when the rehabilitation program was set up] the Army said, if the men don't do well, we'll discharge them. This resulted in a peculiar message to the men: 'If you fail in the drug program, you get discharged, which is what you want.'

"They don't feel they have a drug problem. Even if they feel they have a drug problem, they don't think a program could help them. And even if they think a program could help them, they don't want to take one from the Army."

The exceptions prove the rule. "We have guys," one drug counselor reports, "who come into the rehabilitation program who say, 'Will you help me get off drugs?' We say, 'Sure, why do you want to get off?' And they say, 'Because I'm going to leave the Army.' Then you ask: 'If you were going to stay in the Army would you get off?' And they say, 'Hell no, I'd stay on.' " 29

Most of the dilemmas of military drug programs arise from the stubborn fact that the army is filled with men who hate it. They will take drugs to escape and, paradoxically, some of them will take drug programs to escape.

The history of a program at a domestic Army base illustrates the problem of what psychologists call "secondary gain" and most people refer to as ulterior motives. In September 1971, a halfway house with a bed capacity of twenty-five was opened under the direction of a young psychiatrist with prior experience in a civilian drug program. Initially the patients continued to function in their units while living in the halfway house. Because most soldiers who took drugs did not regard their use as a problem and because of the hidden penalties in amnesty, the program was never even slightly crowded. According to its director, the few who entered it had built up hostility outside and saw the halfway house as a means of escaping pressures in their units. They continued to use drugs, which they bought when they went out during the day. In the director's words, "The men were interested in using this aspect of the system to beat the rest of the system."

In December the program was closed for ten days and then reopened under a more strict format. The residents were isolated twenty-four hours a day so that they would have no opportunity to get drugs. Anyone who entered the program now faced a loss of privileges at the outset and had to work his way up through a system of rewards and punishments. These changes were made to ensure that only the well motivated would be attracted. After the reorganization, fewer soldiers entered the program, but they stayed longer. When they reached the end of their time, however, they still didn't want to go back to the army.

This has been the case elsewhere too. The secondary gains from treatment, particularly insulation from army life, have made therapeutic communities virtually unworkable within the military.

Excerpts from a trenchant and revealing critique by the drug abuse treatment staff of the Continental Army Command indicate the problems:

> The TC's [therapeutic communities] observed thus far have seemed to bear little relevance to the military. . . . When such facilities provide too supportive and too pleasant an environment, it is likely there will be little incentive to "get well" and return to barracks life, in spite of therapeutic efforts of counselors. Such practices as private rooms, elaborate embellishment, staff and clients on a first-name basis, civilian clothes, and virtual withdrawal from the sometimes austere realities of military life would seem likely to reinforce, rather than counter, escapist behavior. . . . Further problems are encountered as members of the participant's unit and his leaders perceive him as living much better than his peers.[30]

Such programs could not meet the needs of the military and the needs of the patients at the same time. The more supportive they were of the patients, the more subversive they were of the army.

The conflict between the needs of the military and the needs of the patients is also evident in the problem of confidentiality. The military has insisted that its interests come before the right of a patient to discuss his problems in confidence with a doctor or counselor. "The physician in the Armed Forces," Assistant Secretary Wilbur has stated, "is a military officer, and his patient relationships are not 'protected' relationships, in that appropriate officials can compel the physician to disclose relevant information he obtains while treating a patient. Such information can be properly used for official purposes and may be introduced at military courts-martial. . . ." [31]

"What this means," Senator Richard S. Schweiker said in response to the Pentagon position at a Congressional hearing, "is that we force men to come in, we force them to take tests, we force them to talk to the doctor, and then we use the information against them; all this in spite of the fact that we know that to cure him he has got to come clean with someone." [32]

Since urinalysis tests and treatment are involuntary, critics have argued that both represent violations of Fifth Amendment protections against self-incrimination. The chief of the department of psychiatry at the Walter Reed Army Institute of Research resigned over this issue, saying, "I felt I could not participate in a program that was unethical." [33]

Confidentiality is an issue in the military primarily because of the ambiguity of its approach to drug abuse. Were it purely medical, there would be no question of compelling psychiatrists and counselors to testify against their patients in violation of professional ethics. But despite considerable evolution, drug abuse in the military still stands in the twilight between the provinces of law and medicine. The army is trying therapy and punishment at the same time in the hope that one or the other will work. Although no "punitive action" can be taken against a soldier on the basis of a urinalysis test or a request for treatment, he is still subject to substantively punitive "administrative actions" and informal harassment, as well as prosecution for crimes divulged in the course of treatment. And if a soldier relapses after an attempt at rehabilitation, drug abuse reverts to its original status as a disciplinary problem. Under these conditions, small wonder that drug users remain unconvinced of the military's commitment to assist them.

The results of military rehabilitation have been as ambiguous as the army's policy. For the majority of men caught, who are not hard-core users, no rehabilitation is really needed, and none takes place. The programs serve to put them on notice that future drug use is risky, because they will be under observation. For the more serious cases (also the least interested in being restored to duty), treatment is a holding action. "There were no real successes," says the director of the program described earlier. "Some guys cut down on heroin or changed to barbs. They'd shape up a little bit, and some went out looking OK. But the treatment of addiction is long-term treatment. We had interruptions in people's lives. You couldn't really call them successes."

What ultimately made a difference was the Army's decision to cut down in size, which made it much easier for soldiers to get discharged. With "qualitative management," many drug users were released. Especially important was the effect on the Personnel Control Facilities, where soldiers facing AWOL charges were housed, and where drug use was usually rampant. The number of men there dropped from four hundred to one hundred in a few months. "So many of the chronic cases of drug use are no longer sitting around the base, and heroin is less available," the director explains.

Where the army has been successful in reducing drug abuse, as it has at this base, the reason has generally not been the success of rehabilitation programs. The military has not "cured" its drug problem; at most, it has discharged it.

To some extent the problem has only been reassigned. Following the withdrawal of troops from Southeast Asia, there were increasing reports of widespread heroin use in West Germany by American soldiers, some of whom had just been transferred from Vietnam.

★ From the Army to the VA: No Rush to Treatment

In the late summer of 1971, the Administration decided that soldiers who were identified as drug users with less than two months of service left would be transferred to the Veterans Administration for treatment. Mandatory referrals were instituted to ensure that no outgoing soldier would be released without thirty days of drug-free experience and to relieve the military of the burden of providing that experience.

An earlier policy had left the decision on whether to undergo VA treatment up to the individual GI. But in mid-September, Dr. Jaffe reported that voluntary treatment "was not working as we had hoped." Since the previous July, when urine tests had just begun, only twenty-three identified drug users had chosen to go to the VA.[34] Dissatisfied, the Administration decided that soldiers would be assigned against their wishes to veterans' hospitals for up to one month before discharge.

Few people at VA hospitals, either staff or patients, seriously believe the treatment is anything more than a formality. Even the goal of thirty drug-free days is not always achieved, since drugs are widely available on VA wards. And because the hospital staffs find many of the Vietnam veterans angry and uncooperative, the soldiers are often quickly released as outpatients and told to come back in a few weeks to pick up their military discharge papers. Meanwhile, the men are able to go home—or onto the streets.

A typical case exemplifies practices under the referral system. Twenty-one years old, identified as a drug user by urinalysis in Vietnam, this soldier insisted to VA physicians that he smoked heroin only now and then, never mainlined it, and had never become addicted.

> Day 1 (initial evaluation): "He is showing at present a very negative attitude toward being on a drug program, as he feels no problem."
>
> Day 7 (progress report): ". . . very negative attitude—all he wants is out—claims he has no drug problem."
>
> Day 8: Discharged.

At some hospitals no attempt is made to keep soldiers involuntarily even this long. At the VA hospital in Battle Creek, Michigan, for example, Dr. Stewart Armitage, a psychologist, runs a drug-free voluntary residential program called January House. In April 1972, thirty-eight servicemen were transferred to his drug unit. "These men," Dr. Armitage reports, "were admitted directly to the January House and thirty-five of these stayed long enough only for the Unit to compile statistical data and for them to request leave against medical advice. In every case these requests were granted. The other three spent the night on the Unit and then left AMA [against medical advice]. None of these men returned to the unit for treatment at a later date." [35]

VA personnel allow soldiers to leave quickly in part because they feel they cannot help someone who does not want treatment, but also because a recalcitrant patient can threaten the progress of others. Returning soldiers often interfere with the normal operation of the program by undermining discipline and bringing in drugs. The staff has little power to control them.

In hospitals where active-duty GIs are held for their remaining time in the service, they are generally kept separate from the regular drug abuse program. "They never want to come in," says Ruth Stoffer, director of a tough residential treatment unit at a VA hospital in Bedford, Massachusetts. "The hospital is responsible for them, but not our program. They go on a psychiatric ward." [36]

The practice of placing drug-using soldiers in wards with older psychiatric patients is bitterly resented by the young GIs, who see themselves as perfectly healthy. "It's hard to get along with them," says one veteran who spent time on a unit with mental patients. "Some of them were slobbering all over their food. You just don't put yourself in that category."

Once they receive their military discharge papers, the soldiers leave VA hospitals—few with fond memories. Although one of the purposes of the referral system is ostensibly to impress upon the men the availability of VA drug programs, the result is more likely to alienate them from the VA and from therapy for a long time. The retention rate beyond the required stay runs close to zero.

"Most of them don't want to stay," admits Dr. William Winick, director of the Brockton, Massachusetts, VA hospital. "We're somewhat disappointed because we went to some lengths to provide a program." [37]

The story is the same everywhere.

"The reality is that most men who are about to be discharged and who have been caught on drugs don't want treatment," says June Swartz, a veterans' assistance counselor in the Baltimore drug program. "The first reason is that many who are caught in urinalysis are not addicted. The urinalysis showed heroin, but maybe they were smoking it. Another reason is that even if they were addicted, a lot of them have no intention of stopping. It's only after they've reached the streets again and experienced the hassle of earning money to get drugs that they want to stop.

"And a third factor is the forced treatment in the army. We've seen this a number of times. A lot of them were forced to detoxify in Vietnam under not very pleasant circumstances. Then they're forced to go through an army treatment program and then the VA. By that time they've had it." [38]

One doctor who ran a drug program at the VA hospital in Vancouver, Washington, describes the soldiers referred from the military as "mostly young volunteers from smaller communities who had smoked or snorted, rather than shot, heroin, and who generally would have stayed with grass had it been readily available. Some had traumatic war stories to tell. All were disillusioned and bitter about their treatment in 'The Green Machine,' and arrived expecting more of the same from the VA in particular, and the government in general." [39]

The resistance to treatment goes beyond mere distrust of the government. At stake is the soldiers' conception of themselves. "They don't want to identify with junkies," says one older addicted veteran. "They feel when they left Vietnam, they left their habit."

At least initially, the veterans do appear to differ sharply from street addicts here. As mentioned earlier, they are generally in good physical condition and show few signs of aberrant behavior. Here is the description of one patient from his medical records:

> . . . comes to us directly from the military . . . admits to starting to smoke pot six months ago as well as smoking some opium. . . . By trade he is a machinist and is a high school graduate. He comes from a stable family. . . . There is no history of any serious physical or emotional trauma . . . well-developed, well-nourished, vigorous . . . deeply sunburned . . . alert, cooperative, and well-oriented. His insight and judgment seem very good. He is motivated to work. . . .

Of course, not all soldiers referred to the VA for drug addiction fit that description, but the mere fact that a number do suggests that their resistance to treatment may not always be irrational.

One key difference between Vietnam returnees and street addicts is the degree to which their lives revolve around drugs. For the returning soldiers, heroin use or even addiction has not represented a total identity as it has for a street addict who has submerged all other aspects of his life. Since drugs were cheap in Vietnam and the army met other needs, the soldiers have not yet had to organize their lives around their habits.

And many may not be willing to do so. Dr. Norman Zinberg, who interviewed veterans after his trip to Vietnam in late 1971, found a strong aversion to both the needle and the junkie life. Twenty-four of twenty-six men he saw stopped on their own.[40] Unfortunately, when a veteran comes home and gives up his habit because of what it would mean to his family, there is no social agency, no class of professionals, no treatment program that can claim him as *their* success.

The probability of natural remission is hard to evaluate. Veterans who stop using heroin, Dr. Zinberg cautions, have not repudiated or even regretted their past use; on the contrary, many of them "speak well" of the drug. They simply find the social barriers to continuing drug use too steep. At this point it is an open question whether their abstinence represents genuine remission or merely a hiatus in drug use. In the face of harsh pressures at home, they may revert to heroin for the same escape it provided in Southeast Asia. Older addicted veterans are skeptical about the younger men. "They might not do it now," says one addict, "but it's a crutch, and they know it's there."

Patterns of post-military drug use can be extremely erratic. "I still go back to shooting heroin now and then for a couple of weeks," says one veteran who smoked heroin in Vietnam and began mainlining several months after he came back. "I get strung out, you know, I catch myself, then I get out of it again." He has already spent time in several programs, including four months at a VA hospital in Illinois.°

There has been a strong temptation on the part of some public officials to call for long-term, involuntary therapy for soldiers certified as heroin users by the military. Several things argue against

---

° In April 1973, the Defense Department released a study, undertaken at Washington University in St. Louis, which indicated that most men who had used heroin in Vietnam had given it up on return home and that the rate of addiction was running at only 1.3 percent. These findings accord with our own impression that natural remission is common, but they seem overly optimistic and unwarranted by the Washington University data. The essential problem with the study was that it was inherently likely to underestimate the rate of addiction among veterans because it was based entirely on reports by veterans themselves interviewed at their homes. The difficulties are twofold: first, veterans who continue to use narcotics are likely to be rather suspicious and reticent when complete strangers come around asking them about it; and secondly, heroin addicts are not the type who scrupulously leave forwarding addresses and turn up promptly at interview appointments. Trying to conduct a census of addicts through interviews is about as practical as trying to count how many foreign spies there are in the country by sending out a questionnaire. The Defense Department concluded on the basis of its study that exposure to drugs in Vietnam had not added significantly to the drug addiction problem in the United States. This seems to us a rather self-serving and disingenuous conclusion.

such a move: the unreliability of the identification process, the situational nature of heroin use in the army, and the tendency of a substantial proportion of veterans toward natural remission or at least dormancy. Furthermore, not only is commitment to institutionalized care an unwarranted breach of the men's individual rights, but it is almost guaranteed to aggravate their problems. On a long-term basis it would serve only to confirm an identity that in many cases may turn out to be ephemeral.

Moreover, the past record of involuntary treatment for drug abuse has been abysmal. Studies of the California Rehabilitation Center have found that only one addict in three is in good standing one year after commitment and only one in six is in good standing three years after commitment.[41] The programs resemble prisons far more than they do hospitals. Many of the soldiers were drafted into the war involuntarily. To hold them for treatment that has been shown to be as fruitless as the fighting itself would be nothing more than a continuation of oppression by other means.

Yet if treatment is to be voluntary, the implications must be faced squarely. Veterans who do continue to use heroin will enter therapeutic programs only after they have run into serious trouble at home. "You don't submit yourself to treatment until you've hit rock bottom," says one addicted veteran, and the pity of it is that on their way to "rock bottom," the men are going to hurt a lot of people, not just themselves.

The hope that mandatory referrals to the VA might prevent that kind of deterioration seems to have little basis. Even if returning soldiers were placed in an ideal therapeutic setting—and the VA is far from that—they would probably still refuse treatment because they reject the society's definition of them as sick. This is a critical impasse not just in the treatment of veterans, but in the treatment of other addicts as well. We have been moving from a penal to a medical approach toward heroin addiction, but the people most directly affected find the medical conception not one whit more palatable. The users and the addicted not only refuse to take part in drug programs; they refuse to accept the ideology behind them. It is only when they encounter the extreme social and physical problems of addiction—created not so much by their dependence on heroin as by their dependence on a vicious black market—that they begin to adjust to the dominant values of the society and accept the premise that they are sick and in need of therapy.

★ *VA Programs: Old Habits and New*

The Chains of Identity

The VA did not move rapidly against drug abuse, and when it finally moved, it had to be pushed. It was not until 1971 that the agency developed any programs specifically for drug patients. The rationale was simply insufficient demand, and indeed, so long as there were no programs, there would not be much demand. Prior to 1971, VA hospitals occasionally treated an addicted veteran on a psychiatric ward, but without any coordinated effort or special expertise. In Buffalo, for example, the directors of the current VA drug program recall that before it was established "at best . . . an attempt might have been made to detoxify [a heroin addict] with methadone and follow this up with a traditional psychotherapeutic approach. The benefits of this type of treatment were almost nonexistent. The recidivism rate was essentially 100 percent, and this type of patient proved to be very disruptive to the ongoing therapeutic approach being used with other hospitalized veterans."[42]

In January of 1971, the VA belatedly opened five drug treatment centers at hospitals in New York, Washington, Houston, Battle Creek, and Sepulveda, California. There was little overall direction at the agency level. Four hospitals chose to set up methadone maintenance programs, while one adopted a drug-free, "problem-solving" approach. Initially the VA planned to authorize five additional programs later in 1971 and ten more in each of the following two years.[43] This timetable was soon overturned. In the spring the VA came under withering attack by the press and Congress for its meager and delayed response to the drug problem. On June 15 Senator Alan Cranston, a persistent critic of the agency, disclosed that the VA was treating a total of 219 drug patients at its five centers. Stung by public criticism and genuinely alarmed, the Administration ordered the agency to embark on a crash program. Instead of opening twenty-five new centers over the next two and a half years, the VA had to open twenty-seven new centers in the next three to four months. It was a task for which the agency was completely unprepared.

"The VA was plunged into the drug treatment business," says Dr. Joel Kantor, now head of education and training for the agency's Alcohol and Drug Dependence Treatment Service.[44] Early growth was chaotic, because there was no time to plan the structure of the program and little relevant experience to draw upon. Typically, a local hospital or clinic was simply authorized to set up a drug center within ninety days, no guidelines or assistance offered. Some ended up with drug-free rehabilitation programs, others with methadone maintenance. The VA had no policy on anything; ignorance was the mother of decentralization.

Chaos from one perspective is diversity from another. The absence of central direction has permitted programs with varying, even antithetical, philosophies to develop within the VA system. At one drug treatment center, methadone maintenance is considered useful and effective; at another it is decried as naïve and debilitating. One VA program seeks to extend as much responsibility to the patients as possible and allows them freedom of movement; another insists that addicts are untrustworthy and must be watched every moment.

Pluralism within the agency, however, does not necessarily mean pluralism on the local level. On the contrary, very often only one kind of treatment is available from the VA in a specific area. In Washington, D.C., for example, the VA hospital offers methadone maintenance, but no intensive drug-free program. Patients seeking such therapy must be referred elsewhere. "There's not a whole lot we can do," says Dr. Norman R. Tamarkin, chief of the Washington unit.

One genuine advantage of VA drug programs is their ability to offer additional veterans' benefits, particularly in education. There are, however, several major institutional liabilities that interfere with their efforts.

The image of the VA as an extension of the military and its orientation toward older veterans make it unattractive to young addicts as a source of assistance. Addicts who voluntarily enter VA programs generally come in off the streets after months or years facing the brutal conditions of addiction in the United States—constant hustling, legal entanglements, imprisonment, family problems, adulterated drugs, hepatitis, community hostility. Suspicious and distrustful, they are reluctant to go to an institution like the VA, fearing that their medical records will not be kept confidential or that they may lose veterans' benefits they are already receiving. "I thought twice about coming here because of government identification," states one patient. And Dr. Winick, director of the Brockton hospital, concedes, "They identify us as a quasi-military organization," an impression which is strengthened by the mandatory referral system.

Limitations on eligibility for treatment represent a second liability. Under present regulations, the VA can treat veterans and no other members of their family for drug problems. But, as one program coordinator points out, "It's damn near impossible to treat a man with an addicted wife." In this case, as in others discussed earlier in Chapter 4, the constraint of exclusivity interferes with effective rehabilitation.

The most serious eligibility limitation has been the restriction of treatment to veterans with good discharges. It is "catch 22" all over again. To get treatment for drug use, one must have a good discharge. But to get a good discharge, one must not use drugs. Therefore the only people who can be treated for drug problems are those who do not have them—or, to be more exact, those whom the military did not punish for having them. One of the reasons VA hospitals responded slowly to the drug problem was that they were barred from treating many of their potential clients.

Legislation that would allow VA facilities to provide drug treatment to all veterans regardless of discharge won the approval of virtually all parties concerned early in 1971, but two years later it was still bottled up in Congress. The House Committee on Veterans' Affairs linked the measure to a provision for judicial commitment of addicts to the VA—a step that both the Senate and the Administration reject. There has also been disagreement as to the extent of services that should be made available to drug abuse patients with bad discharges. Liberals in the Senate fear that unless the services are broad, rehabilitation will be ineffective, while conservatives in the House fear that if addicts with less than honorable discharges receive a wide range of veterans' benefits, the meaning of military discharges will be undermined. Some have already pointed out the paradoxical consequences of the new legislation: An addict with a bad discharge will be able to obtain services from the VA, while an amputee with the same discharge will not.

One of the virtues of an inefficient institution is that it translates misconceived laws into practice as inefficiently as it implements well-conceived ones. Although VA units are unauthorized to treat addicts with bad discharges, many do so anyway. A common practice is to take the addict on as an "emergency" case and then inquire into his discharge status later. Much later. If the VA rules that his discharge precludes eligibility for treatment, an appeal is initiated to persuade the military to reclassify it. This process easily consumes a year and, in the meantime, the veteran receives treatment. If the military finally refuses to make any change, the determination may be moot because by that time either the patient will have dropped out or the VA will have had an opportunity to place him in a community program.[45] On one occasion the agency showed its remarkable talent for the absurd by sending a bill of $4,000 to an addict who had been receiving treatment at the Washington VA drug program for months before it was established that he was ineligible. "I told him not to pay it," says Dr. Tamarkin, director of the program, and of course, the patient never did.[46] One wonders how he might have raised the money were the VA a little more aggressive in its shakedowns.

A final difficulty is the limitation on services that the VA can provide to addicts. The agency has ruled that drug abuse is "willful misconduct" and therefore a "nonservice-connected" disability, no matter where it originated. This ruling bars any disability compensation or vocational rehabilitation assistance. In defense of the VA's position, officials argue that to offer compensation would be an incentive for soldiers to use drugs. Nevertheless, it makes little sense to deny addicts aid for vocational rehabilitation, considering the importance of steady work in the reconstruction of an addict's life.

The liabilities of the VA in treating drug addiction—its inexperience, its image, its statutory restrictions—have been compensated to some extent, occasionally circumvented, but not entirely overcome. What they have cost VA programs most dearly is credibility among their potential patients. Because of the general orientation of the VA toward older veterans, its association with the military, eligibility limitations, and at times bureaucratic intake procedures, many VA drug programs now have a "bad name" on the streets—or no name at all. While the agency has touted its efforts nationally, they generally offer little community outreach or local publicity. Consequently, some programs run well below capacity. The Bedford unit has beds and staff for forty drug users; when we visited it, it had only thirteen patients, virtually all of whom entered the hospital to escape heavy criminal charges. Battle Creek has a capacity of thirty-six for its residential drug program, an average census of eighteen.[47] As of June 1972, the Buffalo program had twenty-three of thirty-five beds filled.[48] The VA's outpatient clinic in Boston, primarily a methadone maintenance program, has been running at half capacity, while other methadone programs in Boston had waiting lists.[49]

Senator Cranston points to the lack of demand for VA drug programs as evidence "that tens of thousands of veteran addicts on the streets today simply have no faith in the VA drug treatment programs." [50] One of the reasons for this, according to the Senator, is the heavy reliance of the VA on methadone maintenance. But the VA programs with the most empty spaces are the drug-free residential treatment units. While an addicted veteran may be willing to take methadone from a VA clinic, he is far less willing to enter a long-term residential program under which the VA will exercise considerably more control over his life.

Residential Programs and Organizational Conflict

On the local level, drug addicts fit into veterans' hospitals about as snugly as a delegation of Black Panthers at an American Legion convention. One program has been described as a "hippie camp amid a Marine bivouac." Relations in most hospitals between the young addicts and other patients are tense; so are the relations between the young drug programs and hospital officials. At the Washington VA, addicts are not permitted to sit in lounges with other patients and watch television. "Even the staff are looked on as lepers," rues Pat Delorme, a social worker.[51]

Hospital administrators typically complain that the addicts make too much noise, refuse to honor rules governing dress and hours for sleeping and visitors (and sleeping with visitors), and roam the corridors disturbing other patients and leaving a trail of missing valuables behind them.[52] Hospitals have used various techniques to manage the conflict. Drug users are segregated on separate wards as much as possible. Security precautions, such as locked doors, are common. In Baltimore, the drug unit has a separate entrance, so that addicts need not pass through the regular outpatient clinic. Some programs hold weekly meetings and invite hospital employees from other departments to improve understanding. A final step, usually mutually appreciated, is physically removing the drug unit to a separate building. Other patients are more comfortable without the addicts, and the drug program is better off apart. To give themselves a sense of identity separate from the VA, the programs sometimes choose a special name: Epic House in Buffalo, January House in Battle Creek.

In some places the conflict has not been managed so well. One of those is the VA hospital in Vancouver, Washington. In July of 1971, as part of its crash program, the VA Central Office authorized Vancouver to develop a treatment center within ninety days. The hospital brought in a young doctor named Charles Spray, who had recently resigned as director of a drug clinic in Portland. At the beginning, Dr. Spray recalls, the program "faced very little in the way of structural guidelines or restrictions. Our mandate from Central Office was simply to create a VA drug rehabilitation program using a fourteen-bed ward and a staff of twelve persons. Filling in the details was clearly defined as our responsibility.

"Plans were made," Dr. Spray continues, "to provide a full range of detoxification, inpatient counseling, and outpatient follow-up services. Most of our patients we could anticipate would be young and would have reasonably short-term habits. Because of this, and because there was an active methadone blockade program within the community, we chose to exclude methadone maintenance from our format."

In shaping the treatment philosophy of the program, Dr. Spray decided to reject "hard-line" policies. "Programs that administered such policies," he believed, "through an established professional power structure managed to achieve a prison-like atmosphere and a wide communications gap between staff and patients. In programs that yielded this power to the people (e.g., patients or ex-addict counselors) professional staff could be found equally isolated but with themselves in the captive position. Furthermore, the authoritarianism exhibited by the empowered group of either type program seemed to repel a significant number of potentially salvagable patients. The challenge as we saw it was to develop a 'soft' program, where power and responsibility—both administrative and therapeutic—would be shared by patients and staff alike in a collaborative fashion." [53]

Dr. Spray's program involved insight therapy rather than action therapy—that is, he was concerned more with exploring motivation than with conditioning patients to socially approved forms of behavior. This voluntaristic, psychotherapeutic approach was consistent with his preference for a more collaborative kind of organization.

There was trouble from the outset. Repeated attempts failed to get the patients to police the ward or to help the staff police it. The hospital administration complained that patients were using, buying, and selling drugs within the hospital, and the staff was soon forced to take counter-measures. But difficulties continued. Dr. Spray allowed the patients to wear their own clothes rather than the prescribed hospital uniform, to bring in women visitors and to keep whatever hours they chose. The hospital administration felt its routine threatened.

"This is basically a hospital designed for the elderly—aging World War II veterans—a nursing home," Dr. Spray explained to a reporter during the controversy.

"Then here comes a group of young people, some hardly out of their teens, who are not physically sick. There is very little recreation available for them—sports or energy-consuming activities. So in its place, the young people roam the hospital and its grounds." [54]

Early in April 1972, Dr. J. Andrew Hall, the hospital director, asked Dr. Spray to resign because his program was overly "permissive," and he had failed to keep proper records. Spray refused, and a decision was postponed pending evaluation of the program by outside authorities. In April and May, teams from the Special Action Office on Drug Abuse Prevention (SAODAP) and the VA Central Office visited the hospital. SAODAP, while remaining neutral, made suggestions to both Dr. Spray and the administration. The VA team came down heavily on the side of the hospital. At the end of June, Dr. Spray was fired, but by that point, the program had been drained of any life. Early in 1972 the ward was filled to its capacity of fifteen, but by the end of June there were only three patients left. "In January," one former patient said, "the atmosphere was calm and conducive to working on a guy's head. It's sure not now." [55]

In the conflict that almost inevitably arises between addicts and the institutions that treat them, Dr. Spray leaned more toward the addicts than the hospital could tolerate. Both the administration and other patients found his unstructured program permissive and threatening. They responded by seeking his dismissal, and were upheld by the VA Central Office. From the drop in the number of patients, it appears that the hospital was accommodated at the price of virtually eliminating the program.

In Brockton, Massachusetts, another loosely structured drug program has also been in conflict with local hospital officials. The program is made up of a residential therapeutic community, located in an attractive cottage on hospital grounds, and a psychiatric ward within the hospital where patients in detoxification or soldiers still on active duty are placed. The cottage residents have all spent some time on the streets before coming into the program, which offers them—in their own words—a "sanctuary." There are no locked doors, and they are able to leave for entire weekends. The loose organization of the program is partly the result of understaffing, but also of the trusting attitude of the psychiatrist in charge. The unique feature of Brockton is a strong emphasis on work; the patients are regularly taken out to labor in a local factory.

But relations with the hospital administration are strained. The director and chief of staff give the impression that they would just as soon do without the drug program. And the addicts in the program make it clear the feeling is mutual. Apparently there is also some resentment among other patients that the young addicts occupy the choicest accommodations at Brockton.[56]

Although the staff and patients deny it, the program appears to have a severe problem of continuing drug use. "I spent two months at Brockton and got thrown out after getting caught in a burglary," says one patient who left the program. "Everybody was shooting dope. It was so loose it was ridiculous. . . . We used to jump out the windows at night and go cop."

The odds are that the Brockton program, like the one at Vancouver, will not survive in its unstructured form. Either the hospital will get rid of it, or it will be reorganized under a more disciplined format.

In nearby Bedford, the VA hospital runs a therapeutic community that is the antithesis of the one at Brockton. The doors to the ward where the program is located are locked, and residents' activities are closely supervised. The minimum commitment to inpatient care is six months. Privileges, such as having visitors, must be earned—and not without considerable effort. No drugs whatsoever are permitted on the ward, not even sleeping pills. Controls are tight: "Even if they go in the bathroom, someone goes with them during their first seventy-two hours," says psychologist Ruth Stoffer, the director. "That's because we don't trust them." [57]

The program operates on a theory of behavior modification. "The more menial lower status chores," a booklet explains, "are assigned to newcomers or as a form of sanction for old residents who have been sliding, or violating some of the family's precepts. The member who does well is rewarded by recognition and promotion up the status ladder. The social system of our community attempts to utilize the motivation of upper status striving as a means to effect behavioral change and control of deviant behavior." [58]

"To come into a program like this," says one patient, "you have to hit rock bottom. If you've got ten years hanging over your head, that's an incentive." Nearly all the patients were, in fact, facing serious criminal charges such as armed robbery before they entered. While in the program, their cases are continued or the charges are dropped.

Daily activities are based on programs like Synanon and Daytop Village: community meetings, encounter groups, seminars, job assignments, and education and training. When the staff and patients consider someone able to leave, he receives day passes to look for work and a place to live outside.

The program has two notable problems: recruitment and follow-up. It is hard to get addicts to enter such a regimented, authoritarian environment, and once they leave, they enter a totally different society. However great an improvement over prisons, it is doubtful that programs like Bedford train men effectively to live in a world that follows very different rules. In the communities to which they return, the open expression of feelings and "upper status striving" are rarely rewarded. Paradoxically, therapeutic communities create new problems of readjustment at the same time as they cope with old ones.

But however serious these problems may be, the Bedford program will probably survive because it does not lead to serious conflicts with the local hospital administration. By maintaining tight control over addicts, the programs that emphasize behavioral conditioning guarantee their own survival regardless of whether they provide successful rehabilitation. The less structured programs, on the other hand, which tend to emphasize insight therapy, generate conflict by intensifying strains in the local environment. Although the VA initially had a wide variety of programs because of the haste in establishing drug treatment centers, it seems likely that the more voluntaristic, unstructured programs will be driven out or reorganized. In the long run, the internal logic of organizational structure will probably lead the initially open VA system into an authoritarian and perhaps ultimately custodial format.

Ambulatory Care and the Strains of Professionalism

To speak of ambulatory drug programs in the VA is to speak primarily of methadone maintenance. A number of veterans with drug problems do take advantage of outpatient counseling or group therapy while abstinent or in detoxification, but most of the active outpatients are maintained on methadone.

In addition to counseling and therapy, the programs offer various kinds of group activities, crafts, assistance in obtaining other veteran's benefits, and limited job referral. It usually takes some time for patients to make productive use of these services, and many never do. But the VA does provide them; it cannot be accused of creating "bare-bones" methadone programs that satisfy only the addict's appetite for drugs and neglect all his other personal needs. At the Baltimore clinic the staff emphasize that "methadone is used as an adjunct to treatment" and that "group and individual therapy, job placement, and helping the veteran to readjust socially are viewed as the major goals of the program." Their outlook is directly contrary to the philosophy implicit in an insulated therapeutic community. "We feel," they declare, "that treating the veteran in the environment and helping him cope with daily stresses that do occur is more desirable than isolating him from such pressures." [59]

Addicts who enter methadone maintenance generally would not fit into a disciplined therapeutic community without its becoming a prison for them. Their tolerance for regimentation is low, as is their motivation to give up drugs. Many have come into the program only because they have tired momentarily of the street life, not because they are ready to stop using heroin permanently.

The requirements for admission are minimal, usually a two-year history of narcotics use and one confirmed attempt at detoxification and abstinence. Low selectivity leads to a high rate of continued drug use. In a typical month at the Boston clinic, urinalysis tests showed that only 41 percent of the patients had stopped taking heroin and other secondary drugs.[60] Out of 141 patients in the New York unit in November 1971, only 27 percent had stayed "clean." [61] Sanctions for illicit drug use are negligible, because few penalties besides severance are available, and the staff would rather keep the patients involved in the programs to whatever extent they can. In cases of violent behavior, trafficking on the premises, and other gross violations of organizational rules, however, patients are "terminated."

Data on the response to VA methadone programs are sketchy. A survey of 104 patients at the Philadelphia clinic in November 1971 indicated that only thirty-three were working.[62] A more sophisticated analysis of 149 patients in the New York drug program showed that about 60 percent were either employed, attending school, or between jobs, whereas only 9 percent had had jobs or been in school on admission to the program. The coordinator claims that "the combination of methadone maintenance, a diversified and flexible treatment approach, and resourceful rehabilitative efforts led to significant lifestyle changes" for a majority of the patients.[63]

The problem of employment is not one the clinics can easily solve, even when a patient is successfully stabilized on methadone. Personnel managers are unreceptive to addicts, whether or not they are being treated. Staff and patients often complain that even agencies of the federal government refuse to consider employing veterans in the methadone programs. In most states, methadone patients are legally barred from holding many licenses that stipulate no drug dependence, in spite of their ability to meet all other physical requirements.

High dropout rates plague VA programs, though many clinics obscure the problem by retaining patients on their rolls long after they have ceased making visits. On the average, VA drug programs seem to list about twice as many patients as they really have. (During an interview, Dr. Edwin Tucker, Acting Director of the

Alcohol and Drug Dependence Treatment Service, called this "a very valid observation." [64]) In some programs, such as those in Philadelphia and Chicago, the ratio of statistical patients to active ones may be three or four to one.

The dimensions of the dropout problem are apparent at the outpatient clinic in Boston, which lists as active patients only those who have come in during the past thirty days. During its first ten months of operation, three quarters of the patients—151 out of 191—dropped out.[65] A large number left during one crisis when the firing of the program's only black counselor triggered the departure of nearly all the black patients. After almost a year, the clinic, which has a full-time staff of twelve, still had an average census of only about forty. "We could double our enrollment," said Dr. Marshall Trubow, acting director. The only trouble is that the addicts won't come.

"To meet our own needs we program out drug addicts," an articulate young counselor explained. "We set up requirements they can't meet, like prolonged intake and motivational testing. That's a hell of a thing for a guy who's been out on the street for a few years." In the name of professionalism, the staff often screens out and drives off the people they are supposed to serve, but who annoy the hell out of them. Without participation by patients in decision-making, that tendency may get out of hand, and the program may end up meeting the staff's needs alone. Significantly, the Boston clinic had no patient involvement in decision-making whatsoever.

Of course, many veterans on methadone are content to take their daily dosage from the program and leave it at that. At some units there is a "day hospital" which, if nothing else, offers a pool table that is in constant use. Instead of hanging out in a local pool hall, a veteran can get "recreational therapy" playing pool with his fellow addicts at the VA day-care center. To the uninitiated, it may look like the same thing, and for many addicts, the only difference is that at the VA they can shoot pool and get methadone for free. In the long run, though, the program may do some good even for these men. To the extent that the VA provides methadone, they are not buying heroin, engaging in street crime, and raising the level of urban terror. Moreover, they have a greater chance to live long enough to outgrow their preoccupation with drugs and assume some responsibility for their families and their own lives. In our culture today, addiction seems strongly related to aspects of the young male personality. As men develop, susceptibility to drug dependence drops off. The assumption behind the creation of drug programs like those in the VA is that professionals offering "treatment" will

somehow cure men of an aspect of their behavior. But the real hope
is that the men will end it themselves as they mature. Meanwhile,
the programs can provide counseling, social services, and stabilizing
doses of narcotics to minimize, though not eliminate, activity on the
black market and harm to others. It is a modest aim, but realistic.

Much of the criticism directed against the VA in the past has
been that it has relied too heavily on methadone maintenance and
has neglected drug-free modalities. But perhaps that only reflects
what the agency can do best. It has limited ability to attract
voluntary patients to residential programs that inherently involve a
great deal of control over daily activities, and it is constrained by
the nature of its hospital system. While drug-free programs should
be available for veterans, the VA should not necessarily operate
them. Were the agency to subsidize independent or ongoing
community programs according to the number of veterans enrolled,
the same purposes could be fulfilled.

Probably the most extraordinary drug program for Vietnam
veterans we visited was an independent operation called the DMZ,
which stood in this case for Drug Mending Zone. Located in the
South Bronx in New York City, one of the most decimated areas in
the country, the DMZ began when veterans in a Puerto Rican
community program named SERÁ (Services for Education and
Rehabilitation in Addiction) moved into a nearby decaying tenement that initially housed mostly addicts and prostitutes. The
following message, which they sent to the executive director of
SERÁ, indicates something of their spirit.

> Operation clean-up is now under way. Under cover of South Bronx
> air pollution, seventeen (17) veterans attacked and secured the fifth
> floor of 1027 E. 167 Street at 1425 hours on 9-17-71. We have now
> established a foothold (which at present is reminiscent of a foxhole),
> and the enemy, shocked and humiliated, is retreating rapidly. The
> entire building should be within our grasp in no time.

The DMZ soon attracted more than eighty Vietnam veterans
with drug problems, making it larger than any drug-free VA
program. But instead of putting the men into "treatment," it
harnessed their energies and organized them for useful and
important work: rebuilding part of the devastated community
where they live. Walls in the tenement were pulled out, beams and
pipes replaced, everything repainted. The program emphasized
remedial education and training in useful skills, brought in teachers

to conduct classes, and sent out residents to attend a local community college. It ran programs for neighborhood children, and even helped negotiate a truce among local gangs, one of which had taken over an entire apartment house across the street for its headquarters.

Early in 1973, however, the DMZ closed after applications to federal agencies for funds had been turned down. The VA said that while the director of its Brooklyn hospital had visited the program and thought it the best of 45 he had seen, the agency could only provide some $99,000 out of a research budget; it had no regular authority to fund residential programs operated outside of its hospitals. Frank Gracia, the director of SERA, says he was under pressure because the state agency funding his program had disallowed expenditures he had made for the DMZ. ("We couldn't allow them to use our money for something we hadn't okayed," explained a representative of the New York State Narcotics Addiction Control Commission. "It [the DMZ] could not be made part of our present contract after the fact.")

But while the DMZ lasted, it offered a remarkable contrast to the VA—a glimpse of how the limits of bureaucratic intervention against addiction might, someday, be transcended. On a drug ward in a VA hospital, the patients are usually lolling in front of a television set, playing pool, or trying to keep themselves busy some other way. In the DMZ, there was none of that lethargy and boredom, which one imagines had something to do with drug use in the first place. Unlike the hospital programs, which place veterans in the passive role of patients, the DMZ, whatever its faults, gave the men a chance to express themselves constructively. It did this not through make-work, phony arts and crafts, or occupational therapy, but by organizing the men into a corps of community workers.

Not just the engaged activity, but the very identity of the people at the DMZ seemed to promise more. All the staff were former addicts; however lacking in academic credentials, they knew their men well and could hold their respect. By contrast, the VA program staff, most of them professionally trained, are strangers to their patients' world. Just before visiting the DMZ, we stopped in at the New York VA hospital and spoke with one of its clinical psychologists. He had worked on the drug abuse ward for a year while finishing his doctorate at Columbia University. In that time, he said, he had managed to develop strong relationships with three patients who saw him weekly. There was just one difficulty: they talked a good deal about personal problems, but never about their problems with drugs. Maybe he would get to that in his second year.

Programs like the DMZ need not be idealized. They have their share of deficiencies—poorly kept records, mismanaged finances—and these aspects require continual scrutiny. But however weak on management techniques, they have an ability to engender respect and cooperation that alien and bureaucratic programs sorely lack. Strong social, political, or religious commitments imbue communities like the DMZ with a kind of motivating force that no government bureaucracy, in its splendid neutrality, can offer. An agency like the VA is limited in its capacity to speak to the men's need for an emotional involvement as deep as their previous involvement with drugs. Recognizing this and other limitations, Congress might well seek to permit, to encourage, and perhaps to require the VA to sponsor independent community drug programs along the lines of the DMZ. For the agency to do so would not be a confession of failure, but a sign of good sense.

Ultimately, of course, the resolution of the addiction problem goes beyond the military and the Veterans Administration. It depends on the nation's capacity for sanity, tolerance and understanding, which the British, at least in this matter, seem to have had in such abundance. We need to understand that most soldiers who used heroin in Southeast Asia will stop using on their own, that those who became dependent need not become criminals, that there is no medical cure for diseases of the spirit and certainly no way of enforcing one, that the strongest antidotes must be at once social and personal and provide a reason for not wanting to escape into loneliness, and that the least we can do is not to complicate the lives of veterans unnecessarily by placing upon them a lifelong stain for what happened to them in the strange crucible of the Vietnam War.

6
Bad Discharges: The Wrong Way Out

To the soldiers who come home with drug problems and to the men who come back physically disabled must be added still another group who carry with them the bitter legacies of the Vietnam War—those who return marked dishonorable and unfit. From the Gulf of Tonkin Resolution in 1964 through the summer of 1972, more than 175,000 soldiers were dismissed with less than honorable discharges.[1] If the reception that other veterans have received has been ambivalent, the homecoming these men have faced has been even more dismal.

Were their discharge papers their only handicap, the prospect for these veterans might not be that serious, but typically a bad discharge is only the most recent problem in a biography of misfortune. Often poor, almost always with limited education, disproportionately black, veterans with less than honorable discharges have a series of strikes against them. Employers who have more than enough jobless veterans to choose from will consider these men last and usually not at all. Even if they had a job before being drafted, the character of their discharge precludes them from asserting legal rights to reemployment upon return.

It is generally assumed that less than honorable discharges also legally bar a veteran from receiving hospital care, educational allowances, and other VA benefits. This is true, however, for only the relatively small proportion of such men who were dismissed through general court-martial. The vast majority of Vietnam veterans with bad discharges received them as a result of administrative action by the military, and the decision to deny these men benefits belongs to the VA. These decisions are made entirely within the agency, without clear statutory guidelines, without a firm set of definitions, and without any opportunity to appeal to the courts. One might also add that the decisions have been made without peer representation, without sympathy, and without any sense of the larger social consequences of compounding the men's problems.

In most discussions of military discharges and their ramifications, the role of the VA is given little attention. The focus primarily centers on the military justice system and discrimination in civilian employment. Our concern here will be to look more closely at the administrative discharge process and at the procedures used by the VA to deny benefits to administratively discharged veterans. As will become evident, these administrative decisions affect a greater number of men than the rulings of the military judiciary and involve the most questionable practices.

★ *The Discharge Hierarchy*

Up until now, we have spoken loosely of "dishonorably discharged" veterans or men with "bad discharges." To understand the discharge system, however, a more precise use of terms is necessary.

Technically, there are five types of discharges the armed services grant to outgoing enlisted men: (1) Honorable; (2) General; (3) Undesirable; (4) Bad Conduct; and (5) Dishonorable.[2] The names can be somewhat misleading to a civilian. For example, both Honorable and General Discharges are granted "under honorable conditions." Hence, when a serviceman is said to have been discharged "under less than honorable conditions," it means he received either an Undesirable, Bad Conduct, or Dishonorable Discharge. It is this group that numbered over 175,000 during the Vietnam War.

Military discharges are distinguished in a second way. The first three discharges (Honorable, General, and Undesirable) are "administrative," whereas the last two (Bad Conduct and Dishonorable) are considered "punitive" and can only be granted after court-martial. In other words, if the military seeks to discharge a man "under less than honorable conditions," it must conduct a court-martial— except in the case of an Undesirable Discharge. To get a little bit ahead of ourselves, what has basically happened over the past few years is that, as constitutional protections have been introduced into the court-martial system, the military has increasingly relied on

Undesirable Discharges as a way of circumventing the legal process. Administrative action is much simpler and can be just as damaging to the veteran.

The vast majority of discharges, over 90 percent in every year, are Honorable. If a soldier has performed "proficiently," he is likely to receive an Honorable Discharge even if he has one or two minor violations of military discipline on his record. If, on the other hand, his record is neither "sufficiently meritorious to warrant an Honorable Discharge" nor sufficiently egregious to warrant a discharge "under less than honorable conditions," the military then grants the man a General Discharge—which is honorable in the general sense of the term, though not Honorable in the strict sense. Soldiers who receive General Discharges have no opportunity to contest, appeal, or answer whatever charges were privately made against them.

The argument for denying the men these rights is that they are still entitled to all their veterans' benefits and therefore have no adequate cause for complaint. Nevertheless, it should be noted that General Discharges do carry some stigma in the labor market and consequently probably do interfere with smooth adjustment to civilian life.[3] During the years of the Vietnam War, the military gave over 200,000 General Discharges, 3 percent of the discharge total.

Bad Conduct and Dishonorable Discharges are much less common, never amounting to more than 1 percent of all discharges in any recent year. Dishonorables may only be imposed by a general court-martial (i.e., one convened by an officer of the rank of general) and are the most severe discharges soldiers can receive. They are rarely imposed and then only in the most serious cases, such as murder, violent assaults, and extensive dealing in hard drugs. During the Vietnam War, a yearly average of only about three of every 10,000 men released were given Dishonorable Discharges. Bad Conduct Discharges averaged about ten times that number during the same period. They are imposed not only by general court-martial, but also by special court-martial, which can be convened by a middle-ranking officer and does not require a formal preliminary investigation.

At the middle of the hierarchy of discharges stands the Undesirable. Like Honorable and General Discharges, it is "administrative," but like Bad Conduct and Dishonorable Discharges it carries heavy penalties in civilian life. It is given most often for drug abuse, frequent acts of misconduct, homosexual acts, and conviction by civil authorities of an offense involving "moral turpitude" or imprisonment for more than one year. Although Undesirable

Discharges are imposed without the formal protections of a court-martial, they are every bit as punitive as the punitive discharges only courts-martial are allowed to impose. In fact, to many civilians, the term "Undesirable" on a discharge paper suggests a deep-seated personality problem, while "Bad Conduct" sounds much less serious—like the comment a school teacher might make on a report card. Part of the handicap of an Undesirable Discharge is that it suggests more than it proves, and this is precisely why it is so dear to the military, which often cannot prove as much as it wishes to suggest.

★ *Outflanking the Law*

The relative importance of Undesirable Discharges is at once apparent from military statistics. During the Vietnam War (fiscal years 1965 to 1972, inclusive), the armed services dismissed 148,194 men with Undesirable Discharges (or six out of every seven who received a discharge less than honorable). Thus to speak of bad discharges is primarily to speak of Undesirable Discharges; to call into question the administrative discharge process is to cast doubt on the legal status of the vast majority of less than honorably discharged veterans.

Further inspection of the Defense Department's data discloses significant increases in the number of Undesirable Discharges in the last years of the war—both absolutely and relative to the total number of discharges. Until 1969 Undesirable Discharges averaged 11,500 annually; in fiscal 1970, they jumped to 22,537, and in 1972 to 40,018. Whereas in 1969 Undesirables represented 1.08 percent of a total of 1,028,951 discharges, in 1972 they represented 4.49 percent of a total of 890,354 discharges. Thus, in spite of a decrease in separations, the number of Undesirable Discharges went up.

This increase is especially surprising because of changes in the military's policy toward drug abuse. As mentioned earlier, in July 1971—the beginning of fiscal year 1972—the Defense Department announced it would not impose Undesirable Discharges on men who were identified as drug users through urinalysis tests or who volunteered for treatment under the amnesty program. If urinalysis testing and amnesty were successful and if the military carried out its professions of good faith, there should have been a decline in Undesirable Discharges. In that light the figure of 40,000 Undesirables for 1972 acquires even more significance.

Part of the increase may have been due to the widespread malaise within the military and the deterioration of discipline and morale.

But a substantial proportion may be traced to increased legal protections extended to defendants in special courts-martial. Beginning in fiscal year 1970 (when Undesirable Discharges first increased 100 percent over the previous year), no soldier could be given a Bad Conduct Discharge unless he was afforded the following rights, in addition to those already present in a court-martial:

1. A defense lawyer. Previously a defendant was entitled to a lawyer only if the prosecutor was a lawyer.
2. A lawyer sitting as the military judge. Previously there was no requirement that any member of a special court-martial panel be a lawyer.
3. A verbatim record of the trial. Previously a summarized record was sufficient.

These changes strengthened the defendant's position in several ways. Lawyers in the military are rarely career soldiers; they identify less with the military as an institution than with the law as a profession. Consequently, as defendant's counsel or as judge, they were more likely to adhere to the explicit dictates of the law than to follow the implicit wishes of a commanding officer. And if the judge did place the demands of the service above the demands of the law, there was always the automatic review procedure that would be more meaningful now that a verbatim transcript was available.

To close some loopholes, however, was only to encourage the military to exploit others more thoroughly. As a result of the reforms in the judicial system, the unreformed administrative system was pressed into heavier service. It was, so to speak, a process of elimination. A commanding officer who wanted to get rid of a man would often send him to an administrative discharge board instead of to a court-martial, where his legal rights might protect him from being discharged. True, some punitive sanctions were sacrificed—the administrative discharge board could not send a malefactor to the stockades—but then, the "right" discharge was likely to come swift and certain.

Members of a discharge board, as the name suggests, do not have a variety of penalties available to them.[4] They have a simple choice: either retain the soldier on active duty or discharge him with an Undesirable, General, or Honorable Discharge. Even before the case begins, they know one thing for certain. The "old man" wants this particular troublemaker out of the service. If he wanted any other punishment, he would have sent the soldier before a court-martial. Board members also have more than an inkling of what kind of discharge the "old man" would like them to impose.

Honorable and General Discharges do not require hearings. If he favored one of those, he would have granted it himself. So even before a word is said at the hearing, the "old man's" verdict is in, and since he happens to be the commanding officer of the members of the discharge board, he gets paid more attention than most old men usually do.

The board will ordinarily have no trouble doing what is expected of them. The soldier facing discharge who attempts to defend himself does not have available many of the most significant rights and protections normally present in a judicial proceeding. He also has a certain incentive to accept the will of the military, since a discharge, even an Undesirable, will at least get him out of the service. "Copping" an Undesirable yields relief of an immediate problem at the cost of shame later in life. Like the tattoo picked up by a young sailor on leave in an exotic port, it will remain with him as a stigma, with little chance of ever being effectively removed.

Soldiers to be brought before an administrative board receive notice that a hearing will be held and must be apprised of the charges against them. If they choose to resist an Undesirable Discharge, they have the right to be represented by a lawyer and to make a personal appearance at the hearing (unless they are confined on a civil charge, in which case they lose that opportunity).

The accused do not have the right to confront all witnesses against them, a right guaranteed by the Constitution in all criminal proceedings, including trial by court-martial. The case against them may be presented solely on the basis of documents. Moreover, the administrative board does not have subpoena power, which makes it all the more likely that witnesses will not appear in person. If, for example, the person who prepared the investigation—usually a military policeman—has left the service or been transferred and is no longer available, the defendant will have no opportunity to cross-examine him on the allegations he has made. Lacking the vehicle of cross-examination, the defense case is often critically weakened.

The defense is weakened in another regard as well. Whereas at a court-martial the government must prove the defendant's guilt "beyond a reasonable doubt," it needs only a "preponderance of the evidence" at an administrative proceeding. This is a much easier standard for the government to meet. Standards of evidence are also relaxed. The rules of evidence applicable at a court-martial are applied only as strictly as the senior member of an administrative board desires. Since he is not a lawyer, he is not required to rule on objections made to the admissibility of evidence; his only duty is to note any objections for the record. But the record is not verbatim, and consequently the objection may never actually be reviewed.

A further problem is double jeopardy. If a commanding officer convenes a court-martial which acquits the defendant on a legal technicality or convicts him but does not impose a discharge, he may simply send the soldier before an administrative discharge board on the same charges. The Defense Department specifically authorizes this:

> No member will be administratively discharged under conditions other than honorable if the grounds for such discharge action are based wholly or in part upon acts or omissions for which the member has been previously tried by court-martial resulting in acquittal or action having the effect thereof, *except when such acquittal or equivalent disposition is based on a legal technicality not going to the merits.*[5]

Among the legal technicalities "not going to the merits" are violations of Fourth Amendment protections against unreasonable search and seizure and violations of Fifth Amendment protections against forced confessions.

Many cases involving drug use hinge on the issue of whether evidence was obtained in violation of the constitutional guarantee against unreasonable search and seizure. Often a commanding officer sends a soldier accused of drug use before a court-martial even when the admissibility of the evidence is doubtful. If the court then decides the search was unconstitutional, the general can convene a discharge board that is more responsive to his wishes.

An actual case will illustrate how the system works.[6] Bill, a corporal in the Marine Corps who had served more than three years without any involvement of a discreditable nature, was charged with five counts of possession of marijuana. His case was referred to trial by a general court-martial, where the maximum sentence would have been twenty-five years in prison. The preliminary investigation indicated there was only enough admissible evidence to charge him on one of the counts, which involved the possession of such a small amount of marijuana that it was actually described in the official charge as "debris." The court found him guilty and imposed a sentence of two months' confinement. Since he had served more than three years without any trouble, the court understandably did not order that he be discharged. By the time the trial concluded, Bill had less than two months remaining on his obligated service, at which time he would have received an

Honorable Discharge. But the general was determined this would not happen. By law, he could not impose a greater sentence than the court had awarded. So he rushed Bill's case before an administrative discharge board, which complied with his desires, snatched Bill's Honorable Discharge from him, and dismissed him as an Undesirable.

It was easier for the board to deprive Bill of his Honorable Discharge than it was for the court, because the board had evidence of all five counts before it. Bill had been tried by the court-martial on only one count, because the preliminary investigation had revealed that evidence on the other four had been obtained in violation of the Fourth Amendment. The board was able to hear this evidence, however, because such protections do not apply in administrative proceedings. Furthermore, the board had read to it the testimony of a confidential informant that the reason only debris had been found was because Bill had been forewarned that his foot locker was going to be searched. Had the government used this statement at the court-martial, it would have had to reveal the identity of the informant. Anonymous testimony was accepted, however, by the discharge board.

Other abuses of the administrative discharge process are more subtle. In Okinawa a few years ago, a soldier charged with three counts of selling marijuana was found guilty by a special court-martial and sentenced to six months in jail and a Bad Conduct Discharge. A review by the general's legal staff, however, indicated that two of the charges were legally deficient. The general's legal advisor doubted whether the court of military review (the first level of review outside of the defendant's chain of command) would uphold the issuance of a Bad Conduct Discharge for a conviction on only one count of selling marijuana. Consequently, the general disapproved the Bad Conduct Discharge, but approved the six months' confinement. He then ordered the soldier before an administrative board, which imposed an Undesirable Discharge.

The issue in these cases is not whether the particular individual involved should have received an Undesirable Discharge. The issue is rather the ease with which the system is manipulated and the lack of protection the average soldier has in administrative proceedings.

★ *A Life Sentence*

Before a soldier receives an administrative discharge, he is counseled by lawyers and others as to what obstacles he may encounter in civilian life. One Army form that he is required to sign before exercising or waiving his right to a hearing includes the following statement:

> I understand that I may expect to encounter substantial prejudice in civilian life in the event a general discharge under honorable conditions is issued to me. I further understand that as a result of the issuance of an undesirable discharge under conditions other than honorable I may be ineligible for many or all benefits as a veteran under both federal and state laws and that I may expect to encounter substantial prejudice in civilian life.[7]

And so he does. An Undesirable Discharge, former California Congressman Clyde Doyle once observed, is "not only a stigma" but "a life sentence, unless it is changed." [8] It is a life sentence, one might add, given to men sometimes only nineteen or twenty years old. Youths who drop out or are expelled from high school have some chance to return and redeem themselves. Youths who are expelled from the army do not.

Very few discharges are changed after a soldier becomes a veteran. Men are discouraged from appealing because the process usually takes years and requires legal assistance beyond their means. They have been told, moreover, that appeals are usually fruitless, and the records bear this out. During a six-year period from 1966 to 1971 the Army Discharge Review Board upgraded approximately 14 percent of the discharges of those persons who appealed to it.[9] Since, at the most, only one out of every five veterans who receives a bad discharge ever appeals, those who had their discharges upgraded probably represent no more than 3 percent of the total.

The difficulties in the discharge review system have been nowhere more evident than in the cases involving drug use. In August 1971 the Defense Department announced that since it was no longer imposing Undesirable Discharges solely for use or possession of drugs, men who had previously received Undesirables on those grounds could have them upgraded. Eight months later the policy was expanded to include the review of drug-related discharges issued by courts-martial. The major purpose of these reforms was to enable such men to qualify for treatment in VA drug programs.

There was, however, no assurance that changes would be made in any particular case, nor were there firm rules on which discharges would be upgraded. During the first year of the policy, 1,893 applications were received from men who received Undesirable Discharges for drug use. Only 909 were upgraded. Each military service was apparently free to apply its own criteria in these decisions; at least, that is what the statistics suggest. While the Navy upgraded 343 out of 385 discharges, the Army was willing to change only 154 out of 911.[10]

Furthermore, although the military announced in two press releases that it would agree to review drug-related discharges, it never bothered to inform the men themselves. There was never so much as a single letter sent to the veterans informing them that their discharges might now be changed. Some men heard about the new policy through newspapers; many others probably never have. One reason the military may not be eager to inform the veterans is the work load it might impose on the review boards. They creep along at the laziest of paces, usually with a long backlog of work. Were the new policy on drug-related discharges to be effective, not only would veterans have to be informed of their rights, but the numbers of boards, or the work capacity of current boards, would have to be increased.

★ The Impassive Protector

Contrary to widespread belief, federal law does not bar the Veterans Administration from dispensing benefits to most veterans with less than honorable discharges. Were the agency to change its own procedures, new legislation would, in fact, not be necessary to permit VA hospitals to offer drug treatment to men with less than honorable discharges. The VA is also in a position to extend educational assistance to veterans who are perpetual unemployment statistics. But because of the way the VA has applied the law and the way it interprets its social functions, the agency has not made such assistance available.

According to the law, benefits are available to all veterans who received discharges "under conditions other than dishonorable." Anyone who received an Honorable or General Discharge is unambiguously entitled to benefits. Anyone who received a Dishonorable Discharge is unambiguously excluded from benefits, as is someone issued a Bad Conduct Discharge by general court-martial. Undesirable Discharges and Bad Conduct Discharges issued by special court-martial constitute the "gray area." If a veteran has one of these—and more than six out of every seven Vietnam veterans with bad discharges do—the VA makes an independent determination whether or not it was issued under dishonorable conditions.

The agency has adopted its own rules on this question. A discharge issued for mutiny, spying, or homosexual acts is automatically considered to be under dishonorable conditions. Mutiny and spying charges appear primarily in war movies, but rarely in real life. Homosexual acts, on the other hand, never occur in war movies but do occur in real life. The categorical position the VA has taken on cases of homosexuality reflects a highly traditional view of moral behavior. Whether it is also constitutionally correct to deny benefits on grounds of extra-legal moral attitudes is another question.

In addition to these specific categories of discharges that the VA has determined to be under dishonorable conditions, the agency has adopted two rather broad and subjective criteria in its eligibility decisions. A discharge is considered to have been issued under dishonorable conditions if it stemmed from an offense involving "moral turpitude" or was the result of "persistent and willful misconduct." What constitutes "moral turpitude" or "persistent and willful misconduct"? Whatever the person ruling on the request for benefits decides. No one that we interviewed in the VA, either in the national or regional offices, could offer any definition. The determination is made on a case-by-case basis without the assistance of any guidelines. An older VA employee in Montgomery, Alabama, may consider smoking marijuana an offense involving moral turpitude, while his younger counterpart in San Francisco would merely be amused. Indeed, the criteria may be applied differently within the same office. The only guidelines would appear to be an unwritten presumption that the services impose bad discharges only for acts of moral turpitude or persistent and willful misconduct, because the VA hardly ever comes to any other conclusion. A recent study by the agency indicated that 93 percent of the veterans with bad discharges who apply for educational benefits are denied them.[11]

A veteran who seeks benefits from the VA applies to his local office, where he will be asked for his discharge papers. If the applicant has a Bad Conduct or Undesirable Discharge, the VA employee will advise him that his application must be sent to the regional office for an eligibility determination. At the regional level an "adjudicator" will examine the applicant's entire file, supplied by the military service involved, and then rule whether the veteran engaged in moral turpitude or persistent and willful misconduct. The adjudicator will base his decree not only on information the military has provided, but also upon any statements submitted by the veteran. Rarely, however, will statements be submitted, since the applicant is not necessarily notified that he can do so. The veteran will probably also be unaware of all the military reports the abjudicator has before him. Although the applicant technically has a right to see his file, he is never advised that he has that right, nor are copies of his file made available to him if he wishes to see it. He must go to the regional office during a weekday and look at the file there.

If the adjudicator determines that the individual is not entitled to benefits, that determination must be approved by an "authorizer." The applicant may then file a "notice of disagreement," in which event the case will be reviewed again, this time by a senior claims examiner and an authorizer. If they agree with the decision of their colleagues, the applicant will again be notified that his request for benefits has been denied; this time, however, he will receive a statement explaining why they have been denied. He will also be advised of his right to appeal, and finally he will be advised that he may submit evidence on his own behalf.

His appeal will be heard by the board of veterans' appeals, which has never had any Vietnam veterans among its members. The board is not limited to reviewing the adjudicator's decision, but can completely reexamine the entire record. However, it also has no guidelines for deciding what is moral turpitude or persistent and willful misconduct.

The veteran has a right to be represented before the board by a lawyer, but it is doubtful that he will be unless a beneficent friend or someone in his family went to law school. Lawyers are limited by statute to receiving $10 for all services they render to a veteran applying for VA benefits. The agency argues that the lawyer's fees would come from the benefits awarded and consequently limit what the veteran receives.

When it is suggested that some benefits may be better than none at all, they note that the various veterans' organizations provide representation. This is true, but the American Legion and VFW have not exactly been in the vanguard of organizations defending such causes as the rights of homosexuals, political dissenters, and drug users. Yet if veterans with bad discharges cannot get help from one of the associations, they are pretty much out of luck altogether. Furthermore, the long participation of the associations in the appeal board procedures has made them part of the VA inner family and so it is unlikely they will seize upon unpopular cases. VA officials note with pride that twenty-five representatives of veterans' organizations have rent-free offices in VA headquarters on Vermont Avenue in Washington, D.C. Their role can probably be better understood in terms of the kinship networks of traditional societies than in terms of the adversary tradition of Anglo-American law.

To ensure that the VA family remains free of outside scrutiny or interference, statutes prohibit appeal to the courts of any decision by the VA granting or denying benefits. Benefits have the legal status of gratuities. The VA can no more be legally compelled to bestow gifts on veterans than children can be compelled to give presents on Mother's Day.

All this contributes to a degree of institutional privacy that one normally finds only in expensive private men's clubs. Both the adjudicator and the board of appeals may issue their decisions without having their notions of morality examined in a public inquiry. The veterans' rights may be unprotected, but the prejudices of agency officials are perfectly secure.

Ordinarily, the VA keeps no statistical records on benefit applications from veterans with Undesirable and Bad Conduct Discharges. A study of a five-month period in 1972, however, noted that only 1,305 applications for educational benefits were received from men with bad discharges. Of these, ninety-one were approved. During this same period, more than 4,000 veterans with bad discharges applied for unemployment compensation. (Although the benefits are dispensed by the Labor Department, eligibility decisions are made by the VA.) Of the 4,000 men who applied, 3,400 were found ineligible. Ninety-seven of the cases involved veterans with drug-related discharges; six of these were approved. As one VA official remarked after seeing these statistics, Undesirable and Bad Conduct Discharges are effectively the same as a Dishonorable Discharge in terms of eligibility for veterans' benefits.

There is some question whether this practice represents the intent of Congress. A veteran, as defined in the law, is a person discharged "under conditions *other than dishonorable.*" Strictly speaking, that means all men who served in the armed forces except those who received Dishonorable Discharges. The VA has taken it upon itself to interpret the definition as excluding nearly all of the men who received Bad Conduct and Undesirable Discharges.

Given the impassive attitude of the VA, very few veterans with bad discharges ever seek to establish eligibility for benefits. The board of veterans' appeals received fewer than a hundred appeals during 1972 involving the character of discharge. One possible explanation for this figure might be that adjudicators were granting eligibility, but as we have seen, favorable decisions at that level are extremely rare.

The infrequency with which the VA grants benefits to less than honorably discharged veterans has left the impression that it has no power to do so—an impression that further discourages men from making appeals. In fact, so widespread is the opinion that the VA has no discretion in this area that several military lawyers contacted answered "absolutely not" when asked whether veterans with Undesirable and Bad Conduct Discharges might be entitled to VA benefits. In that light it is hardly surprising that so few veterans ever appeal to the VA.

★ Simplification, Review, and Reform

Both the military and the VA have vigorously resisted any efforts to change their administrative procedures for granting and evaluating discharges. The military insists the administrative discharge process must remain as it is to maintain discipline and efficiency, while the VA says its administrative procedures protect veterans more effectively than formal judicial processes. The first of these claims is a canard; military discipline can be maintained under a changed administrative discharge process. The VA's argument is belied by its own data, which indicate that the vast majority of veterans with bad discharges are denied benefits on appeal. But whatever the rationale offered separately by each agency, the combined effect of the two administrative systems is to deny entitlement to benefits without basic constitutional protections along the way.

The heart of the legal problem is the Undesirable Discharge. To guarantee veterans their fundamental rights, a critical step would be to deny administrative boards the alternative of imposing Undesirable Discharges. If the military wishes to dismiss a man under "less than honorable conditions," it should have to conduct a court-martial to prove its case. If it does not conduct a court-martial, it should not have the power to impose a discharge that will exclude a veteran from receiving benefits he is entitled to by law. In other words, administrative boards would be restricted to Honorable and General Discharges. The rule on eligibility for benefits would then be unequivocal, leaving the VA no room for discretion and eliminating its entire procedure for evaluating discharges in the "gray area." Any veteran who received an administrative discharge —including one who received an Undesirable Discharge in the past—should be eligible for benefits. Any veteran who received a discharge under dishonorable conditions after court-martial should not.

In addition to this change, the military services should facilitate the process for discharge review. This particularly applies to those veterans who were dismissed for drug-related causes prior to August 1971, when Defense Department policy in that area changed. If someone who received a bad discharge under the old policy would have received a good discharge under the new policy, reclassification should be automatic. Others whose cases may be less clear should be notified of the opportunity for review. To meet the increased work load these reviews would create, the Defense Department should establish additional review boards as needed, possibly on a regional basis so that they would be more accessible to veterans in areas far from Washington.

To raise the issue of discharge review is, of course, to enter upon a much larger matter—one that relates to the Vietnam War and the whole question of amnesty. Emotions on this subject are still intense, and probably only in a more distant and quiet time will the nation find that spirit of charity which characterized Lincoln's attitudes toward the South in a far more divided era than our own. We shall have to ask ourselves then whether a reasonable man might not have been legitimately disaffected in the army during the Vietnam War and led to act in ways that cost him a less than honorable discharge. And even if we reject that possibility, we shall still have to ask whether it is right to mark a man for life for crimes of youthful alienation or merely youthful exuberance. But these, of course, are questions for the distant future. It took us a decade to slip into Vietnam. Surely it will take us at least a decade to slip out.

part three ★ ★ ★
Trials of Peace

The social and economic problems that Vietnam veterans face on returning home are not uniquely their own, but their claims are of a special order. A nation that has found jobs for young men in the army ought to be able to find jobs for the same men in civilian life. A nation that has educated and trained them for military work which, for most, is temporary ought to be able to educate and train them for civilian work in which they will spend the rest of their lives. A nation that has asked of them enormous sacrifices in war ought to be able to make considerable sacrifices for them in peace.

The difference between what is deserved and what has been delivered is even more piquant if one considers what was promised. And nowhere were the promises more glowing and the reality more bleak than for the men who were inducted into the army under a special program of compensatory education called Project 100,000.

7

A Prelude:
How the Great
Society Went to War

"When a military spirit forsakes a people, the profession of arms immediately ceases to be held in honor, and military men fall to the lowest rank of public servants; they are little esteemed and no longer understood. The reverse of what takes place in aristocratic ages then occurs; the men who enter the army are no longer those of the highest, but of the lowest class."

—Alexis de Tocqueville[1]

"Those of our youth who lack education, those who live in the ghettoes, combine the ills of idleness, ignorance, and apathy. Our task is to help cure these ills with education, training, and incentives."

—Lieutenant General Herman Nickerson, Jr., Deputy Chief of Manpower, U.S. Marine Corps[2]

In 1966, at the outset of the war in Southeast Asia, Robert McNamara announced a new Defense Department program to salvage "part of America's subterranean poor." The idea was to bring into the military, and to rehabilitate, 100,000 underprivileged youth each year who previously would have been rejected for failing to meet the army's mental or physical standards. The program, called Project 100,000, would double or triple the men's future income, teach them new skills, and inculcate discipline and self-confidence. It would reduce domestic unemployment and enable the men to receive veterans' benefits. It would also—though its advocates omitted this point—supply much of the manpower needed for Vietnam.

To an Administration trying to fight both a ground war in Asia and a war on poverty at home, it must have seemed a stroke of genius to fight one war with the other. The results of Project 100,000, however, were not as impressive as the ingenuity that went into its conception. In its brief history, which ended quietly with the war's de-escalation, the program provided very little useful training, though it did send several hundred thousand men to Vietnam and several thousand to their deaths. Some career officers came to see it as partly responsible for insubordination and drug abuse in the enlisted ranks; its name now comes up in Congressional hearings on the viability of an all-volunteer army. But perhaps the most volatile aspect of the program was race. Four of every ten of the men it brought into the armed forces were black.[3] This did not trouble its creators. On the contrary, even before McNamara gave Project 100,000 his personal signature, Daniel Moynihan had envisioned it as a means of restoring self-respect to the black American male.

"Military service," Moynihan wrote in his 1965 report on the Negro family, "is disruptive in some respects. For those comparatively few who are killed or wounded in combat, or otherwise, the personal sacrifice is inestimable. But, on balance, service in the Armed Forces over the past quarter century has worked greatly to the advantage of those involved. The training and experience of military duty is unique; the advantages that have generally followed in the form of GI Bill mortgage guarantees, federal life insurance, Civil Service preference, veterans' hospitals and veterans' pensions are singular, to say the least." [4]

Moynihan, then an assistant secretary of labor, argued that the advantages for Negroes serving in the armed forces would be particularly great. Racial equality was not just a legal abstraction in the military; it was closer to realization there than anywhere else. But more than that: "There is another special quality about military service for Negro men: It is an utterly masculine world. Given the strains of the disorganized and matrifocal family life in which so many Negro youth come of age, the Armed Forces are a dramatic and desperately needed change: a world away from women, a world run by strong men of unquestioned authority, where discipline, if harsh, is nonetheless orderly and predictable, and where rewards, if limited, are granted on the basis of performance. The theme of a current Army recruiting message states it as clearly as can be: 'In the U.S. Army you get to know what it means to feel like a man.' " [5]

The logical conclusion was that the government, in its effort to eradicate poverty, should seek to increase the number of black soldiers. Moynihan noted that (as of 1965) Negroes were underrepresented in the Armed Forces. While they constituted 11.8 percent of the population, blacks comprised only 8 percent of the military. He neglected to mention that although blacks were underrepresented in the armed services as a whole, they were more than represented in the front lines. From 1961 to 1966 blacks accounted for 16 percent of the combat deaths in Vietnam.[6] In the year that Moynihan wrote his report, 1965, 23.5 percent of all Army enlisted men killed in action were black.[7]

An added incentive for the policy would be its effect on unemployment levels. "If Negroes were represented in the same proportions in the military as they are in the population," Moynihan pointed out, "they would number 300,000 plus. This would be over 100,000 more than at present (using 1964 strength figures). If the more than 100,000 unemployed Negro men were to have gone into the military, the Negro male unemployment rate would have been 7 percent instead of 9.1 percent." [8]

The core of Moynihan's thesis, however baldly put, was far from absurd. Military service has long been used as an instrument of socialization—witness the choice between jail or the army that judges so often give young offenders. "The discipline of the army," Max Weber once wrote, "gives birth to all discipline." [9] The only trouble was that a war was under way, and it was a war that many Americans, and many black Americans, would increasingly find unsupportable. Rather than instilling discipline, the experience of the next few years would create a level of disorder in the military and American life almost without parallel.

Increasing the number of blacks in the military was neither the first nor the only measure Moynihan had advocated for those who were being rejected by the armed forces. Shortly before his death, President Kennedy established a Task Force on Manpower Conservation under Moynihan's direction to study the one third of the male population that failed to qualify for the Selective Service. The task force found, not surprisingly, that the 600,000 annual rejectees were in large degree the products of impoverished backgrounds and substandard schools. A disproportionate number were black. There were cases of men who were rejected because they had cancer and then merely informed they had been disqualified, without mention of the reason or referral to a doctor. The commission found that four out of five rejectees said they would be willing to accept job training and that three out of four of those turned down for medical reasons would benefit from medical treatment. But the task force did not recommend, as Moynihan himself later would, that more rejectees be drafted so that they might secure the advantages of military training and veterans' benefits. Rather, it proposed to the President "a nationwide manpower conservation program to provide persons who fail to meet the qualifications for military service with the needed education, training, health rehabilitation, and related services that will enable them to become effective and self-supporting citizens." [10]

Less than a week after receiving the report on January 1, 1964, Lyndon Johnson announced that he was directing the Labor Department and the Selective Service System to establish a "voluntary rehabilitation" program for draft rejects. Secretary of Labor Willard Wirtz sounded the trumpet: "This will be the most important human salvage program in the history of our country." [11]

It turned out to be something less than that. Beginning February 17, the letters sent by local draft boards to rejectees informing them they had been turned down by the Selective Service suggested that they stop in at their local employment offices. That was the extent of the program. Within a few months the Labor Department discovered the message was not getting through. By June 134,500 letters had been mailed, but only 23,000 men, or 17.5 percent, had paid the employment service a visit. The wonder is that so many bothered. Of those who came, the Labor Department statistics showed that only 4,900 were referred to jobs and no more than 2,200 placed. One quarter of the placements were for jobs expected to last three days or less. A grand total of 189 had been enrolled in training programs under the Manpower Development and Training Act. [12]

Paul Barton, one member of the task force that originated the program, recalls the group had envisioned that $100 million in MDTA funds would be "earmarked" for training rejectees. [13] But the money never came through, the project was swallowed up in larger programs of the War on Poverty, and ultimately what was to have been "the most important human salvage program in the history of our country" amounted to nothing more than a statistical report.

So passed the Selective Service Rehabilitation Program. The idea that people should be provided services because they failed a test must have seemed so inimical to the American spirit that no one ever suggested a serious program for rejectees again. One can imagine what the Pentagon's reaction would have been had Johnson proposed major benefits for those escaping the draft. Any direct aid to rejectees would have cut sharply into military recruiting. It was implausible from the start.

In any case, other forces were in motion that would make military service itself a preferred, albeit subterranean, avenue for salvaging the poor.

On August 13, 1964, nine days after Congress had passed the Tonkin Gulf resolution authorizing Presidential action in Indochina, the Defense Department announced it would undertake an experimental program of modest dimensions. In the coming year the military would accept and rehabilitate about 11,000 volunteers who were currently being disqualified on mental or physical grounds. The Pentagon stated its objective for the Special Training and Enlistment Program (STEP) with simplicity and candor: "It is intended to reduce reliance on the draft by expanding the pool of qualified volunteers available for enlistment." [14] Also, STEP would give the army experience in training below-standard recruits in case of mobilization. To support the additional training that the new men would need, President Johnson asked Congress to appropriate $16,375,000 for the program in his 1966 budget.

Less out of fiscal prudence than a desire to keep military standards high, Congress refused Johnson's request. But that had little effect on the Administration, which eventually went ahead with the program in spite of Congressional disapproval. While funds had been denied for special training, the Defense Department still had the power to reduce qualification standards on its own. The existing practice was to accept men with scores above the thirtieth percentile on the Armed Forces Qualification Test, as well as men with scores above the fifteenth percentile who passed supplementary aptitude examinations. Legally, however, the military was free to accept anyone with a score above the tenth percentile. When manpower needs increased, the Pentagon could simply take more men with scores in the ten-to-thirty range (called Mental Group IV) and use them for low-aptitude assignments. In November 1965 a small move was made in that direction when certain supplementary tests were waived for draftees and army enlistees who scored above the fifteenth percentile. As a result of this seemingly trivial administrative change, the army took in an additional 30,000 men during the next eleven months.

Throughout 1966 Defense adopted a succession of other measures to meet its rising manpower requirements. Under a "Civilian/Military Substitution Plan," 60,000 civilian workers replaced 75,000 uniformed personnel, freeing the servicemen for transfers to other assignments. In May the Selective Service began administering tests to college students, touching off a furor on the campuses. There was excited talk about activating the reserves for service in Vietnam. And of course there was the draft. In August, just days before Project 100,000 was initiated, the Pentagon announced it would be calling 46,200 for October, the largest monthly request since the Korean War. It was also raising its previously announced September quota by 6,000 up to 37,300 men.

The cynical might be inclined to believe that the Defense Department began to look more favorably upon the idea of upgrading the poor through military service only as its own manpower requirements expanded. The truth appears to be slightly —but only slightly—more intricate. For reasons of domestic social policy that Moynihan and others had articulated, many civilian policy makers, including some in the Defense Department, had long favored a reduction in qualifying standards for military service. But so long as the numerical strength of the army was stationary, it had been impossible for the civilian planners to bring the armed services around. For the generals, a reduction in standards was a bitter pill. Under normal circumstances it would not be accepted. It was only the escalation of the war, and the concomitant manpower crisis and expansion of the army, that induced them to swallow it.[15]

And so it was that on August 23, 1966 to the surprise of a Congress which had only recently voted down such a project, Robert McNamara announced his department was undertaking a massive program to rehabilitate "part of America's subterranean poor." The defunct Project STEP was child's play compared to what McNamara had ordered. The new program would involve 40,000 men the first year and 100,000 each year thereafter— whence the name Project 100,000. Whereas STEP would have lowered standards only for 11,000 volunteers, Project 100,000 would reduce standards for both volunteers and draftees.

"The poor of America," the Defense Secretary told an audience in New York City, "have not had the opportunity to earn their fair share of this nation's abundance, but they can be given an opportunity to return to civilian life with skills and aptitudes which for them and their families will reverse the downward spiral of decay."

Taking note of the vast training resources of the Defense Department ("the world's largest educator of skilled men"), he pointed out that it offered professional training in some 1,500 different skills. Moreover, Defense was "experimenting with the use of carefully designed programmed instruction—matched specifically against actual on-the-job requirements—which allows the student to proceed at his own individual pace, rather than merely be herded along at an arbitrarily determined group pace." A progressive educator, he suggested that the men of Project 100,000 would use their own individual training tapes on closed circuit television.

"I do not believe that the qualifications for military service should now be lowered," McNamara stated. "What I do believe is that through the application of advanced educational and medical techniques we can salvage tens of thousands of these men, each year, first to productive military careers and later for productive roles in society." [16]

Whatever the Secretary believed, the facts proved to be precisely the reverse of what he said. In less than two months his department announced that it would, after all, reduce qualification standards to admit Project 100,000 men. They would be drawn from those who scored between the tenth and fifteenth percentiles on the qualification test. Moreover, it soon became apparent that the special innovative programs McNamara promised could not be introduced for the simple reasons that no money had been allocated to pay for them. Project 100,000 men were absorbed directly into the standard training program. When they had difficulty, they were "recycled," held back to repeat a phase of their training, or else sent to special training companies—including "motivation" platoons, physical conditioning units, and so on—that existed prior to McNamara's announcement. According to one Pentagon official, these units, as a result of Project 100,000, did get "beefed up to handle a somewhat larger load." [17] Also in response to the new program some skill training courses were reviewed and simplified.

The immediate reaction to McNamara's speech was mixed, both outside the military and within. Civil rights leaders lashed out at the plan as an attempt to make blacks and the poor bear the burden of the fighting. On the other hand, F. Edward Hebert, who now heads the House Armed Services Committee, was delighted with McNamara's move. "I applaud his objective," the Louisiana Democrat said. "Maybe now they'll get Cassius Clay." [18] Muhammad Ali had just failed the Selective Service mental exam.

The military press reported that career officers were disturbed about the prospect of an influx of low-aptitude recruits, and the *Army Times* editorialized, "Are the services likely to get any reasonable mileage from such people? Past performances indicate not. . . . Is this any time to require the services to take on a large scale 'poverty-war' training mission? We would think not. The services more than have their hands full with the fighting war." [19]

Not all military men shared that view. One Army officer insisted that rejects would not degrade the service. "These men make the best infantrymen, mortarmen, and mechanics. Practically all will do their best to do a good job. I'd prefer a company of riflemen with fifth-grade educations over a company of college men anytime." [20]

And that, of course, was exactly the choice the Pentagon had made.

"The reduction in mental standards," *The New York Times* reported in October, ". . . will probably ease the pressure now building up, because of the manpower demands of the Vietnam war, to begin inducting college students who are currently being deferred." [21]

Despite McNamara's glowing announcement, which made it seem as if the poor were being sent off to school instead of to war, Project 100,000 soldiers were not about to be assigned to training in the 1,500 professional skills the army offered. For while the Defense Department had reduced aptitude requirements for entering the military, it had no intention of similarly reducing requirements for technical positions within the services. Hence the majority of "New Standards Men" would be barred from the kind of training which McNamara said would "reverse the downward spiral of decay." The result was reported in the *Air Force Times*: "According to Defense officials, about 25 percent of the occupations in the military are suitable for the Project 100,000 men." [22]

The leading occupation, as might be expected, was combat. In the military as a whole today, 14 percent of all personnel are given combat roles; the rest draw support assignments of one sort or another. But among the New Standards Men the proportion going into combat proved to be 37 percent. [23]

Although the Pentagon compiled and released voluminous statistics on Project 100,000, it quite inexplicably omitted data on the casualty rates and combat deaths of New Standards Men relative to other soldiers. Pentagon officials deny that the casualty rates for Project 100,000 soldiers were disproportionately high. [24] One must assume in that case that since they were more likely to go into combat than other soldiers, New Standards Men were better at avoiding bullets and booby traps.

After the infantry, the next most frequent assignment for "100,000" soldiers was service and supply handling. According to a

Pentagon study, 20 percent of the men fell into that slot. While 7.5 percent of personnel in a control group were assigned to electronics equipment repairing, the proportion among New Standards Men was 1.4 percent. The new soldiers did fairly well, however, in the area of electrical/mechanical repairing (e.g., auto service, telephone installation); 16.8 percent drew those jobs. The proportion in the control population was 22 percent.[25]

The promise that McNamara and Moynihan had held out was that Project 100,000 would enable young men with limited education and small resources to acquire skills transferable to civilian life. The proportion who actually did acquire skills in the military has probably been rather small. As mentioned in Chapter 1, a survey of "socially and economically disadvantaged" Vietnam era veterans conducted by the Bureau of the Budget in 1969 found that only 12 percent of the employed veterans had used military-gained training or skills since separation.[26] But of course, as Moynihan might point out, such crude statistics tell us nothing about the number of black youths who may have profited from the experience of living in an all-male environment.

Nor could they suggest how many suffered. With the escalation of the Vietnam War, black attitudes toward the military underwent a remarkable transformation. Initially the black community looked with pride on the achievements of its soldiers, but increasingly civil rights leaders began to note that blacks were suffering a disproportionate number of casualties, that the war distorted national priorities, and that American attitudes toward the Vietnamese—as exhibited in such practices as "free-fire" zones and pacification camps—were nothing but a reflection of the same racism blacks suffered at home. Support for the war plummeted in the black community and black re-enlistment rates dropped by 50 percent between 1966 and 1967.[27] Indicative of the changing sentiment was a speech by Martin Luther King at Riverside Church in New York City in April 1967:

> We are taking the young black men who have been crippled by our society and sending them 8,000 miles away to guarantee liberties in Southeast Asia which they had not found in Southwest Georgia and East Harlem. So we have been repeatedly faced with the cruel irony of watching Negro and white boys on TV screens as they kill and die together for a nation that has been unable to seat them together at the same school. So we watch them in brutal solidarity burning the huts of a poor village, but we realize that they could never live on the same block in Detroit.[28]

As the statistics on Project 100,000 began marching into the Pentagon through the late Sixties, official statements began rolling out acclaiming the program an unqualified triumph. "The plain fact," Robert McNamara told an audience in Denver in November 1967, "is that our Project 100,000 is succeeding even beyond our most hopeful expectations." McNamara noted with pride that the new men were completing basic training at a rate of 96 percent, only two points below other recruits. He made the best of the fact that no special training had been offered: "I have insisted," he declared, "that these men should never be singled out or stigmatized as a special group." McNamara predicted that on their return to civilian life, the earning capacity of Project 100,000 men would be "two to three times what it would have been had there been no such program." [29]

No study before or since that speech supports his prediction. Data reported in 1970 by the Gates Commission, which examined the problem of a volunteer army, indicate that military service has no measurable impact on subsequent lifetime earnings.[30] These findings, of course, contradict the basic assumptions of Moynihan's report and McNamara's public statements.

Project 100,000 men were never informed who they were. The decision to keep their identity confidential probably did help the men's self-esteem, as McNamara contended. (Many soldiers referred to the group as the "moron corps.") But the result was that they never received the special training that was promised, and never will receive any marked attention from the Veterans Administration.

While Project 100,000 soldiers were absorbed into the regular training system, they had the opportunity open to all servicemen to enroll in voluntary educational programs offered by the Defense Department. The Pentagon has released statistics on the experience of the first three years of the program. In that period 246,000 New Standards Men were accepted; of this number, 19,000 were medical remedial cases (men with correctible physical problems), while 225,000 were admitted under the reduced mental standards. According to the Pentagon's records, 12,632 completed reading courses in the Army, 2,019 in the Navy, and 2,554 in the Air Force. In other words, approximately 7.5 percent of the New Mental Standards Men received remedial education.[31]

These courses, which were aimed at raising soldiers to a fifth- or sixth-grade reading level, lasted six to eight weeks. Everyone graduated, whether or not they passed. "Students who fail to achieve a fifth-grade reading level during the six weeks," explained an Army general, "are not recycled, but are assigned to basic combat training." [32] The Marines never offered the literacy program because they believed no real assistance could be given in so brief a period. "We are not impressed with the long-term effects of a short remedial reading program," a Marine Corps general told the House Appropriations Committee in 1970.[33]

The Defense Department also offers an education and training program for outgoing servicemen designed to help them readjust to civilian life. Under Project Transition, 1.3 percent of the New Standards Men took part in educational programs, 2.7 percent received Post Office training, and 2.3 percent were given other kinds of vocational training.[34]

One might think that the institution which gave us the body count would be vexed by the meager statistical results of Project 100,000 education and training. But at least in appearances before Congress, Defense officials have expressed satisfaction with the training programs.

If the military has never doubted that it was promoting the welfare of Project 100,000 men, it has questioned whether Project 100,000 men were promoting the welfare of the military. The sources of disquiet have been many. Since "100,000" soldiers often had to be "recycled" through basic training, the program involved additional expenditures. The Air Force, for example, estimated that it spent 14 percent more to train New Standards Men, only 61 percent of whom completed basic training without "recycling." [35]

A second source of disquiet has been the disciplinary record of Project 100,000 soldiers. According to the Pentagon study cited earlier, they have had a rate of court-martial convictions twice that of a control group (3 percent as opposed to 1.4 percent). The frequency of nonjudicial punishments is also higher among Project 100,000 men (13.4 percent, compared with 8.2 percent for the control population).[36]

These signs would ordinarily be disturbing to military leaders, but they are especially so at a time when rebellion and racial tension plague the army. Moreover, through 1970 and 1971, the armed forces underwent a marked reduction in numerical strength. Had the military maintained the quota of New Standards Men at 100,000, the group would have comprised a progressively larger percentage of new recruits. While the Pentagon insisted that Project 100,000 was good for the poor, its leaders agreed that keeping the program at its original levels would be pushing altruism a little too far.

So it came as no surprise in military circles to learn that the quotas for Project 100,000 were being rapidly scaled down. In 1970 the number of New Standards Men was cut to 76,500 and the following year to under 50,000, making the program's name something of a misnomer. Simultaneously, the services began to eliminate an increasing proportion of the men during basic training. The Marines are a case in point. In 1968 they dropped 6.8 percent of Mental Group IV soldiers during basic training; in 1969, 10.5 percent; in 1970, 33.9 percent; and in the first quarter of 1971, 46.1 percent.[37] Recent legislation now precludes the use of mental group quotas in military recruitment.

But the elimination of quotas for New Standards Men is not tantamount to the elimination of the substance of the program, which was to bring into the army men of certain educational level and social class. While it is true that Project 100,000 was phased out as an experimental program, it has to a large extent been superseded by the volunteer army, which draws upon the same sector of the population. With an all-volunteer army there are no set quotas for New Standards Men; the number that the military accepts depends upon "market forces."

In testimony before Congress, Assistant Secretary of Defense Roger Kelley made it clear that the phasing out of Project 100,000 is only administrative. " 'Project 100,000' as a term," he said, "has pretty well outlived its usefulness. What was Project 100,000 has since become a part of the whole fabric of the personnel management system of the four services. . . . The term is on the way out, but certainly not the utilization of people who are in Category IV." [38]

That the Pentagon intends to use these men for the same tasks it has in the past was evident in a memorandum Kelley sent to the services in March 1971: "The normal flow of Group IV will still enable the Department of Defense to use people with lower mental capacity in jobs that are suited to their talents." [39] Translated into ordinary English, that means combat, supply handling, and simple mechanical work.

What benefit training in such areas has been to Project 100,000 soldiers is a matter of question. They were the men who went into the army with the least education and the fewest skills, and while in the army, they were the most likely to become casualties and the least able to acquire further education. Pentagon studies indicate that about 10 percent of them never finished their service, because they were either killed, disabled, or released with bad discharges[40] —a figure which, to borrow a phrase from Daniel Moynihan, is singular, to say the least. The proportion who receive training in a skill transferable to civilian life has been small. Of course, there are those who argue, or dread, that combat experience will turn out to be transferable back home, but somehow one doubts that is what McNamara and Moynihan had in mind. They are both, as is well known, strictly opposed to the use of violence as a means of social change.

Every society goes to war in its own way; the Great Society was no exception. In countries where justice is of no concern, men are drafted to fight the king's wars simply because they are his subjects and have no choice. In the brutal language of Thucydides, the strong do what they can, and the weak suffer what they must. Such straightforward justifications are unacceptable in our own age. Military manpower policies, like other policies, are now suffused with the aura of benevolence. The poor are drafted not to fight and perhaps to die, but only to be uplifted. The passage from autocratic rule to democratic government was no doubt a great victory for mankind, but the price has apparently been a good deal more hypocrisy.

8

The Unemployed Army

"My son was one of those applying for a county job—was told to come back time after time, finally was told someone else was hired who had worked on roads. My son helped build roads from scratch in Vietnam and also drove all types of equipment. Yet they claim he has no experience. How much more experience do you need? If it takes experience, then why did they send him to war—he had no experience in that."

—Letter from a woman in Racine, Wisconsin.

"Out of the army, out of work, and out of luck" was how many Vietnam veterans put it, and by the spring of 1971 there were more of them in the army of the unemployed at home—about 330,000 strong—than there were in the army in Vietnam. The country was so concerned about "bringing the boys home" that it had neglected what it was bringing them home to. Opportunities to curb unemployment among returning soldiers were missed early in the first Nixon administration. The magnificent flexibility of the military—as the woman from Wisconsin observed, no one asked her son if he had experience in war before taking him in—gave way to the inflexibility of a tight economy where good jobs were scarce, and inflation was hard to control. The men who did the grubby job of fighting only found more jobs like it when they came back.

"Like when I first came home, I was lost, I didn't have nothing to do. Most of my friends were working, and I was just sitting home collecting unemployment compensation. I said, this is stupid, sitting home watching soap operas. I mean I could have gone on collecting fifty bucks a week for thirty weeks, but what are you going to do?

*You spend fifty bucks a week drinking beer, you become a juicer. So
I wanted a job.*

"*And I figured I'd get something decent. I figured like I'd put
down that I'd been a veteran, and it would help, just having your
service out of the way. But no, it was harder than that. When I was
just getting out they had, I forget, some training thing [Project
Transition] where you work on the job after your duty hours. But I
was getting out in only a month.*

"*Then I didn't have the training. There's good jobs if you've got
the training, but I didn't have it. Except what I learned in the
business course at high school. Once I went over to Mattapan, where
they had that OJT [on-job-training] stuff for vets, and I went in and
said, I want to learn a trade. So the guy says, what did you take up
in high school? Business courses. And he told me I should take a
course in bookkeeping. I don't want to do that, right? I want to learn
a trade, I want to make money, I didn't want to sit behind a desk
and take home a hundred and ten dollars a week. So I never got
nowhere with them.*

"*They said I could be a lineman up in Maine. Nice job, right? The
only trade jobs they had had waiting lists a mile long.*

"*Then there were the Employment Service jobs, they were all
about at the minimum wage, no training, no benefits. You could get
them easy, but who wants to work at the minimum wage? That's
where all the bums go, to the Employment Service.*

"*The jobs I got, I mostly got through friends or the newspaper. It
was mainly first come, first serve. Since 1970 I've had five jobs. The
first I got after about a month out, putting in fire systems for a fire
extinguisher place. It was a pretty good job, but you'd have to work
a lot of nights, and everybody's snapping at you all the time. One
thing I can't take, I can't take people snapping at me. Like even my
family, when they get loud, I hate loud people, I really do. Like
where I worked next, that was the best job, in a warehouse
unloading freight. I was only taking home about ninety-one dollars a
week. But the people were good, you know. They didn't yell at me. I
did my work. I mean it's not that I'm a lousy worker, don't get me
wrong. I mean whatever I do I try to do the best I can, you know.
But I hate people–like, in the service–people that make you dig holes
so that you can fill them up again the next morning. At the
warehouse, it was hard work at times, but it was small, it was like a
little family. It could be fun at times, too. The only reason I left
there was because there was no union, no benefits. I'm getting
married in six months, and I had to start worrying about the
benefits. But I stayed at that job longer than any other, about a year.*

"See, when I come out of the service, I'd been taking orders for three years. And I didn't want to take no more orders for a while. But it seems like you have to. That's partly why I went into the service in the first place. When I went in, right, I was nothing, I was a nobody. And like the jobs I had worked at part-time in high school weren't very great ones, either. Like I was a bagger in a grocery store, and then I worked folding boxes in an ice cream factory. You know, the ones I had, if you didn't kiss the boss's ass, you were no good, right?

"So I figured, with the service, maybe you'd go in and you'd earn rank. But that's all shit, too, because if you don't kiss the lieutenant's ass, you were no good anyways. So it's the same as on the outside.

"And now I'm working in a bakery, Wonderland, ITT, right? It's a big factory, I'm just part of a peanut factory. They start me off at three dollars and seventy-two cents, and in three months it goes up to four dollars and two cents an hour. And the work I do, it's really intelligent work. It's like instant replay every night. I work on a machine they call the 'divider,' and they put eighteen hundred pounds of dough in a vat, and the machine divides it into loaves. I have to make sure it runs properly. And most of the time it doesn't. So I'm running around like a chicken with its head cut off. The first night the guy starts the machine, and then he goes. There gets to be dough everywhere. So there's no training at all now. But I'm in the union. Once you're in the union a while—and I mean a while—they start to train you. Then jobs get better. Right now, I'm working six nights a week, including Saturdays, Sundays, and holidays. Every day, I sleep. It sucks.

"I think when I went in the service I had it all planned. But I must have been stupid or something. I came out, all I did was skip around from job to job. I mean, when you was younger, you was looking for something, right? All of a sudden, you get older, you get married, you've got to stop looking. You know, I don't mind hard work. I'd rather work hard than watch the clock run out. But you ought to be learning something, and mostly you're not. Like the job I've got now, at the bakery. The only reason I work at this place is for the benefits, because I'm getting married. I'm getting married, so I've got to take a job I hate.

"I mean, it's not like you, right? Maybe you'd carry that tape recorder around for Ralphy for nothing. Or maybe you're on welfare, you son-of-a-bitch. Like I say, there's good jobs if you've got the training. But I never got it. I mean I fought in Nam for a year and worked in the stateside military for a year after Nam as a file clerk.

That's my training. I can kill people, I can type thirty-five words a minute, and I know what debits and credits are."

★ Background and Setting

Unemployment among Vietnam veterans went from 4 percent in late 1969 to a peak of 11 percent in early 1971, at that time about two points higher than the rate for nonveterans in the same age group. During that period, at least a third of all Vietnam era veterans experienced two consecutive months of unemployment at one time or another. Within the veteran population, the disabled, the young, the educationally and economically disadvantaged, and the minorities did considerably worse. Among black veterans, for example, unemployment increased from 8.5 percent in the third quarter of 1969 to 14 percent two years later and 16 percent in 1972, in one month reaching 22.4 percent for young black veterans. Subsequent improvements in the economy cut that rate substantially, but as of the second quarter of 1973, a boom period, unemployment still stood at 11 percent for all black veterans and 16.3 percent for blacks aged twenty to twenty-four. The boom wasn't reaching them. Overall, those veterans who could least afford to be without work have been without it most often, and those who bore the largest share of the fighting in Vietnam have also borne more than their share of the economic dislocations at home.

Hardships imposed upon veterans by unemployment have been mitigated somewhat by automatic eligibility for unemployment compensation. Veterans receive UCX payments (Unemployment Compensation for Ex-Servicemen) without first having to put in the normally required minimum period of civilian work (six months or more in most states). Some veteran unemployment has been "voluntary" in that servicemen have taken advantage of the opportunity afforded by UCX to relax for several weeks before returning to work. These post-discharge "vacations" probably account for much of the 1 to 2 percent gap that persisted for several years between the unemployment rates for veterans and nonveterans of similar ages.

Still, unemployment compensation doesn't take all the sting out of unemployment. Living off UCX can be pretty dull, especially if preservice friends are working or have moved. More important, UCX fails to make up for lost work experience and needed training. Although some veterans may have left the army psychologically unprepared to return to work, the vast majority have been eager to stop being just veterans and to find responsible employment as soon as possible.

Men returning from a harsh war have a stake in decent jobs that goes beyond the simple need to provide economic security. Especially for those who have served at low wages under draft compulsion, as many did during Vietnam, a good civilian job offers an opportunity to recover training, experience, and income lost to wartime, and to make up for employment advantages, like seniority, gained by those who stayed behind. The post-war job is also critical for more personal reasons. Having lived at the beck and call of a highly regimented military order, many men wish to resume control over the day-to-day decisions that govern their careers. (*"See, when I come out of the service, I'd been taking orders for three years . . ."*) Having learned to handle challenging or dangerous situations in the military, many are reluctant to settle for dull and sedentary civilian jobs. (*"I didn't want to sit behind a desk . . ."*) Veterans care about earning relatively high wages, but they are also concerned about the contributions that civilian employment can make to their sense of responsibility and self-esteem. (*"I figured I'd get something decent."*)

This is just the sort of work they find it difficult to secure. So long as they served in the armed forces, their "full employment" was guaranteed by the war machine, which could find a slot for anyone in reasonably good health willing to obey orders. But an affluent civilian economy has much more discriminating hiring criteria, which returning veterans may have trouble satisfying. Once they leave the military a new, less dramatic, but much more personal battle begins.

A key post-war problem for policy-makers is always accommodating increases in the civilian labor force that result from the return of war veterans, without compromising other economic objectives. For the period immediately following World War II, the transition was aided by several factors. Wartime price controls had restrained inflation, and a backlog of unmet consumer demand helped the economy to recover quickly from the sharp liquidation of war production that followed the Japanese surrender in August 1945. Massive participation in educational programs under the GI Bill helped to withdraw hundreds of thousands of men from the labor force, taking pressure off the private labor market until it could expand to absorb more workers. Returning veterans were also aided in their job-finding by the fact that they were relatively old, compared with the veterans of subsequent wars (twenty-seven years of age, on the average, as against twenty-five for the Korean War and twenty-three for Vietnam). They were aided as well by the withdrawal, between April 1945 and April 1947, of over 3 million women from the civilian labor force, women who often chose, and in some cases were forced, to resume their conventional social roles.

Nevertheless, in the months immediately after demobilization, veteran unemployment reached 14 percent. By August 1946, it dropped to 8 percent, which was still three times the rate for nonveterans. Much of this unemployment was due to the lag between seeking and finding work always encountered by new entrants to the labor force. Although general unemployment was higher during the immediate post-war years than during the war (3.8 percent in 1948, compared with 1.9 percent in 1945), unemployment among veterans continued to fall steadily until it nearly equaled nonveteran unemployment in 1948.[1]

Following the Korean War, a decline in defense spending brought on a recession, and as late as November 1954, veteran unemployment stood at 7.9 percent among the 2 million GIs who had returned home. But 1955 proved to be a better year. Veteran unemployment fell to 4.2 percent as the domestic economy recovered from the post-war slowdown.[2]

In the case of the Vietnam War, veteran unemployment has been complicated by a number of factors, particularly differences in demographic features between Vietnam veterans and their predecessors. The new veterans tend to be younger at the time they are discharged, and young job seekers typically have a much harder time finding stable employment. A higher proportion of Vietnam veterans are black, and blacks often face racial discrimination in hiring practices. Many veterans are politically active or have adopted modes of dress and mien alien to the dominant employment culture. (In 1971, for example, a California state district court ruled that an unemployed Vietnam veteran was ineligible to collect unemployment insurance because he had long hair and so "obviously" could not have been looking for work.)

On the other hand, the readmission of Vietnam veterans to the American civilian economy has been much more gradual than it was for veterans of World War II, which might well have allowed officials to anticipate veteran employment problems and prepare for them. Special appropriations could have been made early; instead, as we shall see, the President actually vetoed critical legislation in 1970 that could have alleviated veteran unemployment. Those federal agencies that have employment programs for veterans might have developed coordination among their local offices and among themselves; instead coordination came late when it came at all. In short, the comparison with unemployment among veterans of earlier wars might well have been made a happier one.

But these opportunities were lost. When President Nixon took office in January 1969, veteran unemployment stood at 3.7 percent. It climbed steadily, reaching 8.9 percent at midterm and peaking at 11 percent in February 1971. The economy then turned upward, and Vietnam veteran unemployment fell along with general civilian unemployment, touching 5.5 percent just before the 1972 elections. In the early months of 1973 veteran unemployment rose to 6 percent and, with inflation more serious than it had been since the Korean War, the economic prospect was clouded.

There is a tendency among some observers to pass off high veteran unemployment as an ineluctable problem at the close of a war. In this case at least, it could have been substantially reduced had the Administration adopted more aggressive measures earlier to combat it. It could be reduced still further if new strategies were accepted aimed at improving the quality of work available to young veterans and other young workers. Veteran unemployment has not been an unpredictable misfortune that sprang without warning from the residuum of war. It was the foreseeable consequence of deliberate decisions made at the very peak of the nation's political system.

★ *The Failure of Economic Restraint (1969–70)*

The main economic objective of the first Nixon administration was to return the nation to pre-1965 price stability. In pursuit of this objective, basic policy choices were made in 1969 that were the roots of subsequent high unemployment rates. Just at a time when Vietnam veterans were returning home at a rate of nearly 1 million per year, the Administration introduced a program to curb inflation by reducing government spending and private borrowing. This could be done, the President reassured the public at his first press conference in 1969, "without increasing unemployment in, certainly, any substantial way." [3] He was wrong, and by the end of the year the Administration's initial optimism was beginning to fade. A November 1969 report from the Bureau of the Budget offered a grim forecast of the impact that disengagement from Vietnam, coupled with the President's anti-inflation efforts, would have on veteran unemployment:

> A decrease of U.S. involvement in Vietnam will obviously affect the nation's economy and the employment situation. More than likely,

there will be serious regional economic dislocations. The employment picture for the skilled and the unskilled, for veterans and nonveterans alike, is not encouraging. . . . The combination of unemployed civilians and veterans looking for jobs will cause special problems for the disadvantaged veteran.[4]

Despite this warning, the Administration continued its policies of economic restraint and during the following year took no measures to provide Vietnam veterans with special job-finding assistance. Two years after the 1968 elections, when both major parties had made platform commitments to aid returning veterans in locating jobs, the Administration and Congress were still relying upon weak and inappropriate traditional programs for unemployed veterans. These programs were reemployment rights, unemployment compensation, preferential hiring in Civil Service positions, and preferential referrals to job openings.° For a variety of reasons, none of these was capable of having more than a marginal impact upon veteran unemployment in a slow economy.

Reemployment rights: The Military Selective Service Act of 1967 provides that "those who serve their country in the interest of the national defense do not lose their jobs and other employment benefits because of such services." This act, administered by the Department of Labor's Office of Veteran Reemployment Rights, permits men who held "non-temporary" jobs prior to service and performed satisfactorily in the military to regain their position without loss of seniority. Veterans who return with disabilities may be rehired in "a comparable position which [they] are qualified to perform." If business conditions make it "unreasonable" for employers to rehire, however, they need not do so.[5]

These rights, unfortunately, have been of little value to Vietnam veterans, because most of them entered the military before they were twenty years old. Consequently, only about one third had any pre-service jobs to which they might return. Furthermore, these were generally "entry-level" positions characterized by low wages, no fringe benefits, poor working conditions, and few training opportunities. This is not the sort of work that many yearn to reclaim.

Unemployment compensation: A second traditional assistance pro-

° A fifth program affecting employment was training under the GI Bill, which will be discussed in the next chapter. For the period we are discussing here, GI Bill benefits were extremely low.

gram guarantees unemployment insurance payments, for up to an average of thirty weeks, to all honorably discharged veterans who have had at least ninety days of active duty (if not disabled). These payments, which are made by the Labor Department's U.S. Employment Service in cooperation with state employment agencies, are intended to provide income to veterans while they are looking for work. The payments vary from state to state; maximum benefits range from $50 to $80 per week for unmarried men. In 1971 about 500,000 Vietnam era veterans who were unemployed at various times during the year drew a total of $310 million in payments, with an average weekly payment of about $52.[6] Compared to the average pre-tax weekly earnings of employed veterans (between $105 and $125 per week in 1969), these payments appear to be low. Actually, since unemployment compensation is tax-exempt, payments usually turn out to be almost two thirds of what after-tax full-time income would be.

Still, these are at best subsistence payments. As noted earlier, they offer no compensation for lost work experience and training. Nor do they offer employers much of an incentive to structure jobs so that young workers have an interest in keeping them. Recent studies in labor economics indicate that many young workers are confined to a "secondary labor market," where available jobs are characterized by high rates of employee turnover, low wages, few training opportunities, and no fringe benefits or seniority.[7] These qualities are not inherent in the work; in many cases, it appears that "bad jobs" might be converted to more stable forms of employment. But so long as employers expect young workers to quit frequently, and also know that those workers will, at some point, have to take an available job to stay eligible for unemployment compensation, they will be less willing to invest in upgrading the work and providing better jobs.

This is not to say that UCX payments should be discontinued. There is ample justification for giving income supplements to the unemployed, veterans or not. In the present labor market, however, these payments effectively subsidize bad jobs and reinforce high rates of turnover. They are certainly no substitute for providing returning veterans with decent full-time employment.

Civil Service preference: The third traditional mechanism for dealing with the employment problems of veterans is preferential hiring for government jobs. In the federal civil service and many state and local governments, this takes the form of adding points to the scores that veterans achieve on competitive examinations. On the federal level, five points are added to the score of honorably discharged veterans who take the "zero-to-one-hundred" Civil Service examination. Ten points are added to the scores of service-disabled veterans. These preference points, however, are only of use to men who already have the basic educational qualifications required to sit for an examination. Otherwise they confer no advantage at all.

The main difficulty with using Civil Service preference as a weapon against veteran unemployment—aside from the fact that those who suffer the most unemployment are also those who lack the prerequisites to sit for exams—is that its impact depends upon the number of government jobs available. During 1970 and 1971 the President imposed personnel freezes on federal agencies and even ordered 5 percent cutbacks in many areas, as part of a plan to curb federal spending. Consequently veterans' preference could have little effect on veteran unemployment. In fact, according to a 1971 report, the proportion of nonveterans aged twenty to twenty-nine holding Civil Service positions was actually higher than the proportion of veterans.[8]

Preference in employment service referrals: The fourth traditional mechanism for dealing with veteran unemployment is preference in referrals to job openings and training programs listed with the U.S. Employment Service and the nearly 2,200 local state employment offices across the nation. With help from the Veterans Employment Service of the Department of Labor, state employment offices also offer unemployed veterans counseling and testing. The Veterans Employment Service itself does none of this directly; it assigns veteran employment representatives to state Employment Service headquarters, primarily to insure that veterans receive the preference to which they are entitled by law.

"Preference in referrals to job openings" does not mean that employers must award open jobs to veterans. If job openings appear for which several applicants are available, the veteran applicants will hear about them first from the employment office. But the employer has the option of screening additional applicants and choosing whomever he thinks most suitable.

The impact of referral preference on veteran unemployment depends primarily on two factors: (1) The degree to which preference is actually carried out by local employment offices, and (2) the number and quality of the jobs that employers choose to list with the Employment Service. Historically, the Employment Service has been more successful in controlling the first factor. Despite its highly decentralized administrative structure (state officials make most policy decisions) and the small size of the Veterans Employment Service, it generally appears that local employment offices have geen putting veterans' preference into effect.[9]

The second factor, the number and quality of Employment Service jobs, has proved more troublesome. In recent years, private employers have grown dissatisfied with the Employment Service. Its referrals are slow and its screening processes inaccurate; many applicants are referred to employers even though they lack specified qualifications.[10] Employers have expressed their dissatisfaction by taking better job openings to private employment agencies, placing more newspaper advertisements, and making greater use of waiting lists. As a result, the Employment Service has gradually lost contact with most of the better jobs in the society. After 1962 the number of new job openings received by the Employment Service declined steadily, reaching a new low in fiscal year 1970—just as Vietnam veterans were coming home in large numbers.[11] Of all new non-farm job openings that became available in the U.S. economy each year, the Employment Service was apparently receiving less than a third. And, as a 1970 study by the Urban Coalition observed, these jobs "tend to reflect the lowest levels of the economy." During fiscal year 1969, out of 5.5 million non-farm job placements made by the Employment Service, professional and managerial jobs accounted for only 6.4 percent. About 60 percent of all placements were for jobs not covered by the minimum wage.[12]

The small numbers and poor quality of Employment Service job listings have undermined its ability to assist veterans. Since 1968 an average of less than 10 percent of those Vietnam era veterans who registered with the Employment Service as "applicants available for work" in any given quarter were placed in jobs during that quarter.[13] No one knows how long they remained on the job. The Employment Service measures its success in "job placement rates," even though many of the placements are for jobs that last only a few days.

Unemployed veterans understand this. They know that Employment Service jobs tend to be inferior, and most of them register with the employment offices as "applicants available for work" only because they must do so to collect UCX payments. Whenever possible, it seems, they try to avoid being at home when the office calls with its list of job "opportunities" or they will go through the motions of applying for job openings to maintain eligibility for UCX payments.

In 1971, under Presidential directive, the Employment Service instituted new procedures to improve the quality and numbers of openings it receives. These changes will be discussed later on.

The traditional mechanisms for dealing with veteran unemployment, therefore, proved to be incapable of doing much for Vietnam veterans in the midst of the 1969–71 recession. By late 1970 the effects were clearly visible. Anti-inflation policies had gotten out of hand, and veteran unemployment soared. Three weeks before the mid-term elections, the President decided to take action. But from an Administration in which the top echelons were populated with former marketing and advertising executives, one might have suspected what kind of action that would be.

★ The Public Relations Gambit: Jobs for Veterans (1970–71)

On October 15, 1970, President Nixon created a Jobs for Veterans Committee headed by seventy-eight-year-old James F. Oates, former board chairman of the Equitable Life Insurance Company, and including representatives from ITT, the Teamsters, Bankers' Trusts, and the International Association of Chiefs of Police. Their job was to mount a national advertising campaign intended to alert employers to the need to hire veterans. The committee also sought to promote the idea of "job fairs," where employers and veterans could be brought together for job interviews and information. It also tried to set up state and local Veteran Task Forces to enlist the assistance of prominent business and government leaders.

To its credit, Jobs for Veterans put together one of the largest public relations drives in recent history. With the help of veterans' organizations, the Veterans Employment Service, the National Alliance of Businessmen, and the National Conference of Mayors, over 300 local task forces were organized. Nearly 500 cities had some kind of promotional activity. The Advertising Council supplied thousands of public service announcements ("Don't Forget, Hire the Vet") in national magazines and media. The American Broadcasting Company made an hour-long film on veterans' problems. Large numbers of corporate executives dedicated their time to the campaign. In terms of billboards raised, speeches made, task force meetings held, and column inches donated, the program was an enormous success. In fact, it succeeded in every respect but one. Veteran unemployment continued to rise. When the program began, it stood at 7 percent; by June 1971 it had risen to 10.8 percent.

Jobs for Veterans failed to reduce joblessness among veterans because, as Undersecretary of Commerce Rocco Siciliano had aptly remarked in June 1970, "It is hard to imbue businessmen with social conscience when business is bad." [14] So long as the economic recession continued, appeals to the business community to provide veterans with jobs would fall on deaf ears.

In February 1971 Jobs for Veterans learned just how deaf those ears could be when it received less than a 2 percent response from a mail appeal to 900,000 employers.[15] Its "job fairs" drew a better response, but their overall performance was insubstantial. At most fairs, the gap between the number of veterans who showed up and the number actually hired was immense. Frustration turned to violence in Chicago in May 1972 as veterans wrecked interviewing stands in anger. Two veterans who attended reported the events in an article in a veterans' newspaper in Milwaukee:

SNOW-JOB FAIR

Of 7,000 veterans who appeared at the May 9th Chicago area "job fair," 88 got jobs. Not bad . . .

John Linton, company man who handled the "fake" for the Illinois Bureau of Employment Security, labeled the ensuing disturbance a "riot." Quoth Linton, "The employers are discouraged by this turn of events. We are closing up. It's too damn bad."

The question, of course, is whether the employers were as "discouraged" as the veterans who attended the fair expecting jobs.[16]

From the American Legion's monthly reports on job fairs, it appears that the average placement rate achieved for veterans who showed up at them has been about 10 percent, comparable to the record of the Employment Service.[17] Even with much higher placement rates, however, job fairs could have had only a slight impact upon veteran unemployment. The total number of unemployed veterans ever reached by them was simply too small.

The continued rise of veteran unemployment even during the most intensive Jobs for Veterans campaigning indicates that if it made any difference, it was only to make veteran unemployment slightly less bad than it otherwise would have been. The basic problem it faced was that the success of its jawboning depended upon its ability to solicit cooperation from private employers, just at a time when those employers, by and large, could not afford to cooperate. A recent study of manpower services to veterans which was sponsored by the Department of Labor summarized the problem this way: "Employers who think veterans should be shown special treatment in employment matters also think that someone else should provide that service." [18]

★ *The President's Veterans Program (1971–73)*

Finally, in June 1971—the same month the Administration acted against military drug abuse—the President decided to take more aggressive action against veteran unemployment. On June 11 he instructed Secretary of Labor James Hodgson to assume charge of a federal interagency task force that would oversee an expanded effort to place Vietnam era veterans in jobs and manpower training programs. This effort was outlined in six points:

1. Increased use of the National Alliance of Businessmen (NAB) to enlist business in the drive to find jobs for veterans.
2. Expanded training of outgoing servicemen under the Defense Department's Project Transition.
3. Increased training opportunities for veterans under existing federal manpower programs.
4. Mandatory listing of all job openings with the U.S. Employment Service by all federal agencies and all private firms holding federal contracts.
5. Improved effectiveness of the U.S. Employment Service in finding jobs and providing counseling services to veterans.
6. Special job-finding services for Vietnam era veterans drawing UCX payments for three months or longer.

President Nixon informed Secretary Hodgson that he assigned the "highest priority" to this Six-Point President's Veterans Program. Nonetheless, he provided no special funding for the program's operation and never requested any from Congress. The President's Veterans Program (PVP) was to be a low-budget operation, financed almost entirely by diverting funds away from existing manpower programs. In practice, this led to conflicts within federal agencies over which special group—veterans, women, blacks, the handicapped, or others—should have the highest "highest priority." These conflicts were exacerbated by inconsistent directives from the White House. For example, though the White House instructed the Employment Service in June 1971 to give unemployed veterans "highest priority" in job placements, in January 1972 it ordered that "highest priority" be given to placement of welfare recipients, as part of its efforts to "take people off the welfare rolls and put them on the work rolls." The Administration's desire to reduce federal spending precluded a budget adequate for the needs of all unemployed people, yet it was unwilling to choose among them. So, as will be evident, PVP's "highest priority" was not very helpful.

During the operation of PVP, veteran unemployment declined substantially. So did all unemployment, because the economy improved markedly after the imposition of wage-price controls in the summer of 1971. To determine what difference PVP made, one must look at each of the program's six points.

Point 1. Use of the National Alliance of Businessmen

The National Alliance of Businessmen is a quasi-public organization created at President Johnson's suggestion in the aftermath of urban riots in 1968 to promote employment among disadvantaged groups. It has since become one of the largest federal manpower efforts. Its board of directors consists of business leaders from more than fifty key metropolitan areas. Their role is to use their contacts with the business community to build private support for employing the poor. Since 1968 NAB has emphasized two projects: Job Opportunities in the Business Sector (JOBS), a program subsidizing on-the-job training for the poor, and a "non-contract" program to locate unsubsidized jobs for disadvantaged workers. Performance under both has been only superficially successful. On October 20, 1972, NAB celebrated its "one millionth hire." One third of these had been recorded by JOBS, the rest by the "non-contract" program. NAB's press releases on the occasion did not mention the other side of the story. Over 40 percent of 1 million poor people hired under NAB programs did not stay with their jobs more than six months; many of the jobs for which NAB claimed credit under its non-contract program would have opened up anyway; and unemployment among the disadvantaged was higher than when the program began.[19]

In any case, when it became apparent to the Administration in mid-1971 that veteran unemployment demanded attention, NAB seemed like a logical ingredient. The Administration believed that NAB's experience in locating jobs for the disadvantaged and its contacts with employers would be useful. So, in June 1971, President Nixon approved a Labor Department plan for NAB participation in PVP. He summoned John D. Harper, Chairman of the Board of Alcoa and NAB's Chairman, and won Harper's hesitant agreement to seek 100,000 veteran job placements in fiscal year 1972 (July 1971 to June 1972). Harper accepted reluctantly, because he thought the veteran program might interfere with NAB's prior commitment to find jobs for 225,000 poor people. To win his consent, two changes were made in the original plan. A provision requiring that a third of the veterans placed by NAB be hired under the subsidized JOBS program was eliminated. Also dropped was a requirement that participating firms hire at least 50 percent of their new employees from the ranks of Vietnam veterans.[20] These changes proved to be significant later on.

After September 1971, when its efforts first began to show effects, NAB operated essentially as an elaborate version of Jobs for Veterans. But while Jobs for Veterans was only an advertising effort run from Washington, NAB had a network of local offices across the nation to contact employers directly, encourage them to hire veterans, and keep some estimates of the number of veterans hired as a result of NAB efforts.

Those efforts appear to have succeeded—much the way that earlier NAB projects appear to have succeeded. NAB claims 125,000 job placements for veterans, compared to its original goal of 100,000. Of all the elements included in the President's Veterans Program, only NAB was able to meet, much less surpass, its internal operating goals for 1972.[21]

A more careful look at these claims raises doubts about them. In certain states NAB has merely taken surveys of the veterans hired by participating employers and then taken credit for those jobs as if they resulted from NAB's own efforts. As the Labor Department's report on manpower services to veterans discovered, in some areas NAB representatives just "asked for reports of the number of recent hires who were veterans so that the employer and NAB could be credited toward achieving national goals on veteran hires. These are cases clearly where there would have been no difference with or without PVP." [22] More than 90 percent of the veteran placements recorded by NAB have been made under its unsubsidized "non-contract" program, and it is arguable that many of these would have been made anyway, since business was improving.

More important, only a small fraction of NAB's veteran placements have gone to those veterans most in need of job-finding assistance. Under the modified requirements for participating in NAB's veteran program, employers can receive credit with NAB for *any* veteran they hire, regardless of his economic status, so long as he is hired under the non-contract program. Charles Collins, an assistant to the NAB Vice President in Charge of Veterans Affairs, reports that only about 6 to 8 percent of all the veterans hired under NAB's campaign have been "disadvantaged." [23] Thus, those veterans who are most likely to be unemployed—the 15 to 20 percent who lack high school educations, or the 11 percent from minority groups, or the more than 200,000 disabled veterans—do not command priority attention from NAB. Unfortunately, NAB collects almost no information on the characteristics of veterans hired under the non-contract program, on the kinds of jobs they have received, or on their rates of retention. So, on the basis of the information available, there is no way to be sure whether the 125,000 veterans who have been hired by NAB employers were hired because of NAB or are better off for its existence. It may well be that, with NAB and fifteen cents, veterans can buy a cup of coffee; with NAB and good qualifications, they can get a decent job.

Point 2. Expanded training of outgoing servicemen in Project Transition

The staggered release of soldiers during the Vietnam War has made it possible for the military to offer them special readjustment and job training programs just prior to discharge. In 1967 the Defense Department set up Project Transition, partly to help the men it was inducting under Project 100,000. With support from Labor Department funding and large private firms, Transition has since been able to provide job counseling and training at roughly half of the military bases located in the United States, and also at many overseas. An average of $14 million in federal funds has been expended on Transition each year since 1968, and in light of this small appropriation, the results appear impressive. Over 250,000 soldiers have received Transition job training, and nearly 1.5 million have been counseled.[24]

As in the case of NAB, however, Transition's statistics merit closer attention. Many of the 1.5 million men who are said to have been "counseled" actually received counseling in large group assemblies. Even individual job counseling conducted under Transition is of questionable value, since it takes place on military bases far removed from the job-search areas to which veterans will be returning.

The job-training aspects of Transition have experienced serious problems from the outset. As mentioned in the previous chapter, Transition training reached only 6.3 percent of Project 100,000 men—the group at which it was originally aimed. In 1969 a review by the General Accounting Office reported that many of the men who were supposed to have completed Transition training never really did. "The criteria used for determining needed training courses were inadequate," the report declared. "Program evaluation could not be adequately performed because of incomplete, inaccurate, or nonexistent training records."[25] The same year, a

Bureau of the Budget survey of disadvantaged veterans disclosed that only 40 percent had ever heard of Transition, only 13 percent had been able to volunteer for it, only 9 percent had actually participated in it, and only 2 percent felt that its training had helped them.[26]

Following the publication of these two reports, the House Appropriations Committee cut $5 million from Transition's budget. "A substantial amount of funds is being expended for very little value," the committee report stated. "Of the total number of personnel being released from active duty, very few participate in the program, and those who participate receive very little training."[27]

This was the program that the President decided to include as Point Two of PVP. To expand Transition, the Administration provided a total of $4 million in additional funds in 1972 to pay for a special drug counseling program, enlargement of overseas counseling, the creation of "skill centers" to help trainees find jobs, and improvements in the regular training program. Few of these plans were carried out. Quite early, Transition fell way behind in meeting the performance goals established for it by PVP.[28] In fiscal year 1972 fewer than one out of ten of all discharged enlisted men were able to participate in Transition's expanded programs. And, of those who actually did participate, a large proportion were retirees, older men who were at the end of their military careers. The Labor Department's study of manpower services for veterans discovered that almost half of the veterans with Transition training whom they surveyed were persons with more than 18 years of active duty.[29] Transition was failing to reach the men for whom it was created. The shortness of training courses (twelve weeks or less) also seems to have limited its impact.

Point 3. Increased opportunities for veterans in federal manpower training programs

This element of the President's plan affected a wide range of federal manpower programs, most of which are administered by the Labor Department. These programs include the Concentrated Employment Program, Manpower Development and Training Act (MDTA) programs, Careers in Public Service, and the newly established Public Employment Program (PEP).[30] To increase the participation of Vietnam era veterans, the Administration instructed each program to set quotas for veterans and to give "absolute preference" to veterans who applied for training so long as the quotas remained unfilled. Coupled as usual with White House unwillingness to provide additional funding, the quotas created serious administrative conflicts. These conflicts, in turn, prevented the programs from meeting the goals that PVP had established for them.

Federal manpower programs, initiated as part of the War on Poverty, have developed strong loyalties to the needs of the least skilled workers, whether or not they happen to be veterans. When quotas on veteran participation were issued without any accompanying increase in the number of training slots, they cut against these loyalties and were deeply resented. Thus, the 1972 PVP goal set for MDTA programs would have reserved 73,000 positions for veterans, out of a total 107,742 training slots available.[31] Since almost all veterans are male, few positions would have been left for unemployed women, unless more slots became available. None did. In the Public Employment Program administrators were told to ensure that 33 percent of new enrollments during fiscal year 1972 were veterans, a quota that made it impossible for PEP to offer enough jobs to unemployed women and male nonveterans so that their participation in the program would approximate their share of unemployment. As a deputy manpower administrator observed in a private memorandum to the Director of the Employment Service in July 1972, "[These quotas] raise serious questions about the distribution of manpower programs in relation to those who need and qualify for them." [32]

Compared to the PVP goals originally established for them for fiscal year 1972, Point Three programs were underachievers. The Concentrated Employment Program, for example, had a target of 25,000 veterans; it actually enrolled about 10,000. Overall, the manpower programs fell about 50,000 short of their 185,000 veteran goal for 1972.[33] This failure was caused largely by the conflict over priorities and resources generated by PVP's penny-wise operation. The July 1972 memorandum cited above underscores this conclusion:

> The disparity between goals and achievement in the Manpower Administration programs . . . is largely the result of difficulties in effectuating administrative changes in eligibility requirements. . . . Many MDTA-Institutional programs were already established in occupational clusters appealing to women or other special interest groups. . . . Low performance in PSC [Public Service Careers] is also due to the program's strong orientation toward the disadvantaged.

For those veterans who have managed to become enrolled in manpower programs, the benefits are mixed. All such programs, except the Public Employment Program, suffer from high dropout rates. At best, less than half of those who enroll in them can be expected to complete training and obtain jobs.[34] The most successful training programs seem to be those that offer direct on-the-job training, with subsidies paid to private employers. Even these, however, have been severely criticized for the quality of training they provide at relatively high cost.[35]

The principal exception to these limitations is the Public Employment Program. After August 1971 it provided more than 60,000 federally subsidized public service jobs in state and local governments to Vietnam era veterans. With its relatively high starting hourly wages, low turnover rate, and wide variety of job opportunities, PEP was by far the most successful weapon in the President's arsenal.[36] Unlike other programs, it seems to have had a direct impact on the number and quality of jobs available to veterans in the economy.

PEP's success is somewhat ironic. Initially, it was part of the 1970 Employment and Manpower Act, which passed Congress in December 1970. This legislation would have provided about $3 billion to pay for public jobs and would have created about 200,000 positions almost immediately. Vietnam era veterans would have had preference for many of these. At that point, despite the fact that veteran unemployment already stood at 9.2 percent, President Nixon vetoed the bill on the ground that it "smacked of old Work Progress Administration makework." Only in July 1971, with veteran unemployment at an even higher level, did the President's sense of the politically necessary override his earlier hesitancy.

Unfortunately, the Emergency Employment Act that he signed then differed in two critical respects from the 1970 bill. First, it provided only $1 billion for jobs, not $3 billion. Second, its lifespan was limited to two years, expiring in late 1973. Terminating the funds meant dismantling a program that probably will only have to be reassembled the next time unemployment rises. Moreover, if anti-inflation policies are to be the wave of the economic future, a built-in PEP-like system would provide insurance to whichever groups—veterans, minorities, the poor—happen to be caught in their pincers. Rather than placing an expiration date on the program the next time it comes up, Congress might well consider a permanent public employment program that would go into effect whenever unemployment passed a threshold level.

Point 4. Mandatory listing of all job openings with the Employment Service by all agencies and contractors funded by the federal government

In its efforts to reduce veteran unemployment, the Nixon administration chose to rely heavily on the Employment Service, which, as noted earlier, had suffered a steady decline during the Sixties in the job openings it received from employers. The aim of mandatory listing was to reverse this trend. Point Four of the President's program provided that all private employers who entered into new contracts with the federal government for values in excess of $10,000 would be required to list all their openings for jobs paying less than $18,000 per year.

Initially, the Administration had high expectations for the impact that mandatory listing would have on veteran job placement. Based on the number of workers employed by federal contractors (over 25 million) and their annual turnover rate (40 percent), the Employment Service estimated that Point Four would yield an additional 10 million job listings each year. These, in turn, would make it possible to place an additional 500,000 veterans annually, more than doubling the total number of veterans placed.[37] Later, under administrative pressure, the expected job listing total was revised downward to 1.2 million for fiscal year 1972.

But even this lower goal proved impossible to meet. Neither the Employment Service nor PVP staff members had anticipated that mandatory listing would prove unpopular with federal contractors. But it did, and mandatory listing quickly became "mandatory" in name only. It ran into heavy opposition from individual firms, construction unions, private employment agencies, and trade associations. Prior to the Labor Department's issuance of final rules on mandatory listing, it acceded to almost all of the modifications recommended by these groups. It also made clear to Employment Service staff members that they "should scrupulously avoid adopting an enforcement posture and should approach subject employers only in the spirit of service to the employer. . . ."[38]

The result of these concessions was to abandon effective enforcement of mandatory listing. In New York, for example, only 31 percent of all federal contractors were reporting their jobs as required, one year after mandatory listing went into effect; in New Jersey, only 10 percent were listing jobs.[39] In Detroit, an Employment Service staff member found that "the biggest problems seem to lie with the employers not being completely honest in their dealings with the ES. Ford and others place orders for journeymen, require eight years of experience in a trade, or request engineers— all with the requirement that the applicant be a Vietnam veteran. The staff believe that many of these jobs do not really exist." [40] A Pennsylvania Bureau of Employment Security director reported in June 1972 that "new placement activity generated by the Executive Order appears to be minimal." [41] And an Employment Service survey of firms that were listing showed that, as of July 1972, of more than 150,000 with sizable federal contracts, only 3,497 had made reports in compliance with mandatory listing.[42] Although failure to comply with mandatory listing requirements is grounds for suspension of federal contracts, no such action has been taken against employers. In short, the Employment Service has "scrupulously avoided assuming an enforcement posture."

Whatever its future, mandatory listing plainly has had minimal impact on veteran unemployment. The total increase in job openings recorded by the Employment Service during fiscal year 1972 was 232,000, far below the original estimate of 10 million, or even the PVP goal of 1.2 million. The number of Vietnam era veterans placed in "mandatory listing job openings," compared with the total number of veterans placed by the Employment Service in all jobs, "is so small as to indicate no significant impact on Vietnam veteran placement." [43]

Point 5. Increased effectiveness of the U.S. Employment Service

Apart from mandatory listing, PVP also hoped to improve the quality of the Employment Service's counseling and job placement efforts for veterans. From the evidence available, this effort also appears to have made a negligible contribution to veteran employment. PVP set a 1972 goal of 376,830 veteran placements. Considering that, during the same fiscal year, over 1.6 million Vietnam era veterans were listed as "applicants available for work" by the Employment Service, this goal seems rather low. Yet the Employment Service failed to meet it; only 304,000 placements were actually recorded. This represents a placement rate of one veteran in five, an improvement over the 13 percent rate recorded for 1971 but nothing to crow about.[44]

The placement rate for disabled veterans was considerably worse. Among the more than 300,000 service-disabled Vietnam era veterans, unemployment stood at about 14 percent in early 1971. In fiscal year 1971, 255,419 disabled Vietnam era veterans registered with the Employment Service as "applicants available for work." But little work was available for them. Less than 2 percent were placed as a result of job development efforts by the Employment Service.[45] When, in June 1972, attention was finally called to the extreme employment problems faced by these veterans, it brought about the production of a twenty-minute employer-oriented color film, a "program letter" to state employment offices requesting their "increased attention and assistance" and a revision of job eligibility requirements in the Public Employment Program, so that disabled veterans would receive priority treatment.

Originally, the Administration hoped Point Five would make a difference in the way veterans were treated when they entered employment offices, in terms of counseling services, testing, and general rapport between veterans and staff members. However, in fiscal year 1971, Vietnam era veterans accounted for 21.5 percent of all Employment Service applicants, but only 17.9 percent of those counseled and 13.2 percent of those tested.[46] In 1972 the figures were about the same. A recent survey of counseling and outreach services to veterans discovered that "only the most impersonal types of outreach efforts were observed in the local ES offices sampled. In all offices, counseling is not a routine service available to all applicants" [47]

Point 6. Special services for veterans drawing unemployment compensation for three months or longer

Point Six called for another kind of qualitative improvement in the Employment Service—the provision of intensive assistance to veterans who have been out of work more than thirteen weeks. For the most part, this "intensive assistance" has amounted to little more than the mailing of letters or the placing of telephone calls to such veterans, encouraging them to drop by. In May 1972, the Employment Service surveyed a large sample of these veterans, reporting that more than 30 percent had not received any "measurable job-related services" whatsoever. This was over ten months after PVP had gone into effect. Among those who had been contacted by the Employment Service, only 9 percent had been tested and 20 percent counseled—about the same rates as for "regular" veterans.[48] This hardly amounts to the provision of "intensive service."

The President's Veterans Program was designed to deal with a crisis in veteran unemployment that government officials had failed to anticipate and that traditional veterans' programs and the Jobs for Veterans campaign had failed to handle. The Administration clung to these initial programs, hoping that a low-cost, *laissez-faire* approach would work. When unemployment continued to rise and threatened to become a political liability, the Administration was forced to adopt more aggressive policies, but these too were limited by its economic and ideological priorities.

The Administration's anti-inflationary economics, which led to high unemployment in 1970 and 1971, also dictated the constraints on federal spending that undermined PVP. The Employment Service, Project Transition, federal manpower programs, and the Public Employment Program have all been frustrated in their efforts to live up to PVP objectives by the Administration's refusal to put money behind its pledges to veterans.

Opposition to government interference with private employers was a second constraint. The President rejected a larger Public Employment Program not only for budgetary reasons, but because it represented an intervention in the private labor market to which Administration officials were ideologically opposed. Only when public employment, like wage-price controls, became politically necessary did the President act. Wherever possible, his administration followed the philosophy outlined by Secretary of Labor George Schultz in 1969:

> The labor market itself must be recognized as a constraint. . . . It is a fact that our economy has lots of jobs that pay low wages. We are not going to be remaking the economy. We can only put people in jobs that exist. . . . We will have to tread our way between our goal of providing good jobs and the realities of the kinds of jobs that are available.[49]

This reluctance to intervene in the labor market effectively limited PVP to programs that relied on cooperation from private employers. The Employment Service and NAB might collect lists of job openings for veterans, but it was up to employers to hire them. Manpower training programs and Project Transition might offer veterans some job training, but it would be up to employers to put it to use. PVP could deal with the "supply" side of the labor market by giving unemployed veterans marketable skills or it could deal with the "efficiency" of the labor market by providing unemployed veterans with more information about job openings. But except for the Public Employment Program, the "demand" side of the labor market was totally off limits. The quantity and quality of jobs available to veterans were left to be determined by the economic needs and interests of employers, not by the needs and interests of the unemployed.

Dependency upon the cooperation of private employers caused many of PVP's key administrative problems. When mandatory listing ran into opposition from federal contractors, it was placed on a back burner. Because NAB and the Employment Service had no power to induce private employers to hire veterans, they were reduced to keeping track of job openings and veterans who had already been hired. Because the disabled, the uneducated and the minorities were not as highly valued in the private labor market, the programs could do little for them. PVP's most serious administrative failings were thus inseparable from its ideological underpinnings.

Nevertheless, it would be wrong to say that PVP had no effect at all. In late 1971 and 1972 unemployment declined among veterans as well as other groups to between 5 and 6 percent. Almost all of this was due to general improvements in the economy. The 1 to 2 percent gap between veterans and nonveterans aged twenty to twenty-nine also disappeared, partly because of PVP and partly because of the declining number of new discharges from the military, which meant that relatively fewer veterans were in the particularly unstable period immediately after leaving the service. Altogether, the six-point program seems to have shaved about one percentage point, probably less, off the veteran unemployment rate.[50] And the element that made the most tangible difference— public employment created by the Emergency Employment Act— was the first scheduled to go out of existence. General cutbacks in manpower programs announced by the President after his reelection may effectively negate the small gains previously made.

★ Unemployment as Discontent

Even after the decline in veteran unemployment in 1972, it remained high, particularly for the younger men back from Vietnam. Among veterans aged twenty to twenty-four, joblessness stood at 9.4 percent in the second quarter of 1973, twice the rate for the general population. This unemployment persisted, because it was of a fundamentally different character from the unemployment the President's program was designed to reduce. It was the result not of an absolute shortage of jobs, but of a shortage of good jobs for young workers.

Even in periods of prosperity in the United States, unemployment among young workers tends to be high. It is responsive neither to changes in economic activity nor to improvements in job-finding services or manpower training programs. At best, these services and programs adapt workers to jobs; they make no attempt to adapt jobs to workers. When Secretary Schultz said, "We can only put people in jobs that exist," he put his finger on the heart of the problem, for the jobs that exist for young veterans are generally not good enough to persuade them to stay employed.

Most unemployed veterans, especially younger men, fluctuate in and out of jobs at short intervals. The average duration of unemployment is relatively short; nearly half are out of work less than five weeks.[51] In 1971 and 1972 more than half of all unemployed veterans were unemployed either because they had quit their last jobs or were returning to the civilian labor force after school or military duty.[52] Thus, a majority initially became unemployed for reasons that had little to do with the absolute quantity of jobs available. Job-losers have consistently accounted for less than half of veteran unemployment.

The incidence of job quitting among young veterans is especially revealing. The number who are unemployed because they quit their last jobs has consistently exceeded the number laid off. Moreover, veterans who quit jobs to take others have been more than four times as numerous as those who quit and then became unemployed. The total rate of job turnover among veterans has apparently been somewhat higher than the 4 percent per month estimated for the industrial labor force at large.[53] Each year almost 50 percent of all employed Vietnam era veterans are quitting their jobs and seeking others. About a fifth of these experience intervening periods of unemployment.

The unemployed veteran population, therefore, is not permanently unemployed but highly active. It appears that, except for the disadvantaged and the disabled, most veterans who have been out of work could find it within a fairly short time. Only at the peak of unemployment was there an absolute shortage of jobs. In general, the short duration of unemployment, high quit rates, and relative unimportance of job-losers' unemployment among young veterans indicate that the problem may not be simply unemployment. It is also an employment problem.

Returning to a civilian economy unscarred by the ravages of war, many young veterans have discovered that their labor is undervalued. There are usually jobs available, but they are "dirt" jobs. They are dull, repetitive, fatiguing, low in wages, and poor in training opportunities. These are not the jobs to which veterans aspired from overseas. These jobs, in fact, remind them of being overseas, on military duty.

Since available jobs are so unsatisfactory, many younger veterans seem to have spent a lot of time moving in and out of them, searching for something better. At their age, most do not have families to support. Also, those veterans who seem to drop in and out of employment most often are least likely to have completed high school and most likely to have had disciplinary problems in the military. These veterans, perhaps unlike others, may be less conditioned to the discipline of the workplace. In any case, large numbers of them have had the freedom to express their discontent by alternating between periods of work and leisure. Unemployment compensation, of course, has helped to make this freedom possible.

Some observers have argued that this pattern stems from the "unrealistic" expectations of young veterans, or their inclination to indulge preferences for leisure over work. From a broader perspective, however, it represents the failure of the larger society to provide many of them—especially the less educated, the minorities, and the disabled—with jobs they would be proud to keep. Disadvantaged veterans, who constitute a majority of the unemployed, might well have liked to go back to work and stay there, but the job opportunities that were available to others were denied to them.

Nor was this simply because these veterans were inferior workers who lacked necessary skills and training. The traditional notion that the ability of workers to perform specific on-the-job tasks is closely associated with their education or pre-work training is breaking down. The key functions performed by high school education and military service are to accommodate young people to routine, disciplined behavior. Disadvantaged, undereducated veterans do, in fact, have more difficulty keeping stable jobs. But this may be less because they are unable to do the work than because they are unwilling to work in bad jobs.

The veteran unemployment problem has, therefore, really been two interwoven problems—first, an absolute shortage of work brought on by the anti-inflationary economic policies of the 1970 recession, and second, discontent persisting beyond the recession with the job opportunities that have been available in the secondary labor market to which many young veterans are confined. This second aspect has proved especially nettlesome to the President's (belated) Veterans Program. Had the two problems been recognized earlier, unemployment might not have reached the proportions it did in 1970 and 1971. Had the needs of returning veterans been given sufficient economic priority, other economic objectives might not have interfered so much. And had the administration program emphasized the quality of jobs as well as their number, an expanded public employment program might have been able to offer both.°

° On July 31, 1973, the Senate passed, by a vote of 75 to 21, a two-year extension of the Emergency Employment Act, including a provision assigning 50 percent of the jobs it created to disabled and Vietnam-era veterans. The House also passed an extension of the act, but without this additional provision. In any case, the Administration said it would veto whichever bill Congress agreed upon.

9

Education
and the GI Bill

"There they stand now and propose to teach us again. But we expect them to set aside some of their dignity. For, after all, what can they teach us? We know life now better than they; we have gained another knowledge–harsh, bloody, cruel, inexorable. . . .

"But for peace? Are we suitable? Are we fit now for anything but soldiering?"

—*Erich Maria Remarque,*
The Road Back [1]

The limited job opportunities available to many Vietnam veterans, especially the unskilled, has lent particular importance to programs for education. Also, for men who feel they have, in some sense, "fallen behind" their friends who have stayed out of the military and gone to college, support for education provides a way of catching up and reentering life at home. Consequently, of all the programs run by the Veterans Administration, none has been more prized by returning soldiers than the education benefits under the GI Bill. Since its reenactment in 1966, over two and a half million Vietnam era veterans (out of a total approaching seven million) have made use of their benefits in some fashion. Asked which veterans' program they consider most valuable, 53 percent of Vietnam era veterans surveyed in October 1971, listed benefits for education. The next most common choices were job placement and training (26 percent) and medical care (20 percent).[2]

Few ventures of the federal government in the past three decades have been so universally designated a success as the GI Bill of Rights. Its virtues are regularly extolled by political leaders of all persuasions, many of whom are indebted to it for their own educations. And indeed, there has been much in the GI Bill to warrant this satisfaction. Since World War II, millions of men have been able to extend their education after military service and prepare themselves for more desirable occupations. The general level of education in the society has been raised significantly. Far from being a mere pay-off to veterans, the GI Bill has aided the development of the whole society, facilitating the transition to a modern service economy through the upgrading of the labor force and fostering the expansion and democratization of the higher education system.

None of these genuine and important achievements should be denied or disparaged. Yet there are serious problems with the GI Bill, some of them new, many of them as old as the program itself. To the large numbers of veterans who are unable to use their benefits because of the way they are structured, it is no solace to know how many other men have used them in the past or are using them now. To the thousands of ex-servicemen who successfully complete a training program "approved for veterans" and then find it is useless for getting a job, it is no comfort to know that others have found their way into better work through GI Bill training. To the man who gets trapped in a correspondence course he was told the VA would pay for and winds up several hundred dollars in debt, it is no relief to be lectured on the generosity of veterans' benefits. To farm workers who have been cut out of the GI Bill, it would be less than reassuring to hear a spokesman of one of the largest veterans' organizations arguing before Congress that VA benefits should be "tailored to [train] someone to operate these really big agribusinesses."

Over the past few years, the major complaint of Vietnam veterans and veterans' organizations has been that the current level of benefits has lagged behind those available after World War II. At that time the VA paid for tuition and fees and provided a basic subsistence allowance of $75 a month to an unmarried student. Under the Cold War and Vietnam era GI Bill originally enacted in 1966, the VA paid only a monthly stipend of $110, out of which the student had to pay for tuition, fees, and subsistence. In 1967 the basic stipend was raised to $130 and in 1970 to $175, still far below the World War II level considering the absence of tuition payment and the inflation in the intervening period.

One consequence of the lower level of benefits was that large numbers of veterans who wanted to return to school felt they simply could not afford it. As a result, the rate of participation in the program lagged behind what it previously had been. In the first thirty-six months of the most recent GI Bill, 20.9 percent of eligible Vietnam era veterans participated. For the first thirty-six months of the World War II and Korean GI Bills, the participation rates were 25.9 percent and 26.5 percent, respectively.[3] Later statistics continued to show the same pattern. As of April 1972, seventy-one months after the current GI Bill began, only 37.3 percent of Vietnam era veterans had taken advantage of their benefits. The participation rate after seventy-one months of the World War II bill was 44.9 percent; for the Korean bill, 39.8 percent.[4]

These figures are especially significant in light of the fact that Vietnam era veterans are released from the military with a higher mean level of education than their earlier counterparts, and all available data indicate that the higher the initial level of education, the greater the likelihood that a veteran will seek more education. The lower rate of participation, therefore, apparently reflected difficulties in the current GI Bill rather than an increased aversion to education. This interpretation was supported by the Harris Survey. Vietnam veterans who had made no use of the GI Bill were asked whether they would do so if benefits were increased. Fifty-three percent said they certainly would; only 7 percent said they definitely would not.[5]

Since the time of that survey, benefits have been raised. Legislation passed in October 1972 increased the basic monthly stipend for an unmarried veteran from $175 to $220. The increase puts benefits closer to World War II levels and goes a long way toward answering the major complaints of veterans regarding the education program. Most officials now expect participation to reach the 50 percent mark set after World War II; by spring, 1973, it was up to 46.1 percent.

In addition to the question of benefit levels and general participation rates, there have been other important issues regarding the GI Bill. These issues have been raised with less publicity and currently stand further from satisfactory resolution. They are worth considering not only because they affect Vietnam veterans today, but also because they may affect many other citizens in the future if the GI Bill becomes—as is quite possible—the model for more general programs of educational assistance. The problems involve such basic questions as: Who gets access to education? How much and what kind of education should they receive? How should programs be approved for benefits and what criteria should be used in their evaluation?

Behind these questions lie basic issues of individual freedom, institutional autonomy, and distributive justice, and important choices as to the kind of society we want to foster.

★ *"Nuts and Kooks"*

The VA's current education program has drawn criticism from a variety of sources: professional educators, veterans' groups, the press, various congressmen, other government agencies. Perhaps the strongest recent critique comes from the National Advisory Council on Extension and Continuing Education, one of many federally sponsored advisory committees. In a March 1972 report,[6] the council decries the VA's inattention to substantive educational issues. "The concerns routinely expressed by VA staff are generally restricted to administrative matters like improved certificate forms and individual and institutional reporting. Expression of concern about substantive program matters involving educational theory and practice are few. These program matters seem genuinely to be beyond the scope and capacity of VA decision makers."

Some would argue that such substantive matters are properly not the business of the VA, but the council points out that one of the consequences of the VA's narrow, technical focus is that the agency has rested content with statutory legislation "somewhat inconsistent with much of what is occurring in higher education today."

"The statutes refer repeatedly to 'credit hours,' 'courses,' 'semesters,' 'attendance,' 'absences,' 'enrollment,' and other terms that reflect only a very traditional and narrow view of what comprises an education program. The language is an impediment to a recognition of other legitimate educational experiences and fails to take into consideration the variety of special educational opportunities for which this language has no meaning."

The report goes on to criticize the VA for its lack of sustained contact with the educational community. It notes that educators have been absent from top decision-making levels and that few educational associations are involved in the planning and policy apparatus of the agency. Although the VA has a Vocational Rehabilitation and Education Advisory Committee, it meets only about twice a year "with no ongoing working agenda, no stated mission, and at the discretion of the Administrator or Chairman."

"If the VA had established a more permanent link to the educational community," the report argues, "and had encouraged the regional offices to do likewise; had a more credible advisory committee; and had gone more routinely to nongovernmental educational associations for professional assistance, then it might at least have realized the inadequacies of the law it has been mandated by Congress to regulate."

In addition to criticizing the process of policy making, the council questions the lack of monitoring over what happens with benefits. "At a given point in time, VA cannot give assurance to the Congress or to the public at large that VA benefits are accomplishing what they were originally intended to accomplish." Virtually the only information that the VA collects is on enrollment. It makes no check to see whether veterans who take a particular training program actually obtain jobs within that training. One wonders what would have been the political consequences, for example, if the VA had traced those of its beneficiaries who have taken flight training in recent years at enormous expense to taxpayers and with negligible results. Or if it had taken the trouble to see whether veterans who have received money for commercial home study had found effective use for those courses. Anyone who has worked in the area of VA education programs will testify as to the paucity of information the agency is able to provide about its own activities.

Finally, the council's report notes that the VA has "lagged behind other federal agencies in responding to the legitimate needs of the educationally disadvantaged." This last matter has been a major concern of Alan Cranston, Chairman of the Senate Subcommittee on Veterans' Readjustment Programs. In 1970 Senator Cranston successfully sponsored a series of amendments aimed at facilitating utilization of GI Bill benefits by educationally disadvantaged veterans. One new program provided tutorial assistance for veterans in academic trouble, another enabled veterans to complete high school without charge to their regular thirty-six-month entitlement, a third provided aid for college preparatory courses prior to military discharge. Two years later, Cranston reported that the programs had been stalled. "I am deeply disappointed," he told the Senate, "that only a handful of the hundreds of thousands of veterans who could have so greatly benefited from these new programs actually benefited from them. The establishment of these programs in colleges and universities has been greatly handicapped by lethargy, delays, and inexcusable foot-dragging and, in some cases, outright resistance by the VA and Defense Department. For example, in the two years since enactment, only 3,954 veterans have utilized tutorial assistance benefits." [7]

Simple operational inefficiency has elicited considerable criticism.

Thousands of letters pour into the offices of congressmen, newspapers, and consumer representatives each month during the academic year from distraught veterans who have failed to receive their checks on time. This is not a matter of mere impatience; the delays occasionally cause great hardship among veterans dependent on them for basic necessities. In April 1972 *Armed Forces Journal*, not a frequent critic of the VA, published the results of its own investigation into the problem. It found that the VA Central Office received over 250,000 inquiries concerning nonpayment of educational benefit checks during 1971. "An average of 917,534 veterans a month were serviced during this period. If the 250,000 inquiries were all from different veterans, this could mean that as many as 27 percent of the veterans had some trouble with their checks." These cases, it should be noted, were formal inquiries that were sent to Washington after attempts at lower levels of authority to resolve them had failed. A survey of one regional office disclosed that the case load there was twice the rate of formal inquiries passed on to Washington.[8]

One of the reasons for the delays and confusion has been the squeeze between rapidly growing enrollment, as more men are released from the military, and a slowly increasing staff. From 1967 to 1972, the number of beneficiaries jumped from under 500,000 to 1.3 million. At the same time, regional offices added about 700 new personnel, bringing the total to 4,500.[9] Staff shortages may account not only for the operational problems, but also for the VA's inability to implement the 1970 Cranston amendments. The problems of delayed payment and uninspired administration of programs for the disadvantaged have both been the subject of new legislation.

In response to criticism of its current program, the Veterans Administration called together a "National Task Force on Education and the Vietnam Era Veteran," comprised of seventy educators, state officials, and VA personnel. In opening the first meeting on January 10, 1972, Administrator Donald Johnson left no doubt as to his own view of the situation. "As far as I am concerned," he said, "the Vietnam era GI Bill education and training program, by whatever yardstick you may use to measure it, is an unqualified success." He then proceeded to cite statistics showing that the current participation rate was only "slightly" below earlier periods, that a considerably higher percentage of Vietnam veterans attend college than did veterans of World War II or Korea (a result of their higher level of education when released from the military), and that more veterans had already been trained under the current GI Bill than were trained during the entire history of the Korean bill (a product of the fact that several million more veterans are now eligible).[10]

The Task Force met in Washington twice and divided into working committees, which then submitted detailed recommendations in various areas to Dr. E. Robert Stephens, a professor of education and consultant to the VA. They were never seen again. In April Johnson told the House Veterans Affairs Committee that he had not received any proposals "in concrete form." The chairman of the House committee at the time, Olin Teague, is reported to have objected to the Task Force recommendations, which emphasized increased utilization of the GI Bill by disadvantaged veterans.[11]

The chairman's views on this matter are well represented by Oliver Meadows, Staff Director of the committee. Meadows denies that the GI Bill has any "social objectives." The GI Bill, he says, "operates on the theory that a veteran is a grown man and can make his own decisions. We've laid it out like a parent. We say we're not going to underwrite your school costs totally; we expect you to work, to get some help."

He criticizes "the socializers who want to socialize the GI Bill with outreach programs to the disadvantaged. . . . They want some government bureaucrat to pursue the veteran, catch him in his lair, persuade him to drop his wicked ways, and go back to school.

"My main mission, and the mission of this committee, is to keep the nuts and kooks from messing up the greatest school program ever devised." [12]

★ The Evolution of the GI Bill

Educational aid for veterans began as World War II ended, originating in the Serviceman's Readjustment Act of 1944. The provisions of the GI Bill of Rights, as it came to be called, included not just education benefits but home, farm, and business loans; unemployment compensation; job placement assistance; and mustering-out pay.[13] It eventually entailed the expenditure of more than $20 billion, two-thirds of which went to education and training.

The benefits for education represented a significant departure from past practice in two important senses. First, government aid for education, beginning with the Morrill Act in 1862, had traditionally been through grants to educational institutions. The GI Bill was the first major federal program that entailed grants to individual students, and today it still remains the largest of federal scholarship programs. During fiscal year 1972, the VA contributed as much to undergraduate student support as all other federal agencies combined.[14]

Benefits for education also represented a major departure as a veterans' program. From the Revolutionary War to World War I, veterans' benefits had primarily been in the form of compensation and pensions. It was between World War I and World War II that life insurance, medical care, and vocational rehabilitation were added. With the GI Bill, however, came the concept of "readjustment benefits" for all ex-servicemen. Unlike the earlier programs, which were either forms of delayed payment or compensation for the disabled, the GI Bill represented a broad investment in human capital.

It was not originally planned quite that way. The first mention of education benefits came in 1942, when President Roosevelt signed a bill reducing the draft age from twenty to eighteen and announced he was appointing a committee to study the needs of young men whose education would be interrupted. The committee recommended education and training benefits for ex-servicemen, but for no more than one year. Under the legislation submitted to Congress, the program inched along; a limited number of veterans selected for their special aptitude would be allowed to receive a second, third, and fourth year of college. In its final form, however, the program provided benefits to all veterans for as long as forty-eight months with virtually no stipulations as to academic performance.[15]

Under the original act, the VA paid the institution where a veteran enrolled up to $500 per academic year for tuition, fees, and supplies. In addition, it provided a monthly subsistence allowance for full-time training of $50 to single veterans and $75 to veterans with dependents (increased December 1945 to $75 and $105, respectively, with $120 for more than one dependent). An amendment permitting veterans to authorize tuition payments in excess of $500, with a corresponding reduction in their period of entitlement, assured most veterans of free tuition and fees at any school they attended.[16] Benefits had to begin within two years from date of discharge and had to terminate by July 25, 1956.

The extraordinarily liberal provisions of the GI Bill were partly the result of an effective campaign led by the American Legion, but more fundamentally the response to a potential economic crisis. Policy makers, sharing the general "depression psychosis" of the time, saw the GI Bill as one means of averting a return to prewar unemployment levels. Furthermore, there was some concern that the war had drawn so many young people away from education that there would be a serious deficit in many professional and technical fields. It was thought that the GI Bill might ease those prospective shortages. Finally, in view of the experience after World War I, there was the hope that the GI Bill would forestall demands for a bonus that would be dangerously inflationary.[17]

As it turned out, each of these three hopes was realized. The GI Bill also had unexpected long-term effects on the strength of the economy and the relationship of the federal government to education.

The idea of sending veterans through four years of college was not universally well received at first. On the right, Congressman John Rankin, Chairman of the House Veterans Affairs Committee and one of the sponsors of the legislation, feared the benefits would channel the nation's heroes into colleges and there subject them to the theories of sociologists. A gifted exponent of the paranoid style in American politics, he declared: "I would rather send my child to a red schoolhouse than to a red school teacher." [18]

A different kind of opposition came from many of the nation's leading liberal scholars. Robert Hutchins, President of the University of Chicago, predicted that the onslaught of unqualified veterans would lead to a reduction in academic standards. "Colleges and universities will find themselves converted into educational hobo jungles," he warned, in the same apocalyptic tones that characterize the current attack on proposals for open admissions at public universities. Labeling the GI Bill "a threat to American education," Hutchins insisted, "Education is not a device for coping with mass unemployment." [19] Harvard economist Seymour Harris took the same view, arguing that "the GI Bill carried the principle of democratization too far." [20] Carrying it to Harvard, at any rate, was carrying it too far.

In the years following the passage of the GI Bill, American colleges underwent the most rapid expansion in their history. In 1945–46 enrollment increased 45.1 percent over the previous year; in 1946–47 it increased 24.1 percent and in 1947–48, 12.5 percent.[21] Almost all of this growth came from veterans receiving aid under the GI Bill. In the fall of 1945 there were 400,000 veterans in college; in 1946, 1.1 million; in 1947, 1.5 million.[22] Had there been no GI Bill, it is quite unlikely that so many men could have attended college on their own resources.

Even more interesting than these figures are the statistics showing the long-range impact on the labor force. Counting only the proportion of students in college and leaving aside the far greater number who took vocational training, the impact was impressive. In 1939, for every hundred persons aged eighteen to twenty-four, there were 9.03 college-level students. Virtually no net change took place during the war. By 1947–48, however, the proportion of eighteen-to twenty-four-year-olds in college rose to 15.93 percent. Thereafter the proportion leveled off, until the mid-Fifties, when it turned up again, though at a slower pace.[23] The World War II GI Bill clearly represented an important turning point. As the historian Frederick Jackson Turner might have put it, education has been America's modern frontier, and the GI Bill has been its Homestead Act. If it is true, as many have suggested, that the Great Depression was never beaten but faded with World War II, and if it is also true that one of the major consequences of an expanded educational system is a constricted labor market, then perhaps more credit for terminating the Depression should go to the GI Bill than is usually given. For not only were large numbers of veterans temporarily withdrawn from the labor force; two long-term changes also took place. The higher education system was pushed through an irreversible expansion, and when veterans re-entered the labor force after further education, many did so in professional and technical fields where manpower was needed rather than in less skilled occupations where they were not.

The GI Bill permitted the federal government to do unwittingly what it was unable to do by design. There was no precedent, and considerable entrenched opposition, to federal aid to higher education. Certainly any proposal to reduce employment by expanding education would have met with derision. Congress could never have been persuaded, on economic and social grounds, to approve such a generous program of educational aid to the general population. Nonetheless, it could be persuaded, on economic and emotional grounds, to provide that aid to veterans. It has often been remarked that mobilization for war is frequently a source of valuable social innovations. More efficient forms of production are suddenly discovered, women shed traditional roles, imagination and ingenuity are in demand, social inequalities are narrowed. What is perhaps less often remarked is that demobilization from war is also a source of valuable innovations. If a society has too few men or too many men to go about its necessary tasks, it has a much better chance of finding its way into improvements than if it has just the right number of men for doing what it has always been accustomed to do, even if it does that badly.

There were, of course, some discomforts. The influx of veterans into the nation's colleges produced quonset hut villages, crowded classrooms, night classes, and summer sessions. But the influx of veterans did not produce the descent into barbarism that Hutchins and Harris had feared. In fact, to their chagrin, one study after another showed that veterans performed somewhat better academically than their comrades.[24] Observers commented that veterans lent a welcome sobriety to campuses more accustomed to fraternity pranks and "gentleman Cs" than serious work.

But the 2.2 million veterans who eventually went to college under the World War II GI Bill were only 29 percent of the total who utilized their benefits.[25] The vast majority took vocational courses. One unintended result of the GI Bill was the spawning of a profusion of shoddy vocational schools set up specifically to rake in VA money. Of the 8,800 schools below college level that were eventually approved for veterans' benefits, 5,600 appeared after the passage of the Serviceman's Readjustment Act.[26] By the late Forties the quality of training in these schools had become a scandal. So had the fact that many veterans were using their benefits to learn dancing, bartending, auctioneering, and other pursuits inimical to the Protestant ethic. After 1948 these courses were ruled unacceptable, and schools were required to have been in operation at least one year (later two) and to have enrolled at least 15 percent nonveteran students before recieving any money under the GI Bill.

By February 1950, a special committee appointed by President Truman and headed by VA Administrator Carl Gray reported that billions had been wasted in the education program. Criticism was directed almost entirely at proprietary vocational schools "operated on public funds but privately conducted for profit by private interests." The committee found that of 1,237 schools involved in some irregularity, 274 were nonprofit and 963 were profitmaking. Of these schools, 329 lost their accreditation: 30 of these were nonprofit, 299 profitmaking.

Prior to the GI Bill, the number of courses offered by vocational schools was limited; most training was provided on the job. "With the VA paying the cost of training, institutions were established to offer classes in vocational trades which would, and could, normally have been furnished basically only as training on the job," the Gray Report stated.

"In other words, the Serviceman's Readjustment Act created a profit incentive for the establishment of many vocational schools to provide a type of training which otherwise would have been provided as on-the-job training at considerably less cost to the government." [27]

In August 1950, the House of Representatives set up a committee to investigate the GI Bill, placing it under the chairmanship of Olin Teague, a young veteran from Texas with a distinguished war record. The report of Teague's committee described the same pattern as the Gray Report:

Schools mushroomed overnight offering any course imaginable, attempting to break into the educational and training field for the purpose of securing the GI dollar. Veterans responded in great numbers to these fly-by-night ventures as it was an easy path for them to pursue to establish eligibility for the generous subsistence payments made available to them under the law. . . . Existing regulations did not question the background or qualifications of any individual opening a school. . . . It is not surprising, however, that in a program of this magnitude there have been abuses, there have been errors, there have been extravagances, there have been isolated instances of corruption and larceny, and there has been administrative inefficiency.[28]

Teague's committee also criticized the VA for making no use of the expertise of the Office of Education and for not employing people with experience in education to direct the program. It found that VA employees had been involved in falsification of data on attendance and costs and overcharging for books and supplies.

As these problems were exposed, the need for new legislation to cover veterans of the Korean conflict emerged. Under Teague's leadership, Congress eliminated the direct tuition payments to institutions, which he argued created the incentive for most of the abuses uncovered. The new law provided a monthly stipend of $110 for veterans with no dependents; $135 for veterans with one dependent; and $160 for veterans with one or more dependents.

The new system soon had unanticipated side effects. Legislated prior to runaway inflation, the payments change had not been expected to reduce enrollment in private colleges. But within a short time it became evident that eliminating tuition payments discouraged veterans from attending private institutions. The data indicate that, while World War II veterans were slightly more likely to attend private colleges than the general population, Korean and Vietnam era veterans have been more likely to attend public institutions. The principal factor in the shift from private to public, however, has been the faster overall growth of public higher education due to factors unrelated to the GI Bill:

PROPORTION IN PUBLIC EDUCATION INSTITUTIONS[29]

	Veterans in %	General population in %
1947–48	47.8	49.4
1956–57	61.8	56.8
1970–71	77.8	73.8

Eligibility for the Korean GI Bill ended in January 1955. The education benefits eventually cost $4.5 billion, compared with $14.5 billion for World War II. The consensus at the time was that most of the flagrant abuses exposed earlier had been brought under control.

Nonetheless, when moves were made in Congress to extend the GI Bill on a more permanent basis during the late Fifties and early Sixties, they were rejected by both the Eisenhower and Kennedy administrations. The Department of Defense had particularly strenuous objections. In 1959, for example, an Air Force representative testified that a peacetime GI Bill should be defeated because it would encourage skilled personnel to leave military service, negate personnel retention benefits in recent legislation, and cost "undue" millions.[30] In his final budget message, President Eisenhower stated that education benefits "cannot be justified by conditions of military service and are inconsistent with the incentives which have been provided to make military service an attractive career for capable individuals." [31]

It was not until 1966 and the escalation of the war in Vietnam that a new GI Bill was passed. Initially President Johnson favored restricting benefits to those soldiers who served in "hot spots" like Vietnam, Berlin, and the Dominican Republic. In its final form, however, the Cold War and the Vietnam era GI Bill made all veterans eligible who had served since the end of the Korean War.[32] To accommodate the Pentagon, benefits were extended to soldiers after they had served two years (reduced later to 180 days), so that they would not necessarily have any incentive to leave the military to take advantage of the GI Bill. The main effect of this change, as we shall see, was to increase the use of commercial correspondence courses, since other forms of education were inaccessible to most servicemen.

Otherwise the new legislation followed the lines that had been established during the Korean War. The system of subsistence allowances to the individual veteran with no tuition payment was retained. So were the benefit levels of the Korean bill, in spite of fifteen years of inflation ($110 a month for an unmarried veteran). Even at face value, the Vietnam era benefits were inferior. Under the World War II bill, the length of entitlement was one year plus time in service, with a maximum of forty-eight months. Under the Korean bill, the formula was one and a half days of benefits for each day of service, with a maximum of thirty-six months. Under the original Vietnam era bill, the formula was one day of benefits for each day of service, also with a thirty-six-month maximum. Within a year, however, the Korean formula (1½ to 1) was restored. Demands continue to be made that the maximum length of entitlement be returned to the World War II level—forty-eight months instead of thirty-six. The argument for extending the entitlement has been weakened somewhat by recent legislation that permits veterans to take pre-college courses without charge to their thirty-six-month limit.[33]

As under the Korean GI Bill, veterans must complete training within eight years after leaving the service. Counseling by VA personnel is optional, except for veterans in vocational rehabilitation programs. Programs must lead to "a predetermined and identified educational, professional, or vocational objective."[34] Notes a VA official: "Taking courses for the sake of personal pleasure or mere self-development, without relating to an objective, is beyond the purpose of the GI Bills."[35] Changes of objective need VA approval. Certain courses, such as bartending, are categorically excluded; others, such as sales management, may be approved only under special circumstances.

Higher benefits—essentially along the lines of the World War II GI Bill—are available for disabled veterans needing vocational rehabilitation, defined as those who are at least 30 percent service-disabled, or, if less, have a pronounced handicap for employment. Disabled veterans receive forty-eight months of support from the VA, including both subsistence allowances and payment of tuition, fees, and supplies.

The initial Vietnam era bill omitted any provisions for on-the-job training, cooperative farm training, or flight training. These were added in 1967. At the same time, the basic monthly stipend was increased from $110 to $130. In 1970 it rose to $175 and two years later to $220, on each occasion over the initial objections of the Nixon administration. The new schedule of benefits for full-time training is $220 for an unmarried veteran (Nixon proposed $190), $261 for a veteran with one dependent, and $298 for a veteran with two dependents, with $18 for each additional dependent. Furthermore, the new legislation calls for a work-study program that will allow approximately 16,000 veterans using the GI Bill to earn an additional $250 for a hundred hours of work per semester in connection with VA programs. The work/study program, like the rate increase, was passed at the initiative of Congress, primarily the Senate, over the objections of the Administration.

★ Vietnam Veterans and the Colleges

Three out of every five Vietnam era veterans receiving benefits under the GI Bill have been attending college-level programs. This proportion represents a marked increase over previous years, due primarily to higher initial levels of education:

VETERANS' EDUCATIONAL LEVEL[36]

	% with high school completion at time of separation	% attending college under GI Bill
World War II	45.4	28.6
Korea	62.5	50.7
Vietnam era	78.9	60.1

As the statistics show, the proportion of high school graduates among separatees has increased 33.5 percentage points since World War II and the proportion of GI Bill beneficiaries at the college level has increased 31.5 percentage points, roughly the same.

Although a higher proportion of Vietnam era veterans are going to college, they represent a smaller proportion of college students than did earlier veterans. In 1946–47, the peak year of the World War II bill, three out of every four male college students was a veteran. In 1957–58, the peak year of the Korean bill, one of every four male college students was a veteran.[37] Today the comparable figure is more like one in every seventeen. Among entering freshmen (males and females) in the fall of 1971, only 2.9 percent were veterans and only 1.5 percent were veterans who served in Vietnam. In the junior colleges, Vietnam era veterans represented 4.8 percent of entering freshmen, in universities 1.0 percent, and in private universities 0.4 percent.[38]

Specific institutions provide a more graphic picture of the change. At Johns Hopkins, for example, in 1947–48 there were 1,751 students and of these, 1,083 were veterans. In 1971–72, Johns Hopkins had 2,020 students and twenty-five of these were veterans. Harvard had 5,600 students in 1947–48, 3,326 of whom were veterans. In 1971–72 Harvard had 6,073 students and eighty-nine veterans. Notre Dame in 1947–48 had 4,220 students including 3,587 veterans. In 1971–72 it had 6,439 students and 108 veterans. Back in 1947–48, Southern Methodist University had 9,011 students and 5,231 veterans. In 1971–72 it had 10,016 students, 505 of whom were veterans.[39]

The extremely small number of Vietnam veterans at major universities is due only in part to the fact that there are not as many of them as after World War II. There are, after all, 7 million veterans of the Vietnam era. If very few have found their way into private universities, that may reflect both changes in the social composition of the armed forces since World War II (namely the absence of the upper middle class) and an indifferent attitude at universities toward veteran applicants. The most important factor, however, is probably the unavailability of tuition payments, which effectively operates to channel veterans into public education, especially the junior colleges, where 43 percent of college veterans may be found.

Veterans from states that lack extensive systems of public higher education have much less opportunity to use the GI Bill. In California, which has the most highly developed system, 49 percent of veterans have used their education benefits, and 36 percent have gone to college. In Pennsylvania, on the other hand, just 29 percent of veterans have used the GI Bill, and a mere 14 percent have gone to college. All the states with high GI Bill participation rates are in the West and have extensive state college systems. In the East, where private colleges are more numerous and tuition fees high, the use of the GI Bill is low.

The original purpose of eliminating tuition payments was to curb abuses primarily at the vocational level, but its effect has been to penalize veterans from states where low-cost college education is limited. There are many who argue that at least partial tuition payments should be provided to restore some balance.

Because of their small numbers at most universities, veterans have been almost as invisible on the campus as they have been in the society at large. Even at a school like Fairmont State College in West Virginia, which has 300 veterans out of about 3,600 students, an attempt to form a veterans' club never really got off the ground. "We had meetings," says Ronnie Caldwell, one of its founders. "Nobody would ever come. Most of the veterans are married. If they're married, they don't have time to come to meetings or to get away. . . . And the single guys just hated the service and wouldn't have nothing to do with veterans." [40]

★ *The GI Bill and the Disadvantaged*

One of the virtues of the World War II GI Bill was that it provided scholarship money for young men from working-class and lower middle-class backgrounds who would otherwise have had little opportunity for further education. On the surface, the GI Bill enacted in 1966 seemed to do the same thing, but in reality, the level of benefits was so low that participation was greatly restricted for veterans from lower class families who lacked additional resources to draw upon for support.

Even when it was raised to $130 and then to $175, the stipend was inadequate to cover costs. The VA recognized this and pointed to statutes that said plainly the GI Bill was only a partial subsidy for education. By that very fact, it operated against those poorer veterans who could not afford to make up the difference on their own. Officials urged disadvantaged veterans to work part-time as they went to school, but in a period when any job at all was hard to find, convenient part-time jobs were even scarcer.

Social class differences in GI Bill participation showed up in one survey after another. A 1969 Bureau of the Budget study indicated that veterans with some college were twice as likely as high school graduates and more than four times as likely as high school dropouts to use the GI Bill in some way:

Education Prior to Discharge	% GI Bill Participation
1 to 3 years of college	55.7
high school graduates	27.9
high school dropouts	13.0

This correlation held up *even when controlling for ability,* as measured by the Armed Forces Qualfication Test. For example, considering only those who scored in the top two deciles, the participation rate was about 60 percent for those with some college, 40 percent for high school graduates, and 25 percent for veterans with less than twelve years of school.[41]

The problem finally received recognition in 1969 in the Report of the President's Committee on the Vietnam Veteran. "Available survey data," the report stated, "show that participation in GI Bill training is inverse to need. Nearly 50 percent of the veterans who already have college training at the time of discharge and therefore have the best prospects for immediate employment seek to upgrade their education under the GI Bill. On the other hand, those who have serious education deficiencies show participation rates as low as 10 percent." [42]

One reason for this low participation, the report noted, was that payments began only after enrollment—and even then were long delayed. "The effect of this after-the-fact method of payment can be to discourage program participation by the veteran who cannot afford the initial outlay required by most schools for prepayment of fees, tuition, books, and the necessary money for subsistence for himself and his family until the first payment is received. The intent of the program is thus jeopardized."

As its first recommendation, therefore, the committee proposed "an advance education assistance payment" to help veterans meet the initial cost before the first regular payment arrives. Simple as this idea was, it would be four years before any change would be made. Passed by the Senate in 1970, but blocked by the House Veterans' Affairs Committee that year, the advance education payment finally received full Congressional approval in October 1972, to become effective August 1973.[43] (That it should take less time for a student to pass through college than it has for an *advance* payment proposal to pass through Congress is a measure of the speed at which the federal government has responded to the needs of Vietnam veterans.)

Other proposals of the President's committee have also faced considerable foot-dragging. As its second recommendation in the area of education, the committee suggested a program to assist soldiers on active duty to prepare for post-secondary training. Third, it urged improvements in providing information about colleges to outgoing soldiers and help in bridging the transition from military to school. Fourth, the committee suggested that in making awards to institutions for programs for the disadvantaged, the Commissioner of Education take into account whether the schools gave special attention to veterans. Fifth, it proposed GI Bill payment for individual tutorial assistance when the school certifies it is necessary to overcome educational deficiencies.

Of these four additional proposals, not one has yet had any substantial impact on the educational opportunities of Vietnam veterans. Two of them were enacted into law in 1970, but initially administered under such restrictive conditions and with so little enthusiasm that few veterans were affected. Nonetheless, they do provide some basis for improvement in the future, particularly because of amendments added in 1972.

The two programs that were enacted in 1970, primarily under the leadership of Senator Cranston, were the predischarge educational program (PREP) and tutorial assistance. That same year Congress passed amendments enabling veterans to take remedial and re-fresher courses without charge to their thirty-six month entitlement and placing upon the VA "the affirmative duty" of seeking out eligible veterans to encourage them to make use of educational benefits.

In the first two years after their enactment, the PREP and tutorial programs were shackled by extremely rigid requirements. Soldiers in PREP programs had to have twenty-five hours a week of classes to be considered full-time participants, and, of course, few base commanders were willing to release soldiers for even half that length of time. Dr. John Mallan, director of the veterans' program of the American Association of Junior Colleges and the man outside the government most in contact with PREP programs, estimates that in the first two years no more than 2,000 men received schooling under the program. During that period about 2 million men were released from the armed services.[44]

Says Senator Cranston: "The Defense Department, the individual armed services, and the individual base commanders have never taken steps to make PREP available to large numbers of servicemen. The complete failure of individual base commanders to publicize PREP, to establish and promote PREP programs, or to encourage their men to participate has been particularly frustrating. . . . That this cooperation has not been forthcoming in any uniform sense is not really surprising in view of the fact that no official in either the Department of Defense or the Veterans Administration has even been given the specific responsibility to implement and oversee PREP."[45]

New amendments sponsored by Senator Cranston and passed by the 92nd Congress now require the VA to designate an official responsible for coordinating PREP programs with the Department of Defense. They also direct the military services to meet with representatives of education institutions in the vicinity of installations to set up new PREP programs and to release servicemen for at least part-time participation when not against the interests of national defense. Most significantly, through technical changes in the law, the number of hours required for PREP has been cut in half. These changes will almost certainly increase use of the program. Ironically, however, the main reason PREP may expand is that the Pentagon is contemplating phasing out financial support for General Education Degree (GED) programs. The net effect may not be a growth of in-service education, but simply a transfer of budgetary responsibility from the Pentagon to the VA.

Like PREP, the tutorial assistance program begun in 1970 has faced severe problems getting off the ground. During its first two years only 3,954 veterans were able to make use of it. Restrictive regulations, lack of publicity, and administrative lassitude were responsible. Typically a veteran needed a signed statement from a professor saying he was failing a course before he could qualify for tutorial assistance, but since grades are not posted before mid-term, and the application process took time, it was almost impossible to use the program. The difficulties arose partly because the original legislation said tutorial aid was to be awarded only in cases of "marked" academic deficiency, and the VA chose to interpret that rather strictly. Recent amendments have deleted the word "marked," and the change promises to make tutorial assistance more widely available.

Similar obstacles slowed use of the provisions for remedial education. The requirement of twenty-five classroom hours a week was unfeasible for many veterans who worked part-time, nor was it supported by college educators, who would prefer to see more independent study encouraged. In 1971 the American Association of Junior Colleges initiated discussion of a new remedial program to be called Upward Bound for Veterans. "Several colleges—for example, a distinguished black college in North Carolina—were very interested in the idea, but reported that they simply did not have college funds to carry the educational costs of such a program and also provide the subsistence costs which $175 would not cover." [46]

Since the time of that report, the situation has improved considerably. Not only have GI Bill benefits been increased, and the twenty-five-hour requirement reduced, but in 1972 the Office of Education in the Department of Health, Education, and Welfare allocated $5.8 million to Veterans Upward Bound. "Special emphasis will be placed on the unemployed veteran who does not have a high school diploma or equivalency certificate," HEW announced.[47]

One highly praised remedial education project for veterans that predates Veterans Upward Bound is being conducted at the University of California at Los Angeles. Begun in 1969 on the initiative of an associate dean of students, the program has enrolled veterans with high school records so poor they had no chance of getting into any college. Their average age is twenty-three, about one-third never finished high school, and many of them read at the seventh-grade level. The tuition is $500, but UCLA provides scholarships covering 80 percent of the cost for 60 percent of the students. The program consists of twelve weeks of intensive work in English, speech, psychology, study skills, reading, and mathematics. According to an article in *American Education*, 89 percent of those who start the program have successfully completed it; 83 percent of the graduates have gone on to college; average reading scores have improved by three grades; and the students evaluate the program overwhelmingly as "the most valuable educational experience" of their lives.[48]

Rosalind Loring, who developed the curriculum, and Edward Anderson, the program's original coordinator, have outlined some of the problems the UCLA project has encountered. They describe the students as highly motivated, but anxious about their age and prone to impatience with their progress. The men want to be respected for their experience and accomplishments in the service, but at the same time they lack self-confidence in academic skills and consequently may use "elaborate defenses" to hide their learning problems. Veterans react ambivalently to the authority of the teachers, sometimes challenging it, at other times seeking "specific assignments, explicit standards, and stated expectations for behavior." They are more accustomed "to external discipline than self-discipline" and even though older than other students, they often lack career plans. They express "dissatisfaction with the American system," and in many cases insecurity spilling over from general readjustment problems affects their ability to learn. To meet these difficulties, the UCLA program has provided extensive tutorial and counseling assistance, encouraged student evaluation of instructors and course material, continually adjusted the curriculum, and employed its own graduates in counseling and administrative roles.[49]

Programs like the one at UCLA are precisely the kind the VA should be encouraging. Nonetheless, the agency has taken no action to mobilize colleges and universities in that direction. It has construed its mandate in the narrowest sense. Its "outreach" activities in the past few years, spread extremely thin across the country, have been aimed at providing veterans with information about their benefits—a necessary and important function, but not enough. For as almost any Vietnam veteran will point out, virtually every veteran, disadvantaged or otherwise, knows that he is entitled to education benefits. The problem is not primarily awareness. Rather, veterans are worried that they cannot get into school and that, once there, they will not fit in socially or be able to handle the work. Clearly the institutions best able to allay those fears are not the offices of the VA, relying on form letters and pamphlets, but the local colleges and universities. The critical step, therefore, should have been to mobilize concern in the educational community and encourage the development of programs on the UCLA model. But, as the National Advisory Council on Extension and Continuing

Education pointed out, the VA has been almost completely isolated from educational institutions and associations.

What can happen when a college makes an effort was illustrated in 1971, when Fordham University in New York placed a single advertisement in the *Daily News*: "Veterans—Would You Want a Second Chance for Education?" The response was considerable: 800 veterans applied, and 300 were admitted.[50]

Most institutions have shown little interest in enrolling veterans, though that may change with Veterans Upward Bound. It may also be affected by amendments to the Higher Education Act of 1972, which provide "cost of instruction grants" to schools that increase their veteran enrollment during the first year by 10 percent, provide veterans counseling, and offer outreach, work/study, PREP, and remedial programs for veterans. The grants would amount to $300 per veteran plus an additional $150 for every disadvantaged veteran. Funds for the program were impounded by the Nixon administration, then ordered released by a federal court.

Another key area is the expansion of part-time employment opportunities. One of the first programs of this kind, Veterans in Public Service (VIPS), sought to provide jobs for GI Bill beneficiaries as part-time teacher aides. The program was defeated by the veterans' lobby, however, because it was administered by the Office of Education and not the VA. Subsequent programs have fared better. A project funded by the Office of Economic Opportunity called Veterans Education and Training Action Committee (VETAC) has promoted the idea of "split jobs." That is, instead of having one veteran work full-time in a government agency, two veterans who are going to school share the position, working part-time and supplementing their GI Bill allowance.

Hopeful as the new programs for the disadvantaged are, the situation still remains rather bleak. According to the VA, as of June 1972, the GI Bill participation rate among the educationally disadvantaged was still only 19.6 percent.[51]

Even this low figure overstates the extent of educational benefits. It says nothing about the kind of training disadvantaged veterans enter, its duration, or its value. The majority of working-class and poor veterans have no access to college and use the GI Bill instead to enroll in career and correspondence schools. These are the two areas of education still dominated by proprietary institutions and, twenty-five years after the scandals of World War II, they continue to be the most subject to abuse. Their record as educational institutions has consistently been the worst of any. In a survey conducted by the Census Bureau in 1955, the proportion of GI Bill beneficiaries indicating they had not used their training at all was 11 percent for veterans who went to college; 31 percent for men who took on-farm training; 41 percent for those who went to vocational schools; and 51 percent for those who took correspondence courses.[52]

We shall focus here on correspondence schools. Since the enactment of the current GI Bill, more than 700,000 Cold War and Vietnam era veterans—21.7 percent of all participants—have received money from the VA for home study courses.[53] Among educationally disadvantaged Vietnam veterans receiving benefits, the proportion taking mail-order courses has been 30.2 percent (51,383 out of 170,113 as of June 1972).[54] What value the courses have been to these men is open to serious question.

★ *Correspondence Schools and the VA*

> Easy home study plan prepares you for exciting career in conservation and ecology. Many Forestry and Wildlife men hunt mountain lions, parachute from planes to help marooned animals or injured campers. Catch breakfast from icy streams. Feel and look like a million.[55]

The advertisement is for the North American School of Conservation and it points out in large type that the school has been approved for GI Bill benefits. Literature from North American promises exciting job opportunities and high incomes. A form letter from its executive director, Charles Leichert, affects a personal, folksy tone: "You see, I am in this work because I love it—not just for a pay check, even though it is quite a good one. I want to help *you* get started toward a profitable, exciting career that will bring a lifetime of pleasure and satisfaction to *YOU*—and *just as important* to help the cause of conservation by training men who are properly fitted for it." The letter speaks of jobs in government hunting ("As I write this letter, *twenty-one states* employ full-time Government Hunters"), wildlife protection ("Excellent pay, with most jobs starting well above the average"), forest conservation ("The Ranger's badge of authority is familiar to every . . ."), and so on. The course costs $460 or $495, depending on payment plan, and a veteran learns that if he chooses the lower payment plan and completes the lessons, the VA will cover 90 percent of the cost. It sounds as though there's nothing to lose.

But you can lose and, in fact, most veterans who take correspondence courses end up in debt to the school. For those who enroll, the odds against obtaining work with correspondence school credentials are enormous.

North American School of Conservation is a case in point. Although it suggests that jobs are available, even begging, for its graduates, the Society of American Foresters has testified before hearings of the Federal Trade Commission that it knows of no state forest service that will employ persons who have taken correspondence courses. Referring specifically to North American and the National School of Conservation (another home study operation approved for VA benefits), the chairman of the society's Committee on Professional Employment Services stated: "Whatever a school may claim, we know of no professional level career opportunities for people whose training in forestry is completion of the course work offered by these schools." [56]

The testimony is interesting not only because the advertising used by the home study schools suggests opportunities are available, but also because it is supposedly VA policy only to support programs "generally accepted as necessary to fulfill requirements for the attainment of a predetermined objective." [57]

"This pragmatic test," says a VA official, "rules out courses pretending to teach the skills of an occupation, when it is manifest that hardly any practitioners of that occupation have taken such courses." [58]

North American School of Conservation is not a fly-by-night operation. It is part of a large family of correspondence schools operating out of Newport Beach, California. Its siblings include the North American Institute of Data Processing Sciences, the North American Institute of Systems and Procedures, and the North American Schools of Drafting, Advertising, Recreation, Surveying and Mapping, and Travel. All of these are approved for GI Bill benefits and all of them are owned by the National Systems Corporation, a member of the American Stock Exchange. According to a 1971 prospectus, 18 percent of the students in the North American Correspondence Schools are receiving aid under the GI Bill. [59]

This proportion is not unusually high. The Cleveland Institute of Electronics, another correspondence school, states that it has an enrollment of about 49,500 students, including 8,500 veterans and 15,000 active duty personnel studying under the GI Bill. [60] Advance Schools, Inc. claims an enrollment of nearly 100,000 students, of which 60,000 to 70,000 are veterans and servicemen. [61]

The large number of active-duty servicemen taking correspondence courses through their veterans' benefits is a new phenomenon, made possible by changes in the most recent GI Bill. Of the 267,000 soldiers who have used their education benefits, 166,000, or 62.3 percent, have used them for mail-order courses.[62] This new market has drawn a swarm of correspondence salesmen to military bases across the country. Says Colonel Hazel Benn, Education Officer for the U.S. Marine Corps: "We have tremendous problems with correspondence study salesmen. Our military police have substantial problems policing salesmen of all types, but the correspondence salesmen are among the worst. One school, JETMA, insists that it can teach jet engine mechanics through the mail. I personally think that is incredible." [63]

Until recently, there were few hard statistics on correspondence training under the GI Bill except the data on enrollment. The Veterans Administration could not say how many veterans completed correspondence courses, how many ever received counseling from the VA, or how many actually obtained work with their training. Although GI Bill benefits are by law only provided for an "identified educational, professional, or vocational objective," the agency could not indicate—nor did it show any interest in learning—to what extent the intention of the law was being fulfilled.

In March 1972, however, the General Accounting Office, the investigating arm of Congress, released the results of a study of its own. Examining VA records from June 1966 through June 1970, GAO found that 75 percent of veterans who had enrolled in correspondence courses did not complete them. The dropout rate passed 90 percent in several fields: in electronic operation, 91 percent; electronic technician training, 91 percent; drafting, 93 percent; accounting, 93 percent; commercial art, 96 percent.

GAO also conducted a questionnaire survey of 1,000 randomly selected veterans. The survey revealed that of those veterans who failed to complete the courses, 84 percent ended up paying the correspondence schools for lessons they never took and for which the VA would not reimburse them. Most of the veterans said they had enrolled in courses to learn new skills or improve old ones to obtain better jobs. Asked whether they had achieved their objective, 6 percent said they had; 27 percent said they had in part; and 67 percent said they had not achieved it at all.

Of those who had finished the courses, 44 percent said they had looked for jobs on the basis of their training, and about half of those said they had been able to find them. Veterans who finished the courses and found jobs represent about 6 percent of the total who enrolled.[64]

Particularly galling to veterans who successfully complete correspondence courses is the attitude of the federal government. "The FBI, Secret Service, CIA, and the several other agencies do not recognize a correspondence school credential," writes Albert L. Maise, of Northglenn, Colorado, "yet the same parent government is paying out funds promoting such study." [65]

All courses for which veterans receive GI Bill benefits must be approved, but the function of approving courses is actually not carried out by the Veterans Administration itself. Legally, that function has been delegated to the states, but in reality it is divided between the states and private trade associations. Under the law, agencies appointed by state governors determine which courses are eligible. If a school has been accredited by an accrediting agency recognized by the U.S. Office of Education, state approval is perfunctory. If not, a course must meet certain standards set by statute and administered by state approval agencies. The VA does not supervise the state agencies; it contracts with them for services. Although it is well known that many of the state agencies, especially in the South, have neither the personnel nor the expertise to undertake serious reviews of vocational and correspondence schools,[66] the VA has never withdrawn funds or threatened to withdraw them for failure to enforce adequate standards.[67]

In the field of correspondence education, the officially recognized accrediting agency is the National Home Study Council (NHSC). About 88 percent of the veterans who have enrolled in mail-order courses have enrolled in courses accredited by the council (rather than by state approval agencies).[68] It was NHSC, for example, that accredited the North American School of Conservation and enabled it to advertise that it was "approved for the GI Bill." NHSC also accredited the school that trains jet engine mechanics by mail.

The National Home Study Council serves two functions. On the one hand, it is a trade association representing the interests of its members, lobbying for favorable legislation, and resisting regulatory controls. On the other hand, it is an accrediting agency, determining which schools meet proper standards and qualify for GI Bill benefits. "I wear two hats," said David Lockmiller in an interview, "executive director of the council and secretary of the independent accrediting commission." [69] The independence of the commission is open to question.

The council claims that while four of its members are from the

home study industry, five are public representatives. Among the
public representatives, however, have been Jack C. Staehle, a
director of Lasalle Extension University; Herold Hunt, a Harvard
professor who is also a trustee of a correspondence school; and
Lawrence C. Derthick, a retired official of the National Education
Association and a director of Intext, one of whose three divisions is
International Correspondence Schools.[70] Asked about the affiliations
of the public representatives, Henry Wellman, assistant to the
director of NHSC, replied that the issue had come up a number of
times. "We thought this would strengthen the commission," he
stated, "because they would have some involvement in the home
study industry." Did he feel that it was deceptive to call such men
"public" representatives? "We have never felt that it was." [71]

The high dropout rate from correspondence courses is not an
accidental flaw in the home study industry; without it, many schools
would perish financially. In July 1970, Jessica Mitford published a
devastating article in *The Atlantic* on the Famous Writers School, a
correspondence operation (approved, of course, for veterans) that
claimed to provide would-be writers with hints and personal
criticism from Famous Writers like Bennett Cerf, Rod Serling,
Bruce Catton, Red Smith, and others. None of these writers, of
course, ever saw a student's paper; they merely lent their names for
a handsome fee. The reading was done instead by less famous
Connecticut housewives. Had all 65,000 students enrolled at the
time completed all their lessons, the school's fifty-five instructors
would have been swamped. With awesome regularity, however, the
dropout rate approached 90 percent. "We couldn't make any
money if all the students finished," Famous Writer Phyllis McGin-
ley candidly told Ms. Mitford.[72]

If the students had finished, the school would have had to invest a
great deal of money in education, which it studiously avoided.
Famous Writers School belonged to FAS International, which also
owned the Famous Artists School and the Famous Photographers
School, all approved for GI Bill benefits. According to the latest
figures Ms. Mitford was able to obtain (from a 1966 annual report),
FAS had been spending about twice as much on "advertising and
selling" as it had on "grading and materials." This pattern does not
appear to be unusual. The National Systems Corporation, which
owns the North American Correspondence Schools, reports that
during 1971 it spent $3,771,119 on "course materials, service, and
instruction costs" and $6,054,112 on "selling and promotion." [73]

"I think mail-order selling has several built-in deficiencies," the
late Bennett Cerf, a founder of the Famous Writers School and

head of Random House for many years, told Ms. Mitford at an off-guard moment. "The crux of it is a very hard sales pitch, an appeal to the gullible. Of course, once somebody has signed a contract with Famous Writers, he can't get out of it, but that's true with every business in the country."

Asked how many books by Famous students Random House had published, Cerf replied, "Oh, come on, you must be pulling my leg—no person of any sophistication, whose book we'd publish, would have to take a mail-order course to learn how to write." [74]

The cost of the Famous Writers course was about $900, or, as Ms. Mitford found, roughly twenty times the cost of comparable, if not better, correspondence courses offered by state university extension divisions. Probably none of the 2,000 veterans taking the course through the GI Bill at the time had ever been advised that the extension courses existed. The GAO study found that only 1 percent of veterans taking correspondence courses received any counseling from the VA.[75] The state university programs naturally tend to be less known because they never advertise, which is also partly the reason they cost a fraction of the fees charged by commercial schools.

The National Home Study Council not only accredits schools; it also sets the standards that the schools are supposed to follow. Under the law, only those courses that are nonaccredited but approved by state approval agencies must meet detailed VA standards (which are often not enforced). Accredited schools need only satisfy very minimal criteria to get GI Bill approval. Among other things, they were until recently exempt from following VA standards on refund policies.

It was this aspect of the law that has caused many veterans unexpected debts to correspondence schools. The VA does not provide a subsistence allowance to home study students; rather it reimburses them on a quarterly basis according to the number of lessons they have completed. The schools accredited by the National Home Study Council, however, charged students according to the amount of time elapsed since enrollment. After three days, for example, the charge would be $50 plus 15 percent of the full tuition; after 180 days, the charge would be the full tuition, no matter how many lessons were completed. If most veterans completed correspondence courses, the disparity between the VA's payment policy and the schools' refund policy would have been irrelevant. With all the lessons completed, the veterans would have been reimbursed in full. But because most veterans sought to terminate their contracts after completing a fraction of the lessons, the difference usually left the men in debt. The GAO found that of the veterans who did not complete correspondence courses, 84 percent paid the schools for uncompleted lessons. These payments ranged from $10 to $900 and averaged $180.[76]

Correspondence schools not accredited by NHSC but approved by state agencies, on the other hand, had to meet federal guidelines, which required that they follow a *pro rata* refund policy, i.e., that they charge only for courses completed and refund any other money paid. Oddly enough, veterans who enrolled in the supposedly inferior schools denied accreditation by NHSC were less likely to get bilked.

In July 1970 the Federal Trade Commission issued proposed guidelines for vocational and home study schools which, if adopted, would require all correspondence schools to follow a *pro rata* refund policy. The VA moved in the same direction. Legislation introduced by the Administration in the 92nd Congress and passed by the Senate would have made a *pro rata* refund policy mandatory for all correspondence schools approved for GI Bill benefits. The House Veterans' Affairs Committee, however, balked at the proposal, finding the counterarguments of National Home Study Council persuasive. The council contended that correspondence schools must charge dropouts more than a *pro rata* refund policy would allow them because of "basic economics." According to NHSC, it costs an average of $80 just to get a new student started, and research and review costs amount to $200 per student.[77] It is unclear whether the council included all the costs for advertising and promotion in estimating how much it costs "to get a new student started."

But let us suppose these claims are correct—that the "start up" costs of commercial home study make a *pro rata* refund policy economically unfeasible. In that case, if state universities are able to offer the same courses for a fraction of the cost through their extension divisions, the implication is that the commercial correspondence schools are noncompetitive and are only sustained by intense promotion—"an appeal to the gullible," as Bennett Cerf so honestly phrased it. The danger of arguing from "basic economics" is that it calls into question the basic economics of the industry.

In any case, anticipating a crackdown, the National Home Study Council decided to modify its position and retain what advantages it could. It promulgated a new refund policy that would still allow its member schools to collect money for uncompleted lessons, though probably somewhat less than under the earlier policy. The NHSC position was supported by Olin Teague and in House-Senate conference in late 1972 it replaced the VA and Senate-supported *pro rata* refund requirement.

The new policy is as follows. No enrollment agreement in a correspondence course is to be effective unless the GI Bill beneficiary notifies the VA affirming the agreement within ten days. To recover any money paid, the veteran must notify the correspondence school immediately and return any materials he received. (This provision protects the veteran who succumbs to a salesman's hard sell, but soon regrets having enrolled.) If he wishes to drop the course after ten days, he will be charged 10 percent of the tuition or $50, whichever is less. If he wishes to terminate the course after completing one lesson but less than 25 percent of the total, he will be charged 25 percent of the tuition plus the registration fee (10 percent or $50). If he wishes to terminate after completing 25 percent of the lessons but less than 50 percent, the school may keep 50 percent of the tuition plus the registration fee. After he has completed 50 percent of the lessons, the school need make no refund.

To see how the system works, consider a veteran who enrolls in the North American School of Conservation under the cheaper payment plan and who decides to drop the course after doing five out of the hundred lessons. According to the new refund policy, he will be charged 25 percent of the tuition ($116.25) plus a registration fee ($46.50). From the VA the veteran will receive one twentieth of 90 percent of the tuition, or $20.92. He ends up owing the school $141.63. What is he paying for? Primarily two things: first, the cost of the school's advertising budget (i.e., the cost of his own deception) and second, the cost of having had Olin Teague as Chairman of the House Committee on Veterans' Affairs.

Considering the data on drop-out rates presented to Congress by the GAO, the hearings on deceptive practices held by the Federal Trade Commission, and the numerous complaints of individual veterans, the Congressional response has hardly been adequate. In the period after World War II there was a scandal because of manipulation of the GI Bill by profit-making vocational schools. Today the situation is essentially the same, except that it no longer involves fly-by-night operations but correspondence schools owned by large corporations with a well-financed lobby in Washington and a sympathetic ear on the House Veterans' Affairs Committee. The question is whether Congress will do today to large companies what it did when faced by abuses in small businesses.

Moreover, correspondence schools use their "GI Bill approval" like a U.S. Government Seal of Inspection, making the VA an accomplice in defrauding thousands of other Americans who think "approved for veterans" means they are safe.

On the basis of its study, the General Accounting Office recommended that the VA compile and make available to veterans information on enrollment and dropout rates in various correspondence subjects. The VA agreed to do so.[78] But a comprehensive response to the problem would go further. Four measures are warranted:

1. As the Administration and the Senate originally proposed, all correspondence schools should be required to follow *pro rata* refund policies.
2. The function of accreditation should be taken out of the hands of the National Home Study Council, a private trade association operated for private interests, but with the power to determine which members of its industry are eligible for public funds.
3. The VA should compile, make public, and distribute data on enrollment, course completion, job placement, and student satisfaction for each of the programs approved for benefits. (GAO proposed it compile data only on dropouts by subject.)
4. This information should be used in reviewing the accreditation of the programs and developing new standards. To qualify for GI Bill benefits, correspondence schools using future-service contracts should be required to maintain minimum completion and job placement rates (where jobs are promised). This would eliminate GI Bill approval for ineffective training courses. It would encourage schools with completion rates under the required minimum to raise the quality of their courses and to pre-test applicants to see whether they are able to handle the work. Finally, it would fulfill the intent of the law.

The correspondence schools argue that they serve an important function, enabling people who work or cannot leave their homes to take further education. The premise that these services are needed is accurate, but the conclusion that it justifies the home study industry, as currently structured, is not. Universities are becoming more involved in extension education, and there has been considerable talk of imitating the British "open university," which enables people not in school to take courses via correspondence, television, and community seminars and ultimately to qualify for degrees.

The current system has very little to do with education or training. The correspondence schools appear to spend more on promotion than on educational services. By playing to the fantasies of people lacking ready means for education and advancement, they trap large numbers of people into long-term contracts. Veterans sign up in unusually large numbers because they are led to expect the VA will cover the cost. Once signed up, however, they find the courses are not what they expected; often they are unprepared, or they simply lose interest. With only a fraction of the lessons completed, they learn that they owe the school more than the VA will pay them. Or, if they do complete the course, they find that no one takes the credentials seriously, not even the government that financed the program in the first place.

★ *The Future of the GI Bill*

Our criticism of various aspects of the GI Bill should not obscure our basic conviction that it has been an extremely worthwhile program—the best, without any doubt, available to Vietnam veterans. Many of the deficiencies of the original Cold War and Vietnam era GI Bill have been remedied. When benefits for education were restored in 1966, they were worth less, their duration was shorter, and the options available under the program narrower than they had been under the World War II or Korean GI Bills. But in the years since then, benefits have been upgraded to the point where they are now very nearly comparable to earlier programs. As the benefit levels have risen, so has the rate of participation in the program, and it now seems likely that it will reach the 50 percent level set after World War II. Whether we should be satisfied with that mark is another question. Education has become far more important in the economy in the years since World War II, and although much of this emphasis arises out of a rampant mania for credentials, its effects on veterans' chances of employment are no less real.

The utilization of benefits has been spread very unevenly, with the least use occurring among those veterans who need education and training (and certification) the most. Although Congress has responded to this problem by approving a series of programs for disadvantaged veterans, the Nixon administration has never given these programs any priority or serious commitment. The VA, in particular, has failed to generate interest and concern in the educational institutions where the problems ultimately get resolved.

The way the Administration has handled programs like PREP, tutorial, remedial aid, and outreach do not inspire confidence in the way it will handle new programs like Veterans Upward Bound or the work-study program passed over its objections. The attempt to impound funds for veterans' cost-of-instruction grants is probably just an omen of more to come.

Nonetheless, the passage of these programs has signaled an important change in Congressional intent. Whereas earlier legislation treated veterans as if they all had the same resources, the more recent legislation recognizes that some stand at an economic and social disadvantage and need special assistance to make use of their educational benefits. Whereas the earlier legislation sought only to make up for opportunities missed because of military service, the new legislation seeks to open up opportunities for those who never would have had them even if they stayed home. This shift in the emphasis and rationale of the program has taken place in spite of a hostile committee chairman in one house of Congress and an indifferent administration. As yet it has only been a shift of paper. The low participation rates of the "educationally disadvantaged" indicate that the programs have yet to bear significant results.

Much of the discussion of participation rates seems to proceed on the assumption that all utilization of GI Bill benefits is equally desirable. The participation rates have almost always been used as the principal indicators of the success of the program. In some areas, however, high utilization indicates not success, but an extraordinary amount of wasteful expenditure on useless training. We have dealt with the problems of mail-order courses subsidized through the GI Bill, a phenomenon that has grown enormously because of the extension of education benefits to active-duty servicemen in 1966. A study of career schools and flight training, we think, would disclose a similar pattern of useless expenditure and consumer fraud. The Veterans Administration has shown almost no concern over these problems, hiding behind the legal arrangements that delegate the function of approving courses for the GI Bill to the states. Although it provides funds for the state approval agencies, it has never threatened to withdraw them for failure to enforce adequate standards. It does not even have any procedures to review decisions the state agencies make.

Although changes in the structure of the GI Bill made at the time of Korea eliminated some of the more egregious frauds, the basic problems persist because their roots have been left untouched. In the United States we now have a dual system of post-secondary education: Proprietary schools dominate the vocational and correspondence area, whereas nonprofit and public institutions predominate at the college level. Under the current GI Bill, 76 percent of the college-level beneficiaries have attended public institutions, while 87 percent of the below-college trainees have enrolled in private, mostly profit-making, institutions.[79] This is the meritocratic equivalent of socialism for the rich and private enterprise for the poor.

There has been so little public concern about the vocational area—except, perhaps, in the community college movement—that regulatory functions have been almost entirely ceded to accrediting associations established by the industry itself to look after its own interests. The role of the National Home Study Council is typical in this regard. Neither students nor professionals—nor a combination of the two—have been charged with the responsibility for evaluating the schools. Instead that function has been handed to trade associations that conveniently double as accrediting agencies gifted with Olympian detachment. Their evaluations, like the judgments of gods, are made secretly, never explained, and never reviewed by anyone else. So long as the problems of regulation and accountability remain unresolved, the GI Bill and programs like it will end up being used to profit the schools rather than the students.

This issue may assume greater importance as the nation moves toward general financial support for post-secondary education. On the one hand, a national entitlement to post-secondary education that excluded vocational training would result in a substantial overinvestment in higher education and function as a regressive form of income redistribution (since the better off will have greater access to college). On the other hand, a national entitlement that includes vocational training will open the door to the kind of abuses that have taken place under the GI Bill, magnified several times because of the new program's greater size. The only way to avoid this Hobson's choice is to make changes in the educational system, not just in its financing.

This may go against the grain. The attractiveness of the GI Bill, as a form of educational assistance, is that it leaves the educational system, as well as individual students, remarkably unfettered by the federal government. It is primarily this feature that has led the Carnegie Commission to recommend the GI Bill as a model for federal aid to education. In a recent report, the commission calls for "a new Educational Bill of Rights, modeled on the successful program for GI's after World War II, which would provide students from low and modest income families with the financial resources required for college attendance, and would also provide a cost-of-education supplement going along with these students to the institutions of their choice." The report notes that such a national entitlement would permit aid to colleges with religious affiliations, whereas direct grants to those colleges might raise Constitutional issues. Direct grants to state colleges would also encourage state legislatures to reduce the level of their support. "These several considerations," the commission concluded, "have led us . . . to favor the GI Bill of Rights approach, since it makes the greatest contribution to national welfare, provides substantial support to nearly all institutions without running major risks of constitutional challenges for many of them or of reduced state support for still others, and preserves to the maximum the freedom of choice for students and the autonomy of state systems." [80]

These views were decisive in the formulation of the Higher Education Act of 1972, which authorized Basic Opportunity Grants (BOGs) for students from low- and middle-income families. It is unlikely, however, that the program will receive adequate funding for some time.

In the long run, two developments will influence the future of the GI Bill. One is the growth of general assistance for post-secondary education. The other is the volunteer army. To attract sufficient new recruits and to retain its men, the military has increased salaries and bonuses enormously. This increase in manpower costs produces a natural response to look for related expenses that might be eliminated. As the Pentagon opposed extension of the GI Bill after Korea because of its alleged impact on re-enlistment, so it may oppose its extension after Vietnam. The recent increases in GI Bill rates, which make the program even more expensive, will probably strengthen the Pentagon's hand.

No direct moves have yet been made, but one senses what the arguments will be. For example, Alfred Fitt, former Assistant Secretary of Defense for Manpower, recently told the *Washington Post*, "It seems to me that if you end the draft you really ought to end such things as the GI Bill, because you don't have to compensate them [volunteers] for interrupting their careers." [81] The cruel irony of such a move would be that the volunteers may be drawn from just those sectors of the population that stand most in need of education when they leave the military. Many of them will not be career soldiers, but short-term enlistees.

Oddly, then, just as the Carnegie Commission is suggesting that the GI Bill be used as a model for general educational aid, and the Congress is moving in that direction, the Pentagon may seek to eliminate the real GI Bill. In the long run—if it is a peaceful long run—a national entitlement will probably gain ground as educational benefits for veterans decline. What veterans will be entitled to under a general entitlement is unclear, since grants will be based on family income, and veterans are generally no longer dependent on parental support. It will probably be necessary, therefore, to seek a separate benefit structure for veterans within the new legislation. The old GI Bill, even if it is disowned by the military, may still find a home with its children.

part four ★ ★ ★ ★
Conclusion

10

Escalating
the Peace

★ *A Preamble*

In thinking about human problems and social policy, there are two
complementary hazards. On the one hand, there is a temptation to
deal only with the institutional reality—the world as it is reflected
in official records and reports. On the other hand, there is a
temptation to focus narrowly on personal experience—the world as
it is reflected in the lives of individuals. We have tried, wherever
possible, to keep a balance between men and institutions: in
discussing the experience of Vietnam veterans, not to lose sight of
the social realities that frame their experience; in discussing
institutions like the VA, not to lose sight of the people for whose
benefit the agencies and programs were established.

This is a difficult task. The bureaucratic reality is attractive in
that it superficially seems much more "objective." But as we have
often seen in the preceding pages, information processed by a
bureaucracy is often systematically incorrect and misleading. For
example, the VA's statistics on how many drug cases it treated we
found to be vastly inflated because of various record-keeping
practices. Whenever questioned on the progress of drug treatment,
top VA officials would point with satisfaction to the swollen
statistics, and reporters who had no reason to doubt the data would
pass them along to the public. So do bureaucratic fictions become
established facts. One begins to penetrate beyond the veil of official
facts only by seeking out reality on the bottom level, as it is seen by
ordinary people in their daily work.

But relying on their perceptions can also be misleading. Just as the bureaucratic perspective superficially seems more objective, so the personal perspective superficially seems more authentic. Many of the veterans, doctors, drug counselors, and others we interviewed could be extremely perceptive about things which took place in their immediate vicinity. But they often had only the vaguest idea of where policies originated. So far as many of them knew, the rules came from "Washington." They rarely differentiated among Congress, the Executive Office of the President, the VA Central Office, or even local officials. (Most commonly, the VA would be blamed for policies that actually were matters of law.) When it came to suggesting changes, they often had sound instincts about how things ought to work, but were at a loss about how to make that happen, where to cut into the institutional reality, who or what to blame for irrational rules and practices they confronted daily. If this report has given them a better understanding of the institutional reality, we will consider our efforts well spent—even if they disagree with our conclusions, which they may well do.

In moving from analysis to recommendations, the needs and behavior of both men and institutions must be kept in focus. There is a danger of suggesting changes that reduce the problems of an institution but actually complicate the problems of its clients. Conversely, there is a danger of proposing reforms that at first sight meet human needs but that call forth counterproductive institutional responses.

One must also keep a balance between recommendations for the long and short run. In focusing too sharply on immediate problems, one often loses sight of the changing context of policy. To avoid that requires a sense of history. Conversely, in emphasizing too strongly long-run changes, one may lose sight of immediate reforms that could concretely ameliorate existing conditions. To avoid that requires an appreciation of the seriousness of people's daily needs. Our bias is toward the long term, but we try never to suggest that veterans' immediate needs be sacrificed for the sake of far-off (or far-out) reforms.

★ A Recounting

We have covered much ground: in Part One, the odyssey of Vietnam veterans and the overall operation of federal veterans' programs; in Part Two, the problems of the severely injured, the compensation system, veterans' hospitals, drug addiction programs, and less than honorable discharges; in Part Three, the economic and social problems of readjustment and the operation of the GI Bill. There is more that we could have covered—housing, for example, is a major omission—and doubtless much that we have not treated within those areas that we did cover.

The major recommendations from Part Two concern the VA hospitals. There we suggested that as health insurance programs are developed on the national level, the VA system be phased out in favor of a program of insurance credits graded according to the level of service-connected disability and number of years since military discharge. We made this proposal for many reasons, three of which are particularly important. First, an insurance system would provide veterans—particularly young veterans who may not be enthralled with the character of VA hospitals—with a wider choice as to where they can receive free medical care. Second, it is our belief that the nature of the VA as a system essentially of chronic care facilities on the periphery of American medicine cannot be altered by any statutory reforms. Third, if the VA remains an independent hospital system, it will make regional coordination among health services that much more difficult. There will be unnecessary duplication of facilities and equipment, discontinuities of care, artificial barriers that prevent patients from getting to the institution that can best handle their problems (as in the case of spinal cord injury). All these considerations militate against the maintenance of a separate system of veterans' health services— which, as we have pointed out, deviates from all other veterans' programs in that it involves a separate *institutional system*, not just separate financing, as in the GI Bill.

The theory of the VA hospital system is that its principal task is to care for all service-connected medical problems. Second, because the nation owes a special debt to wartime veterans, it treats their most serious nonservice-connected conditions (i.e., those which require hospitalization) on occasions when they cannot afford treatment themselves. The trouble with this reasoning is that it leaves VA patients half in the system and half outside. This makes no sense medically or economically. The proposal for insurance credits, on the other hand, would allow veterans to receive all their medical care from one institution, if they so wished. This would be consistent with the new emphasis on health maintenance organizations. The proposal preserves—or rather, restores—the proper role of veterans' benefits. It provides permanent aid for those with permanent service-connected disabilities and readjustment assistance for those who are not disabled.

In the area of disability compensation, our chief concern was to see that the power to make disability evaluations be removed from individual federal agencies—particularly the armed services—and transferred to an Independent Medical Board. Two considerations prevailed here. First, there is abundant evidence from separate sources to indicate that the military has for years given unjustifiably high ratings to officers as a retirement bonus. Second, the proliferation of disability benefits among three different agencies has produced a great deal of duplication in examinations that wastes valuable resources and causes unnecessary paperwork both for beneficiaries and the federal government. A coordinated system with a unified evaluation board and judicial appeal would eliminate conflicts of interest, provide adequate safeguards, save money, and simplify procedures for distributing benefits. It would not mean a less generous compensation program. On the contrary, more resources could be concentrated on those that have legitimate injuries.

In addition, we proposed that military disability retirements be submitted to a critical review and that in cases where evaluations are found to be inflated, benefits be reduced. We also suggested that in the treatment of behavioral and psychiatric problems, the VA's disability compensation system often works at cross-purposes with the goals of therapy, discouraging early release from institutional care. To reduce the degree of institutionalization, reforms are needed not only in compensation, but in the orientation of VA facilities. The large poorly staffed mental hospitals located in small towns far from the homes of most of their patients should be converted to other purposes. Increased emphasis should be given to outpatient services and transitional communities, such as halfway houses.

This has particular relevance to the treatment of drug abuse and addiction. Again, we favor an insurance system that would provide funds for the treatment of veterans in community drug programs. But so long as the VA is involved, it should develop outpatient services, transitional communities, and residential drug programs removed from its hospitals. In addition, the regulations preventing treatment of addicted veterans with bad discharges must be removed. All necessary funds for vocational rehabilitation should also be made available. Legislation in the Senate has included provisions that would restore GI Bill entitlements to veterans with bad discharges who, after a year in rehabilitation, continue to "stay clean." This is sound as an incentive and as a means of providing aid necessary to help the men reconstruct their civilian lives. The Senate bill also calls for active efforts on the part of the VA and other agencies to find employment for veterans in drug programs; we can think of no item more critical.

Veterans who experienced drug problems in the military have received discharge papers marked with special code numbers. The meaning of these numbers is known to businessmen, and they have cost many veterans good jobs. Considering the Defense Department's own view that most veterans do leave drugs behind, it should be the first to favor erasing these code numbers.

Military discharges require further action. We have advocated simplifying and reforming the system by eliminating the Undesirable Discharge, which effectively deprives a veteran of his lawful benefits, although it is issued as a result of administrative rather than judicial proceedings. Only men receiving discharges under dishonorable conditions after court-martial should be denied eligibility for benefits. The rules on eligibility would then be unequivocal, leaving the agency no opportunity to exclude men, as it has in the past, on moralistic and extralegal grounds.

The employment problem has two principal sources—the Administration's anti-inflationary economic measures, which were set in motion just as Vietnam veterans were returning in greatest numbers, and the discontent veterans have felt with the work available in the secondary labor market to which they have been confined. The former led to a shortage of jobs, the latter to a high rate of job turnover. Ultimately, resolution of these problems depends on policies able to curb inflation without raising unemployment, and on reforms of the labor market. Among the programs introduced specifically to combat veteran unemployment, the most effective seems to have been the Public Employment Program created by the Emergency Employment Act. Although Congress has been willing to extend this measure, with an additional provision assigning 50 percent of the jobs to Vietnam veterans, the Administration finds it ideologically unpalatable.

In the area of education and training, our suggestions fall into three categories: those that concern the overall shape of the GI Bill, those that are aimed at increasing participation in the program by disadvantaged veterans, and those that would place tighter regulatory controls on career and correspondence schools.

With the increases in GI Bill benefits voted in 1972, stipends approach World War II levels. But the question nevertheless remains: Why should benefits for Vietnam veterans be lower at all? Realistically, it is highly unlikely at this point that Congress will vote further increases in monthly subsistence allowances or that the Administration will accept them. Indeed, defenders of the GI Bill will probably have a hard time just seeing that the program is extended for veterans after Vietnam. Nonetheless, we think consideration should be given to restoring at least partial tuition payments and extending the length of entitlement, in certain cases, from thirty-six to forty-eight months, as it was after World War II. A cost-of-living escalator is also needed.

Liberalization of benefits would probably improve use of the GI Bill among veterans from poorer backgrounds. But other measures are warranted as well. As we have repeatedly noted, these are the men who had the least education when they entered the armed forces, ended up on the front lines and casualty rolls in the greatest numbers, and came home with the highest rates of psychological distress and the fewest transferable skills. If anyone deserves priority treatment from the VA, it is these men. The agency must implement more aggressively the progressive measures adopted by Congress in 1970—tutorial assistance, remedial education, outreach, and PREP. Amendments by the 92nd Congress should facilitate that process.

The position of disadvantaged veterans (and others) needs to be strengthened in another regard. The vocational and home study schools that prey on the unwary must be placed under tighter controls. The extremely loose system for approving programs gives an official stamp of approval to operations that have little educational value. The VA should begin reviewing the decisions made by state approval agencies and, where performance has been inadequate, withdraw its subsidies.

The failure of the VA to initiate action in this area has wider relevance. It illustrates how too great an emphasis on one measure of an agency's performance often fosters negligence in related fields. Beginning in 1969 the VA was under continual attack in the press and in Congress because of the low rate of participation of Vietnam era veterans in the GI Bill. In its eagerness to see participation rates increase, the agency abdicated its regulatory functions and allowed wasteful programs to flourish. A truly prudent and fiscally conservative administration would never have allowed mail-order courses in particular to reach the proportions they have. But the more than 700,000 young veterans and servicemen who have enrolled in correspondence courses have raised the index on which the VA's performance was being evaluated. Consequently, the agency had no incentive to take forceful action.

Congress has a responsibility not only to see that regulatory controls are tightened, but to insist on more discriminating performance measures on the GI Bill. The VA has failed to monitor its readjustment programs adequately. While the agency has long had a substantial and distinguished program of medical research, it has had nothing comparable in the area of education. This is particularly odd, because much of the medical research is tangentially related to the VA's functions, whereas research on readjustment programs would be eminently relevant. Here we see the pressures of the market place at work. The VA has been forced to spend increasing amounts on medical research to attract physicians to its hospitals. It has had no similar need to spend anything for research on its education programs. The only people who might have benefited from that would be young veterans, many from lower-income families, and they have not been particularly well represented in the agency's decision making.

This gets close to the heart of the problem. The orientation of the VA has been, and continues to be, toward older veterans. It is evident in the veterans' hospitals. It is evident in the VA's budget. It is evident in the VA hierarchy. The price of lifelong veterans' programs is less concentrated readjustment assistance. The demands of the new veterans are an intrusion into the operation of the VA. That is precisely the reverse of how it ought to be. Their demands should be the VA's first concern. The demands of older veterans who have long passed the period of readjustment should be subordinate, except for those veterans who have permanent service-connected disabilities. This is a point we made at the outset. And it is a point we return to at the conclusion.

Concomitant with reform of civilian employment pensions, the system of nonservice-connected veterans' pensions should be abolished. More than 90 percent of veterans qualify for social security. Their military service counts for social security. Years after that service is completed, they should not be placed in a status above other citizens in similar circumstances. Ultimately it is an issue of equity: People in equal circumstances should not be treated unequally. Nonservice-connected veterans' pensions violate that principle. This was the view of Franklin Roosevelt, it was essentially the position of the Bradley Commission in 1956, it was the judgment of a 1971 report by the Brookings Institution, and it is our position as well.

Furthermore, as we have already indicated, nonservice-connected medical care for veterans should be replaced with a comprehensive health insurance plan for all Americans, whether or not they are service-connected. There is a legitimate place within such an insurance system for permanent credits for men who are permanently service-disabled and for temporary credits for all other veterans in the years after discharge. The changes would return veterans' benefits and the VA to their proper functions: readjustment assistance for all veterans and permanent aid to those who have suffered permanent losses on account of military service. The reforms would permit more concentrated efforts where they are needed.

One way to have those efforts made is to have them made by young veterans themselves. The tremendous energies and commitment of Vietnam veterans to each other need to be harnessed. In a number of cities, funds from the Emergency Employment Act and grants from the Office of Economic Opportunity have been used to finance programs in which veterans aid one another through counseling, hot lines, special houses, and publications. These programs generally creep along for want of adequate resources, coordination, and guidance. These are things that the VA should provide. It does not provide them now.

★ *A Last Word*

The scars of Vietnam go deeper than any set of programs can ever reach. There is a certain dishonesty even in using words like "compensation." Of course, there never really is any compensation for the loss of an arm or an eye, a mind at rest, or a husband. And with a war like Vietnam there will always be a sense of absurdity and uselessness that makes it all hard to put away. To continue discussing benefits and programs seems at times like mistaking points of irritation for the deeper sources of distress. But men continue to be hurt by bad discharges, drug problems, and lost jobs, and so one goes on despite the beckoning false wisdom that it is all beside the point. Veterans have been left with a sense of being unclean, as if the unworthiness of the war they fought somehow reflected on them. We have an obligation to show that we feel their actions and their honor are separable from the conflict. The challenge is to meet the need for respect without falsifying the past, and to meet the need for special assistance without creating a special social status and special privileges that place inordinate burdens on the future.

Those of us who approved sending troops to Vietnam cannot now abandon them after they have returned. And those of us who fought against the war need to demonstrate that we have never been against those who fought the war. This is a time not so much for guilt and shame as for genuine sorrow that such things ever happened to our people and to others, and for genuine determination that, so far as we can help it, they shall never happen again.

Notes

CHAPTER 1.   DIFFERENT WAR, INDIFFERENT PEACE

1. U.S. Senate, *Impact of the Vietnam War*, A report to the Committee on Foreign Relations, June 30, 1971. Later statistics were provided periodically in the "Southeast Asia Casualties Statistical Summary," Office of the Assistant Secretary of Defense (Public Affairs).
2. Michael Useem, *Students Against the Draft* (tentative title). New York: John Wiley & Sons, Inc., 1973, Ch. 3.
3. *Ibid.*
4. J. Ronnie Davis and Neil Polomba, "On the Shifting of the Military Draft as a Progressive Tax-in-Kind," *Western Economic Journal*, VI, 5, December 1968, pp. 150–53, Table 1, Row 8.
5. John A. Sullivan, "Qualitative Requirements of the Armed Forces," in *Studies Prepared for the President's Commission on an All-Volunteer Armed Force.* Washington, D.C.: Government Printing Office, November 1970.
6. A 1964 survey of veterans by the National Opinion Research Center indicated that their motives for enlistment had been as follows: draft-motivated, 36.9 percent; personal, 28.8 percent; self-advancement, 23.1 percent; patriotic, 11.2 percent. (See Charles Moskos, *The American Enlisted Man.* New York: Russell Sage, 1970, p. 199.) In 1969, a Defense Department-funded survey of high school and college students' attitudes toward enlistment indicated the pattern had not changed. Among those students who seriously considered enlisting (24 percent of the total), "almost one-half . . . identified educational and training benefits. These included job and skilling, schooling on the job, the GI Bill, and career security. Another quarter said they had seriously considered enlisting in order to get their military obligation over with; i.e., to avoid the draft. The remaining quarter identified a number of personal reasons such as 'get away from the confusion in my home' and a 'chance to grow up.' Only 3 percent felt that they wanted to enlist out of a sense of duty to their country." (See Jerome Johnston and Jerald Bachman, *Young Men and Military Service*, Volume V of *Youth in Transition.* Ann Arbor, Mich.: Institute for Social Research, 1972, p. 143.) Finally, in 1971, another Defense Department-sponsored study found that nearly half of the young men surveyed would not enlist no matter what

inducement was offered. Among those who said they would or might enlist, economic and personal reasons again predominated. See *Attitudes Toward Military Service: Results of a National Survey Conducted in May 1971,* prepared by the Human Resources Research Organization (HumRRO) for the Office of the Assistant Secretary of Defense (Manpower and Reserve Affairs).

7. *Statistical Abstract of the United States 1972.* Washington, D.C.: Government Printing Office, 1972, p. 260. In 1971, as the number of combat deaths went down, the proportion of draftees did also (to 33 percent).

8. U.S. House of Representatives, *Extension of the Draft and Bills Related to the Voluntary Force Concept and Authorization of Strength Levels,* Hearings Before the Committee on Armed Services, 92nd Cong., 1st Sess., 1971, p. 172.

9. "Draftees Shoulder Burden of Fighting, Dying in Vietnam," *National Journal,* August 15, 1970.

10. Friedrich Nietzsche, *The Genealogy of Morals,* Chs. VII, XXVIII. See *The Birth of Tragedy and The Genealogy of Morals,* tr. by F. Golffing. Garden City, N.Y.: Doubleday, 1956, pp. 200, 298.

11. See Moskos, *supra,* note 6, pp. 51, 139, 202.

12. Morris Janowitz, *The Professional Soldier.* New York: The Free Press, 1960, p. 21.

13. Frances Fitzgerald, *Fire in the Lake.* Boston: Atlantic–Little, Brown, 1972, p. 343.

14. Memorandum for Secretary of Defense, May 4, 1967, *The Pentagon Papers,* IV, 462, cited by Helmer (see next note).

15. John Helmer, *Bringing the War Home: The American Soldier in Vietnam and After,* doctoral thesis, Harvard University, 1972, pp. 41–42.

16. Veterans World Project, *Wasted Men: The Reality of the Vietnam Veteran.* Edwardsville, Ill.: Southern Illinois University Foundation, 1972, p. II-5.

17. This was reported to us independently in five different interviews. It may be a myth, but it is certainly widely believed among veterans.

18. Fitzgerald, *supra,* note 13, p. 370.

19. Moskos, *supra,* note 6, pp. 148–9.

20. Joseph Neilson, "Survey of American Veterans," *Congressional Record,* May 17, 1971, at E 4471–73. Cited in Helmer, *supra,* note 15.

21. J. J. Dowling, "Psychological Aspects of the Year in Vietnam," *USARV Medical Bulletin,* II: 45–58 (May–June), 1967: H. Spencer Bloch, "The Psychological Adjustment of Normal People During a Year's Tour in Vietnam," *The Psychiatric Quarterly,* October, 1970. Reprinted in *The Vietnam Veteran in Contemporary Society.* Washington, D.C.: Veterans Administration, May 1972.

22. Peter G. Bourne, "The Viet Nam Veteran," in *The Vietnam Veteran in Contemporary Society, ibid.*

23. Ronald J. Glasser, *365 Days.* New York: Bantam, 1971, pp. 26–27.

24. Michael Casey, "A Bummer," in Larry Rottmann, Jan Barry and Basil T. Paquet, eds., *Winning Hearts and Minds.* New York: McGraw Hill, 1972.

25. Shelby Coffey III, "Back Home With Three Vietnam Casualties," *The Washington Post, Potomac,* July 19, 1970, p. 23.

26. *The New York Times,* October 26, 1972. The scene was a hearing on veterans' problems in Newark, New Jersey.

27. New York State Chamber of Commerce, "Drug Abuse as a Business Problem," cited in *Ramparts,* November, 1971, p. 10. See also Carol Mathews, "The Drug Stigma on Vets," *New York Post,* May 24, 1971.

28. *Wasted Men, supra,* note 16, pp. I: 1, 2.

29. Bourne, *supra*, note 22, IV: 84.

30. Catherine Breslin and Mark Jury, "America's Human Time Bombs," *The Philadelphia Enquirer, Today*, August 20, 1972; "The Violent Veterans," *Time*, March 13, 1972.

31. Perhaps some additional comments on the "brutalization" hypothesis are in order. The few empirical studies that we have of Vietnam veterans' psychological problems tell a somewhat different story. There is, first of all, some mildly suggestive evidence that Vietnam veterans do have a somewhat greater tendency than did veterans of earlier wars at the same age to "act out" their problems. A study at the Minneapolis VA hospital, comparing patients after World War II, Korea, and Vietnam, found that while the diagnosis of "personality disorder" had been made in only 7 percent of cases after World War II, it was made in 36 percent of the cases of Vietnam era veterans, with psychoneurotic symptoms on the decline. "To a much greater extent than previously," the authors concluded "today's young veteran is expressing maladjustment in the form of 'acting out' behavior, rather than by internalizing anxiety into neurotic symptoms." The implication is that there has been an increase in suicides, assaults, and accidents. It should be noted that this study did not separate out combat veterans, so that many of those referred to as Vietnam veterans did not in fact serve in Vietnam.

    On the other hand, we have a study by two military doctors comparing fifty patients who developed psychiatric problems after tours of Vietnam combat duty with a group of patients who had not been in Vietnam. They concluded that "although Vietnam returnees face significant readjustment stress, their reactions are generally internalized, and their potential for violent aggression is no greater than in those without Vietnam experience."

    If one thinks about these two studies carefully, they turn out to be quite consistent. What they suggest, however, is not that Vietnam has left its veterans on the edge of violence, but that there have been general shifts in our culture since World War II—breakdowns in traditional controls over behavior —which permit both Vietnam veterans and others to "act out" their problems more than before. But passive expressions of disorientation remain the dominant pattern. This conclusion may not satisfy those who wish to ascribe to the war the responsibility for violence at home, but it seems more consistent with this admittedly meager data. See G. A. Braatz, G. K. Lumry, and M. S. Wright, "The Young Veteran as a Psychiatric Patient in Three Eras of Conflict," *Newsletter for Research in Psychology*, XIII: 1 (February 1971) and W. Goldsmith and C. Cretekos, "Unhappy Odysseys: Psychiatric Hospitalizations Among Vietnam Returnees," *Archives of General Psychiatry*, 20: 78–83 (January 1969).

32. Bureau of Labor Statistics, Monthly Reports.

33. Moskos, *supra*, note 6, pp. 53–4.

34. Paul A. Weinstein, "Labor Market Activity of Veterans: Some Aspects of Military Spillover," Final Report of the Military Training Study, University of Maryland, June 1969, p. 143.

35. Bureau of the Budget, "A Survey of Socially and Economically Disadvantaged Veterans," November 1969, p. 21.

36. U.S. House of Representatives, *Survey of Government Operations, Part 12–Veterans Administration*, Hearing Before a Subcommittee of the Committee on Government Operations, 90th Cong., 2nd Sess., June 18, 1968, p. 23.

37. *Ibid.*, p. 43.

CHAPTER 2. THE MACHINERY OF GOVERNMENT

1. Michael March, *Veterans' Benefits and the General Social Welfare Benefits: A Study in Program Relationships*, doctoral thesis, Harvard University, March 1962, p. 103.
2. President's Commission on Veterans' Pensions, Staff Report No. IV, pp. 137–8. Cited in March, *ibid.*
3. Louis Harris & Associates, "A Study of the Problems Facing Vietnam Era Veterans: Their Readjustment to Civilian Life," Conducted for the Veterans Administration, October 1971, p. 237. The notable difference here is the greater importance attached to employment assistance to returning veterans.
4. Veterans Administration, "Budget in Brief: Fiscal Year 1974," p. 21. The figures refer to column 3, lines 2, 3, and 12.
5. Administrator of Veterans Affairs, *1971 Annual Report*, p. 14.
6. Administrator of Veterans Affairs, *1972 Annual Report*, p. 115 (single page seen in pre-release draft).
7. Office of the Comptroller, Veterans Administration. Vietnam era veterans represented only 9.4 percent of the VA's patients in a hospital census taken October 20, 1971—a lower proportion than they represent of hospital discharges because of their shorter average length of stay. In using the higher rate, we are trying to be as generous as we can to the VA.
8. "Budget in Brief: Fiscal Year 1974," *supra*, note 4, p. 21. The totals for compensation and pensions, medical care, and readjustment benefits refer to column 1, lines 2, 3, and 12.
9. We put the percentage at 12 to 15 because we presume Vietnam veterans are receiving the greater part of compensation payments, although they are almost certainly getting less than half of readjustment benefits. The estimate is generous. The real figure may be below 10 percent.
10. "Budget in Brief: Fiscal Year 1974," *supra*, note 4, p. 3. Vietnam era veterans numbered 5,976,000 out of a total of 28.8 million living veterans.
11. March, writing in 1960, made an estimate of $12 billion. We have adjusted his figure to take account of subsequent increases in pension rates. If anything, the figure is an underestimate.
12. Statement of Professor James L. Clayton, *The Military Budget and National Economic Priorities*, Hearings Before the Subcommittee on Economy in Government of the Joint Economic Committee, 91st Cong., 1st Sess., June 1969, pp. 145–47. Benefits for veterans of the nation's first five wars cost three times as much as the wars themselves. Later benefits cost somewhat less.
13. Veterans Administration Information Service, "America's Wars," December 31, 1970. The secret of the longevity of veterans' benefits: old warriors on their deathbeds marrying young maids, who live to ninety and collect VA benefits for all those many years.
14. James L. Clayton, "Our Mortgaged Future," *Playboy*, April 1970, reprinted in U.S. Senate, *Impact of the War in Southeast Asia on the U.S. Economy*, Hearings Before the Committee on Foreign Relations, 91st Cong., 2nd Sess., Part 1, April 1970.
15. See Davis Ross, *Preparing for Ulysses*. New York: Columbia University Press, 1967, p. 18.
16. See below, "Education and the GI Bill."

17. Willard Waller, *The Veteran Comes Back.* New York: The Dryden Press, 1944, Part Two.
18. Veterans Administration Information Service, "GI Bill of Rights: 25th Anniversary, 1944–1969," p. 11.
19. *Statistical Abstract of the United States 1972.* Washington, D.C.: Government Printing Office, 1972, p. 248.
20. See testimony by representatives of Aircraft Owners and Pilots Association and Air Transport Association in U.S. Senate, *Cold War GI Bill Amendments of 1967,* Hearings Before the Subcommittee on Veterans' Affairs of the Committee on Labor and Public Welfare, 90th Cong., 1st Sess., 1967.
21. "Vietnam Veterans' Education Project Lobbied to Death," Associated Press, September 7, 1970.

CHAPTER 3.　A TRADE IN SCARS

1. U.S. Senate, *Oversight of Medical Care of Veterans Wounded in Vietnam,* Hearings Before the Subcommittee on Veterans' Affairs, Committee on Labor and Public Welfare, 91st Cong., 1st and 2nd Sess., p. 93.
2. Veterans Administration, *The Vietnam Veteran in Contemporary Society* (Department of Medicine and Surgery, May 1972), "Wounded Army Personnel Separated for Disability—Percentage Distributions of Specified Residual Disabilities," p. III–33. The statistics for Vietnam are based on 1,000 disability separations of wounded Army personnel in 1966 and 1967. The authors caution that "no firm conclusions would be justified."
3. Veterans Administration, "Data on Vietnam Era Veterans," n.d., p. 29.
4. U.S. Senate, *Oversight of VA Hospital Crisis,* Hearings Before the Subcommittee on Health and Hospitals, Committee on Veterans' Affairs, 92nd Cong., 1st Sess., pp. 47, 50.
5. *The Wall Street Journal,* July 24, 1969.
6. *Oversight of VA Hospital Crisis, supra,* note 4, p. 46.
7. Veterans Administration, "The Vietnam Era Veteran: Challenge for Change," 1971, p. 64. The 9.4 percent figure comes from the hospital census, October 20, 1971.
8. Administrator of Veterans' Affairs, *1971 Annual Report,* p. 13.
9. See Sidney E. Cleveland and Fred Lewis, "Attitudes of Vietnam Era vs. WWII Era Veterans Toward VA Hospital Practices," and Anne W. Florell, "Young Veterans' Perceptions of VA Hospital Treatment," *Newsletter for Research in Psychology,* XIII: 3, August 1971.
10. See below, Chapter 4.
11. Sidney Cleveland and Fred Lewis, "Attitudes of Vietnam vs. WWII–Korean Era Veteran Employees Toward VA Hospital Practices," *Newsletter for Research in Psychology,* XIII: 4, November 1971.
12. Robert A. Burt, "Admission and Release Processes of Veterans Administration Psychiatric Hospitals," A Report Prepared for the Chairman of the Administrative Conference of the United States, March 1972, pp. 1, 70.
13. See Cecil P. Peck, "The Vietnam Veteran," in *The Vietnam Veteran in Contemporary Society, supra,* note 2.
14. *Oversight of Medical Care of Veterans Wounded in Vietnam, supra,* note 1, pp. 273–4.
15. Housing grants to eligible disabled veterans have since been raised to $17,500.

16. "On Disbelieving Atrocities," in *The Yogi and the Commissar*. New York: Macmillan, 1945. Cited in Nevitt Sanford and Craig Comstock, eds., *Sanctions for Evil*. Boston: Beacon Press, 1971, p. 111.
17. The following account is based on unpublished materials and an article in *The New York Times*, August 11, 1972.
18. *The New York Times*, April 29, 1965.
19. Letter from the Comptroller General of the United States to Senator William Proxmire, August 23, 1972.
20. President's Commission on Veterans Pensions, Staff Report No. VIII, p. 89. (House Committee Print No. 281, 84th Cong., 2nd Sess.)
21. Brooke Nihart, "Disability Retirement: Some Facts," *Armed Forces Jounral*, November 1972.
22. President's Commission on Veterans Pensions, Staff Report No. VIII, p. 76.
23. Ray Cromley, *Benefits for U.S. Veterans*. New York: Bantam Books, 1971, p. 87.
24. Burt, "Admission and Release Processes of Veterans Administration Psychiatric Hospitals," *supra*, note 12, p. 40.
25. *Ibid.*, p. 43.
26. *Ibid.*, p. 44.
27. Cited in Michael March, *Veterans' Benefits and the General Social Welfare Benefits: A Study in Program Relationships*, doctoral thesis, Harvard University, March 1962, p. 172.

CHAPTER 4.   VETERANS' HOSPITALS: NEW INJURIES AND OLD

1. Mary C. Moran and William E. Davis, "Viet Nam Veterans and AMA Discharges: A Brief Note," *Newsletter for Research in Psychology*, XIII: 1, February 1971.
2. Gerald J. Mozdierz, "Vietnam Era Veterans and AMA Discharges: A Further Look," *Newsletter for Research in Psychology*, XIV: 2, May 1972.
3. *Journal of the American Medical Association*, 129: 1189, December 22, 1945. For the extreme AMA position, see H. H. Shoulders, *et al.*, "VA Medical Care: A Contest for Survival between the Civilian and Government Hospital Systems," *Journal of the Tennessee State Medical Association*, 44: 439, October 1951. Dr. Shoulders was President of the AMA in 1945–46.
4. Administrator of Veterans Affairs, *1971 Annual Report*, p. 13.
5. Veterans Administration, Public Information Office.
6. U.S. House of Representatives, *Veterans Administration Hospital Funding and Personnel Needs*, Hearings Before the Subcommittee on Hospitals of the Committee on Veterans' Affairs, House of Representatives, 91st Cong., 2nd Sess., 1970, p. 2913.
7. *Ibid.*, and *1970 Annual Report*, p. 11.
8. U.S. House of Representatives, *HUD-Space-Science Appropriations for 1972*, Hearings Before a Subcommittee of the Committee on Appropriations, 92nd Cong., 1st Sess., 1971, p. 117.
9. U.S. House of Representatives, *Medical Care for Veterans*, House Committee Print No. 4, 90th Cong., 1st Sess., April 17, 1967, p. 214.
10. Interview, October 1971.
11. For a general discussion of the conflict between academic and clinical

orientations in a hospital setting, see Raymond S. Duff and August B. Hollingshead, *Sickness and Society*. New York: Harper & Row, 1968, Ch. 4.

12. U.S. Senate, *Federal Role in Health*, Report of the Committee on Governmental Operations, made by its Subcommittee on Executive Reorganization and Government Reorganization and Government Research, 91st Cong., 2nd Sess., Report No. 91–809, 1970, pp. 18–19.

13. National Center for Health Statistics, *Illness, Disability, and Hospitalization Among Veterans, United States, July 1957—June 1961*, Series 10, No. 14, U.S. Department of Health, Education, and Welfare, Public Health Service, 1965, p. 18.

14. U.S. House of Representatives, *Survey of Veterans' Health Insurance Coverage and Preference for Hospital Care*, House Committee Print No. 2, 91st Cong., 1st Sess., April 3, 1969, p. 4.

15. *Illness, Disability, and Hospitalization Among Veterans, supra*, note 13, p. 22.

16. A. J. Jernigan and Ronald Kidd, "Interview Survey of 220 Vietnam Era Patients," *Newsletter for Research in Psychology*, XIV: 1, February 1972.

17. John W. Walsh, "Planning Health Care for Veterans," *American Journal of Public Health*, 59: 2209–14, December 1969. Dr. Walsh is a VA hospital administrator.

18. *1971 Annual Report, supra*, note 4, p. 13.

19. *Illness, Disability, and Hospitalization Among Veterans, supra*, note 13, p. 25.

20. Administrator of Veterans' Affairs, *1971 Annual Report*, p. 15; "The Nation's Hospitals: A Statistical Profile," *Hospitals*, 45: 462, August 1971.

21. We are indebted to Dr. A. Gerson Hollander, Chief of Staff, Boston VA Hospital, for collecting these data.

22. U.S. Senate, *Oversight of VA Hospital Crisis*, Hearings Before the Subcommittee on Health and Hospitals of the Committee on Veterans' Affairs, 92nd Cong., 1st Sess., 1971, p. 126.

23. Interviews with staff personnel, St. Martinsburg, Va., September 12, 1972.

24. U.S. House of Representatives, *Medical Care Programs of the Veterans Administration*, A Report to the Committee on Appropriations, March 1973, p. 2.

25. *Hospitals*, 45: 462, August 1971.

26. Veterans Administration, "Final Report—Staffing Ratio Study," submitted by Chief Medical Director's Advisory Committee of Hospital Directors, in U.S. Senate Report No. 93-57, 93rd Cong. 1st Sess., March 2, 1973.

27. U.S. House of Representatives, *Operations of Veterans Administration Hospital and Medical Program*, House Committee Print No. 1, 92nd Cong., 1st Sess., February 17, 1971, pp. 282–83.

28. Department of Medicine and Surgery, *The Future of the VA Medical Program, 1970–1990*, Veterans Administration, March 1970, p. iii.

29. *Medical Care Programs of the Veterans Administration, supra*, note 24, p. 28.

30. *Operations, supra*, note 27, p. 257.

31. *Ibid.*, pp. 264–65.

32. *HUD-Space-Science Appropriations for 1972, Supra*, Note 8, p. 502; *Hospitals*, 45: 454 (August 1971).

33. *HUD-Space-Science Appropriations for 1972, ibid.*, p. 437; *Hospitals, ibid.*, p. 437.

34. U.S. House of Representatives, *HUD-Space-Science Appropriations for 1971*, Hearings Before a Subcommittee of the Committee on Appropriations, 92nd Cong., 1st Sess., 1970, p. 440.

35. *Operations, supra*, note 27, p. 283.

36. U.S. Senate, *VA Health Care and Health Manpower Training Legislation,* Hearings Before the Subcommittee on Health and Hospitals, Committee on Veterans' Affairs, 92nd Cong., 1st Sess., August 4, 1971, p. 330.
37. Interview, October 7, 1972.
38. *The Future of the VA Medical Program, supra,* note 28, p. 50.
39. Kenneth Boulding, *The Organizational Revolution.* Chicago: Quadrangle Books, 1968, pp. 30–31.
40. *1971 Annual Report,* p. 14.
41. Walsh, *supra,* note 17.
42. Interviews with Dr. Pat Suzman, fellow in endocrinology, and Dr. Ronald Weingut, senior resident in medicine, November 12, 1971.
43. Interview, December 20, 1971.
44. *VA Health Care and Health Manpower Training Legislation, supra,* note 36, p. 243.
45. *Congressional Record,* October 13, 1972, at S17947.
46. *HUD-Space-Science Appropriations for 1972, supra,* note 8, p. 83.
47. *Ibid.,* p. 424.
48. Members of a prepaid health plan, like Kaiser Permanente, pay a flat sum annually for all medical services including hospital care. It is then in the interests of the institution to catch medical problems early so that hospitalization will be unnecessary. A series of studies comparing such programs with private insurance plans have shown that they substantially reduce the rate of hospitalization. Critics argue that the programs sometimes also withhold necessary services. See Sidney Garfield, "The Delivery of Medical Care," *Scientific American,* April 1970; Judy Karnory, "Kaiser. You Pay Your Money and You Take Your Chances," *Ramparts,* November 1970; and Anne R. Somers, ed., *The Kaiser-Permanente Medical Care Program: A Symposium,* New York: The Commonwealth Fund, 1971.
49. U.S. House of Representatives, *Operation and Funding of VA Medical Program and Legislation Related Thereto,* Hearings Before the Subcommittee on Hospitals of the Committee on Veterans' Affairs, 92nd Cong., 1st Sess., 1971, p. 558.
50. U.S. Senate, *Oversight of Medical Care of Veterans Wounded in Vietnam,* Hearings Before the Subcommittee on Veterans' Affairs of the Committee on Labor and Public Welfare, 91st Cong., 1st and 2nd Sess., 1969, 1970, p. 222.
51. *American Medical News,* March 8, 1971, pp. 8–9. Dr. Musser is a former director of the Regional Medical Program in North Carolina. For a more extensive presentation of his views, see Marc J. Musser, "Unified Health Plan Needs VA Linkage," *U.S. Medicine,* January 15, 1971.
52. Leonard P. Ullmann, *Institution and Outcome.* New York: Pergamon Press, 1967.
53. *1971 Annual Report,* p. 70.
54. U.S. Senate, *Oversight of Medical Care of Veterans Wounded in Vietnam,* Hearings Before the Subcommittee on Veterans' Affairs of the Committee on Labor and Public Welfare, 91st Cong., 1st and 2nd Sess., 1969, 1970, p. 43. The ratio of psychologists to psychiatric patients was 1 to 107.
55. *1971 Annual Report,* p. 84.
56. *Operations, supra,* note 27, p. 61.
57. Interview, December 20, 1971.
58. Data supplied by Dr. Donald Watkin, January 10, 1973.
59. Interview, February 3, 1972.
60. See R. Sommer and H. Osmond, "Symptoms of Institutional Care," *Social*

Problems, 8, 254–63, and Erving Goffman, *Asylums.* Garden City, N.Y.: Doubleday, 1961.

61. Eliot Freidson, "Disability as Social Deviance," in *Sociology and Rehabilitation,* American Sociological Association, 1965, p. 87.
62. *Operations, supra,* note 27, p. 271.
63. *Proceedings of the Conference on the Medical and Consumer Problems of Paraplegics and Quadriplegics,* June 24, 1971, p. 5.
64. Graham J. Sharman and Kenneth A. Owen, Jr., *Spinal Cord Injury.* A Report to the National Paraplegic Foundation concerning the New England Region, September 1970.
65. Dr. John Young, "A National Network of Regional Spinal Injury Care Systems, A Plan for the 70s," in *Proceedings, supra,* note 66, pp. 21–23.
66. National Advisory Commission on Health Manpower, *Report of the National Advisory Commission on Health Manpower.* Washington, D.C.: Government Printing Office, 1967.
67. *American Medical News,* March 8, 1971, pp. 8–9.
68. *Survey of Veterans' Health Insurance Coverage and Preference for Hospital Care, supra,* note 14, p. 10.

CHAPTER 5. WAR ON DRUGS: THE LIMITS OF INTERVENTION 1: ORIGINS

1. U.S. House of Representatives, *Inquiry into Alleged Drug Abuse in the Armed Services,* Report of a Special Subcommittee of the Armed Services Committee, 92nd Cong., 1st Sess., April 23, 1971.
2. U.S. House of Representatives, *The World Heroin Problem,* Report of a Special Study Mission by Representatives Morgan F. Murphy of Illinois and Robert H. Steele of Connecticut, Committee on Foreign Affairs, 92nd Cong., 1st Sess., May 27, 1971.
3. See Alfred McCoy, *The Politics of Heroin in Southeast Asia.* New York: Harper & Row, 1972; Frank Browning and Banning Garret, "The CIA and the New Opium War," *Ramparts,* May 1971; and "Heroin and the War," editorial in the *Washington Post,* July 26, 1972.
4. U.S. Senate, *Staff Report on Drug Abuse in the Military,* Report of the Subcommittee on Drug Abuse of the Committee on Armed Services, 92nd Cong., 1st Sess., p. 8.
5. Stewart Alsop, "Worse than My Lai," *Newsweek,* May 24, 1971.
6. Peter G. Bourne, "The Vietnam Veteran," in *The Vietnam Veteran in Contemporary Society,* Department of Medicine and Surgery, Veterans Administration, May 1972.
7. *The World Heroin Problem, supra,* note 2, p. 18.
8. U.S. Senate, *Military Drug Abuse,* Hearings Before the Subcommittee on Alcoholism and Narcotics of the Committee on Labor and Public Welfare, 92nd Cong., 1st Sess., June 9 and 22, 1971, p. 6 and elsewhere.
9. *The Washington Post,* September 12, 1971.
10. *Senate Staff Report, supra,* note 4, p. 21.
11. Allen H. Fisher, Jr., *Preliminary Findings from the 1971 DOD Survey of Drug Use,* Human Resources Research Organization Technical Report 72–8, March 1972.
12. Richard S. Wilbur, "How to Stamp Out a Heroin Epidemic—Army-Style," *Today's Health,* July 1972.

13. *The Washington Post*, September 12, 1971.
14. "Profile of Drug Abusers in Vietnam," Department of Defense, Office for Health and Environment, ca. December 1971.
15. Norman E. Zinberg, "Rehabilitation of Heroin Users in Vietnam," manuscript, p. 2. Published as "GI's and OJ's in Vietnam," *New York Times Magazine*, December 5, 1971.
16. "Profile," *supra*, note 14.
17. "The Viet Nam Veteran," *supra*, note 6.
18. *Ibid.*
19. Zinberg, "Rehabilitation of Heroin Users in Vietnam," *supra*, note 15, p. 6.
20. See "Black Power Group in Vietnam Fights the Enemy Within: Heroin Addiction," *New York Times*, August 12, 1971.
21. Seymour Halleck, *The Politics of Therapy*. New York: Science House, 1971, p. 72.
22. Zinberg, "GI's and OJ's in Vietnam," *supra*, note 15.
23. Troy Duster, *The Legislation of Morality*. New York: Free Press, 1970, Ch. 1.
24. *Marijuana: A Signal of Misunderstanding*, Report of the National Commission on Marijuana and Drug Abuse. Signet, 1971.
25. "Concerning Drug Laws," Interview with Dr. David Musto, *Yale Reports*, October 29, 1971.
26. See, for example, advertisement in *The Medical Mirror*, April 1900, reprinted in "Concerning Drug Laws," *ibid.*
27. Duster, *supra*, note 23, pp. 9–13.
28. See L. Lasagna, J. M. von Felsinger, and H. K. Beecher, "Drug-induced Mood Changes in Man," *Journal of the American Medical Association* 157 (1955), 1006–1020.
29. See Charles B. Towns, *Habits That Handicap, The Menace of Opium, Alcohol, and Tobacco, and the Remedy*. New York: The Century Company, 1916. Writes Towns: "Drug habits may be classified in three groups: The first and largest is created by the doctors, the second is created by the druggist and the manufacturer of proprietary and patent medicines, and the third, and smallest, is due to the tendency of certain persons toward dissipation.
    "The major importance of the first two groups is due to the fact that they include by far the greater number of cases, and to the pitiful fact that such victims are always innocent."
30. Cited in Alfred Lindesmith, *The Addict and the Law*. Bloomington, Indiana: Indiana University Press, 1965, p. 21.
31. Cited in *Marijuana: A Signal of Misunderstanding*, *supra*, note 24.
32. Lindesmith, *supra*, note 30, p. 20.
33. Duster, *supra*, note 23, p. 16.
34. "Remarks of the Honorable Stephen G. Porter in the House of Representatives," February 26, 1923, p. 14.
35. On the clinics, see Duster, Lindesmith, Musto, and Charles E. Terry and Mildred Pellens, *The Opium Problem*. New York: Bureau of Social Hygiene, 1928.
36. For the subsequent legal history of medical involvement in treating drug addiction, see Lindesmith, *supra*, note 30.
37. I. Pierce James, "The Changing Pattern of Narcotics Addiction in Britain—1959 to 1969," *The International Journal of the Addictions*, Vol. 6, No. 1, March 1971, pp. 119–134.
38. Griffith Edwards, "The British Approach to the Treatment of Heroin Addiction," *Lancet*, April 12, 1969, pp. 768–72.

39. Edgar May, "Drugs Without Crime," *Harper's,* July 1971.
40. Richard Hofstadter, *The Age of Reform.* New York: Random House, 1955, p. 292.
41. R. Glasscote, J. N. Sussex, J. H. Jaffe, J. Ball, and L. Brill, *The Treatment of Drug Abuse.* Washington: The Joint Information Service of the American Psychiatric Association and the National Association for Mental Health, 1972, p. 27.
42. Perry London, *Behavior Control.* New York: Harper & Row, 1969, pp. 56–82.
43. Glasscote, *et al., supra,* note 41, p. 40.
44. *Ibid.,* pp. 30–35.
45. We do not mean here to preclude the possibility that such consequences may be demonstrated in the future. The treatment of drug abuse is an area where none of the alternatives is free of costs. Eliminating methadone maintenance now would only cause grave social and personal harm in the name of preventing potential physical damage. If, at some point, serious long-term harmful consequences are demonstrated, it may become advisable to curb maintenance programs, but that point has not been reached.

CHAPTER 5. WAR ON DRUGS: THE LIMITS OF INTERVENTION II. REFLEX AND RESPONSE

1. *Inquiry into Alleged Drug Abuse in the Armed Services, op. cit.,* p. 2174.
2. *Military Drug Abuse, 1971, op. cit.,* p. 108.
3. "Report of the Drug Abuse Control Commission Task Force," reprinted in the *Congressional Record,* December 3, 1970, at S19314.
4. "Illegal or Improper Use of Drugs by Members of Department of Defense," October 23, 1970.
5. *Inquiry into Alleged Drug Abuse in the Armed Services, op. cit.,* p. 2212.
6. *Senate Staff Report, op. cit.,* p. 15. See also "Memorandum for the Assistant General Counsel, Department of Defense, from the Office of Judge Advocate General, Department of the Navy," April 28, 1972: "It must be explained to the Exemption applicant that he is not required to identify drug abusers as a condition *precedent* to his obtaining Exemption; however, it should also be explained that if he has knowledge of drug abuse activities of another person he may be required to testify about such activities before an official board of investigation, court-martial, or other such body *after* being granted Exemption." (emphasis added)
7. See Samuel A. Simon, "The Catch in Amnesty," *The Nation,* October 4, 1971; *Senate Staff Report,* pp. 15–16.
8. "Case histories from files of Subcommittee on Alcoholism and Narcotics on members of the military with drug problems and how they were dealt with," *Military Drug Abuse, 1971, op. cit.,* p. 294.
9. *Senate Staff Report,* p. 15.
10. See "Chronology of Action Involving Drug Abuse in the Military," *Congressional Quarterly,* January 22, 1972, p. 146.
11. "Memorandum of the Secretary of Defense on the Military's Drug Abuse Treatment Program," June 17, 1971, reprinted in *The International Narcotics Trade and its Relation to the United States,* Report of a Special Study Mission

283

by Seymour Halpern, New York, Committee on Foreign Affairs, House Report No. 92–836, 92nd Cong., 2nd Sess., February 17, 1972, p. 141.
12. Data from the Department of Defense.
13. See "Transcript of News Conference of Dr. Jerome Jaffe, July 17, 1971," reprinted in Halpern Report, *supra*, note 11, pp. 134–40.
14. Richard S. Wilbur, "How to Stamp Out a Heroin Epidemic—Army-Style," *Today's Health*, July 1972, p. 10.
15. *Medical World News*, September 3, 1971.
16. News briefing with Dr. Richard S. Wilbur, Friday, January 7, 1972. Transcript reprinted in U.S. Senate, *Drug Abuse in the Military*, Hearing before the Subcommittee on Drug Abuse in the Military of the Committee on Armed Services, 92nd Cong., 2nd Sess., 1972, p. 148.
17. See "Urinalysis Accuracy Rates of Commercial Laboratories Performing Under Army Contracts," *ibid.*, p. 5.
18. Letter from General John K. Singlaub, Deputy for Drug and Alcohol Abuse, to the Honorable Les Aspin, June 19, 1972.
19. *Drug Abuse in the Military, supra*, note 16, pp. 288–301.
20. *Ibid.*, p. 296.
21. Norman Zinberg, "Rehabilitation of Heroin Users in Vietnam," *op. cit.*, p. 23.
22. Bob and Carol Spencer, "Abusing drug abusers: The military solution," *Civil Liberties*, Fall 1971.
23. *Medical World News*, September 3, 1971.
24. Wilbur, "How to Stamp Out a Heroin Epidemic—Army-Style," *supra*, note 14.
25. Statement of Dr. Jerome Jaffe, *Drug Abuse in the Military, supra*, note 16, p. 168.
26. Data from the Department of Defense.
27. Letter from S. Sgt. Frank B. Poyas, Non-Commissioned Officer in Charge (NCOIC), Long Binh Drug Treatment Facility, South Vietnam, to LTC A. Carl Segal, MD, MC, Acting Director, Division of Neuropsychiatry, Walter Reed Army Institute of Research (WRAIR), August 24, 1971.
28. *Senate Staff Report*, p. 5.
29. *The Washington Post*, September 14, 1971.
30. Project Assist, Headquarters, U.S. Continental Army Command, Ft. Monroe, Va., April 5, 1972, p. 37.
31. *Drug Abuse in the Military, supra*, note 16, p. 34.
32. *The New York Times*, June 23, 1971.
33. *The New York Times*, June 2, 1972.
34. *The New York Times*, September 14, 1971.
35. Letter from S. G. Armitage, Unit Administrator, August 9, 1972.
36. Interview with Dr. Ruth Stoffer, May 17, 1972.
37. Interview with Dr. William Winick, May 16, 1972.
38. Interview with June Swartz, June 22, 1972.
39. Letter from Dr. Charles Spray, July 12, 1972.
40. Conversations with Dr. Norman Zinberg, May 1972.
41. Cited in *New Perspectives on Urban Crime*, A Report by the American Bar Association Special Committee on Crime Prevention and Control, ms., p. 41. See also John C. Kramer, "The State Versus the Addict: Uncivil Commitment," *Boston University Law Review*, 50:1 (Winter 1970), pp. 1–23.
42. Peter D. Russell and Solomon L. Frumson, "Drug Dependent Treatment Center Protocol," Veterans Administration Hospital, Buffalo, New York, January 4, 1972, p. 1.
43. Interview with E. Holt Babbit, March 28, 1972.

44. Talk by Dr. Joel Kantor, George Washington University School of Medicine, July 27, 1972.
45. "A Study of the Army Drug Abuse Program," A report by the American Bar Association Special Committee on Crime Prevention and Control, ms., pp. 68–70.
46. Interview with Dr. Norman R. Tamarkin, June 15, 1972.
47. U.S. House of Representatives, "Veterans Administration Drug Dependence Program—April 1972," Committee on Veterans Affairs, p. 2.
48. Letter from Peter D. Russell, Coordinator, Drug Dependence Treatment Center, June 12, 1972.
49. Interview with Dr. Marshall Trubow and other members of the staff, Outpatient VA Drug Clinic, Boston, May 23, 1972.
50. Speech by Senator Alan Cranston on Veterans' Drug Problems, Institute for the Study of Health and Society, Mayflower Hotel, Washington, D.C., June 16, 1972.
51. "A Study of the Army Drug Abuse Program," supra, note 45, p. 83.
52. Talk by Dr. Joel Kantor, supra, note 44.
53. Charles Spray, "A Developmental History of the Drug Dependency Treatment Center, Veterans Administration Hospital, Vancouver, Washington," May 1, 1972.
54. "Doctor faces new battle on treating drug addicts," The Oregonian, n.d.
55. "VA Hospital Drug Chief Fired," The Oregon Journal, July 1, 1972.
56. Visit to Brockton Veterans Administration Hospital, May 16, 1972.
57. Interview with Dr. Ruth Stoffer, May 17, 1972.
58. "A Description of the Treatment Philosophy and Program of the Drug Dependency Treatment Unit," Veterans Administration Hospital, Bedford, Massachusetts, n.d.
59. "Veterans Administration Drug Treatment Program, Baltimore, Maryland," ca. June 1972, pp. 1–2.
60. "Drug Dependence Treatment Center," Boston, Mass., May 11, 1972.
61. Robert Derman and George V. Mascia, "The Addicted Veteran: A Report on Response to Methadone Maintenance," ms.
62. "A Study of the Army Drug Abuse Program," supra, note 45, p. 32.
63. Derman and Mascia, supra, note 62.
64. Interview with Dr. Edwin Tucker, August 15, 1972.
65. "Drug Dependence Treatment Center," supra, note 61.

CHAPTER 6. BAD DISCHARGES: THE WRONG WAY OUT

1. "Types of Discharges Issued To Enlisted Personnel By Fiscal Year 1950–1972," Office of Assistant Secretary of Defense (Manpower and Reserve Affairs), August 31, 1972. Unless otherwise noted, all statistics relating to discharges are from this report.
2. The types of discharges are not usually capitalized. We have done so in hopes of minimizing some of the confusion. When the type of discharge is capitalized, it is being used in the purest sense as a specific type of discharge issued in a particular proceeding, as opposed to a reference to a category of more than one type of discharge.

3. "Since the vast majority of discharges from the armed forces are honorable, the issuance of any other discharge stigmatizes the ex-serviceman. It robs him of his good name. It injures his economic and social potential as a member of the general community." *Sofranoff* v. *United States*, 165 Ct. Cl. 470, 478 (1964).
4. Even the Defense Department directive on the subject of administrative discharges provides that before a serviceman can be given an Undesirable Discharge he has the right to present his case before an "administrative *discharge* board." Department of Defense Directive, Number 1332.14, December 20, 1965, as amended. (Emphasis added.) The name does not convey open-mindedness on the subject.
5. *Ibid.*
6. This case and others were related to us by military lawyers.
7. Army Regulations 635–212, p. 9.
8. U.S. Senate, *Constitutional Rights of Military Personnel*, Hearings Before the Subcommittee on Constitutional Rights, Committee on the Judiciary, 87th Cong., 2nd Sess., 1962, p. 315.
9. "Discharges Reviewed by the Army Discharge Review Board," supplied by Major Shurtleff, Recorder of the Army Council of Review Boards.
10. Office of the Assistant Secretary of Defense (Public Affairs), October 26, 1972. The statistics cover the period October 13, 1971, to September 30, 1972.
11. Letter from Mr. Stratton Appleman, assistant director, Public Information Office, Veterans Administration, to Raymond Bonner, dated January 18, 1973.

CHAPTER 7.   A PRELUDE: HOW THE GREAT SOCIETY WENT TO WAR

1. *Democracy in America*, tr. by Henry Reeve. New York: Schocken, 1961, Vol. II., p. 320.
2. *The Marine Corps Gazette*, August 1968, p. 30.
3. "Project One Hundred Thousand: Characteristics and Performance of 'New Standards' Men," Office of the Assistant Secretary of Defense (Manpower and Reserve Affairs), December 1969, p. 14.
4. "The Negro Family: The Case for National Action," Office of Policy Planning and Research, U.S. Dept. of Labor, March 1965. (Hereinafter referred to as Moynihan Report.) Reprinted in Lee Rainwater and William L. Yancey, *The Moynihan Report and the Politics of Controversy*. Cambridge, Mass.: The M.I.T. Press, 1967, p. 42.
5. *Ibid.*, p. 42.
6. Charles C. Moskos, Jr., *The American Enlisted Man*. New York: Russell Sage Foundation, 1970, p. 116. For 1967–68, the proportion of black combat fatalities fell to 13–14 percent, still above their representation within the military and society as a whole.
7. *The New York Times*, October 16, 1966.
8. Moynihan Report, p. 42.
9. Max Weber, "The Meaning of Discipline," in H. Gerth and C. Wright Mills, eds. *From Max Weber: Essays in Sociology*. New York: Oxford University Press, 1958, p. 261.
10. Task Force on Manpower Conservation, "One Third of a Nation, A Report on Young Men Found Unqualified for Military Service," January 11, 1964.

11. *The New York Times*, January 5, 1964.
12. *The New York Times*, June 19, 1964.
13. Interview with Paul Barton, Policy Planning Council, Department of Labor, Executive Director of Task Force on Manpower Conservation, August 5, 1971.
14. *The New York Times*, August 14, 1964.
15. Interview with Harold Wool, Dept. of Labor, formerly director of Project 100,000 in the Department of Defense, August 11, 1971.
16. *The New York Times*, August 24, 1966.
17. Interview with Irving Greenberg, Assistant Director of Recruiting and Retention, Department of Defense, August 9, 1971.
18. *The New York Times*, August 24, 1966.
19. *The Army Times*, September 14, 1966.
20. *The New York Times*, September 4, 1966.
21. *The New York Times*, October 25, 1966.
22. *The Air Force Times*, January 25, 1967.
23. "Project 100,000: Characteristics and Performance," *supra*, note 3, p. xvii. The figures for each service are interesting: Army, 41 percent; Navy, 33 percent; Air Force, none; Marine Corps, 56 percent. The reason for the reversal in the Air Force is that it is the only service where high status roles are also combat roles. Lower ranking men are like medieval squires.
24. Interview with Irving Greenberg, *supra*, note 18.
25. "Project 100,000: Characteristics and Performance," *supra*, note 3, p. 28.
26. Bureau of the Budget, *A Survey of Socially and Economically Disadvantaged Veterans*, November 1969, p. 21.
27. James Fenrich and Michael Pearson, "Black Veterans Return," *Trans-Action*, March 1970.
28. *Ibid.*
29. Robert McNamara, "Social Inequities: Urban's Racial Ills" (*sic*), *Vital Speeches of the Day*, XXXIV: 4, December 1, 1967, pp. 98–103.
30. David B. Kassing, "Military Experience as a Determinant of Veterans' Earnings," *Studies Prepared for the President's Commission on an All Volunteer Armed Force*. Vol. II. Washington, D.C.: Government Printing Office, 1970.
31. "Project 100,000: Characteristics and Performance," *supra*, note 3, pp. 47–48.
32. U.S. House of Representatives, *Department of Defense Appropriations for 1971*, Hearings Before a Subcommittee of the Committee on Appropriations, 91st Cong., 2nd Sess., 1970, Part II, p. 64.
33. *Ibid.*, p. 314.
34. "Project 100,000: Characteristics and Performance," *supra*, note 3, p. 50.
35. U.S. House of Representatives, *Department of Defense Appropriations for 1972*, Hearings Before a Subcommittee of the Committee on Appropriations, 92nd Cong., 1st Sess., 1971, Part III, p. 1159.
36. "Project 100,000: Characteristics and Performance," *supra*, note 3, p. 43.
37. *Department of Defense Appropriations for 1972*, *supra*, note 35, p. 933.
38. *Department of Defense Appropriations for 1972*, *supra*, note 35, p. 87.
39. *The Air Force Times*, March 24, 1971.
40. "Project 100,000: Characteristics and Performance," *supra*, note 3, p. 54. The percentage refers to a rate of attrition after an average service of eighteen months, not to a final attrition rate, which should be higher.

CHAPTER 8.   THE UNEMPLOYED ARMY

1. *Monthly Labor Review*, 63:5 (November 1946), pp. 673–674; 68:2 (February 1949), pp. 172–3. See also Dale W. Berry and Steven van Dresser, *Evaluation of Special Manpower Services to Veterans*, draft final volume, prepared for the Office of Policy, Evaluation and Research, Manpower Administration, U.S. Department of Labor, July 1972, by Kirschner Associates, Inc. (hereinafter referred to as the Kirschner Report.), p. 17.
2. Kirschner Report, p. 17. See also *Monthly Labor Review*, "Employment Situation of Vietnam Era Veterans," September 1971. Reprint 2758.
3. *The New York Times*, January 29, 1969.
4. Bureau of the Budget, *A Survey of Socially and Economically Disadvantaged Vietnam Era Veterans*, November 1969, p. 6.
5. Elizabeth Waldman, "Vietnam War Veterans—Transition to Civilian Life," *Monthly Labor Review*, November 1970, Reprint 2702, p. 27.
6. *Monthly Labor Review, supra*, note 2.
7. See Martin S. Feldstein, "Lowering the Permanent Rate of Unemployment," Discussion Paper No. 259, Harvard Institute of Economic Research, Cambridge, Mass.; also Peter B. Doeringer and M. J. Piore, *Internal Labor Markets and Manpower Analysis* (Lexington, Mass.: D. C. Heath and Co., 1971); more generally, R. E. Hall, "Why Is the Unemployment Rate So High at Full Employment?" *Brookings Papers on Economic Activity*, 1971:3, pp. 659–701.
8. *Monthly Labor Review, supra*, note 2.
9. Kirschner Report, p. S-18.
10. National Urban Coalition, *Falling Down on the Job: The United States Employment Service and the Disadvantaged*, June 1971, p. 3. See also Hall, *supra*, note 7, pp. 667–668, and Kirschner Report, pp. 77–80.
11. U.S. Department of Labor, "State Employment Service Activities, Fiscal Year 1970" ("Green Sheet"), September 1970.
12. *Falling Down on the Job, supra*, note 10, p. 3.
13. Kirschner Report, p. 77.
14. *The New York Times*, June 28, 1970.
15. *Congressional Record*, June 17, 1971, p. S 9295. Statement by Senator Alan Cranston.
16. *The Honeybucket*, Summer, 1972.
17. *The American Legion Magazine*, January–July, 1971. "Monthly Reports of Job Fair Activity."
18. Kirschner Report, p. 84.
19. Interview with James M. Ritch, Vice President, National Alliance of Businessmen, August 24, 1972.
20. U.S. Dept. of Labor, "NAB/JOBS for Veterans: A Strategy for Coordination." June 3, 1971.
21. President's Veterans Program. "Monthly Review and Analysis Report, Period Ending December 31, 1971," p. 6. U.S. Dept. of Labor, Manpower Administration, PVP Task Force.
22. Kirschner Report, F-8.
23. Interview with Charles Collins, National Alliance of Businessmen, July 31, 1972.
24. Interview with Frank McKiernan, Director, Project Transition, September 22, 1972.

25. *Air Force Times*, December 31, 1969.
26. Bureau of the Budget, *supra*, note 4, p. 24.
27. *Air Force Times*, December 17, 1969.
28. Special Evaluations Group, Division of Program Evaluation, Manpower Administration, U.S. Department of Labor, "An Evaluation of the Tooling-Up Phase of the President's Veterans Program." DSE Report No. 21, December 1971, p. 21. See also President's Veterans Program, "Monthly Analysis," June 31, 1972. Manpower Administration.
29. Kirschner Report, p. 47. See also Memorandum to Paul J. Fassner, Deputy Assistant Secretary for Manpower, U.S. Dept. of Labor, from Merwin S. Hans, Acting Deputy Associate Manpower Administrator, "Subject: Project Transition," June 1972; and "Monthly President's Veterans Program Memorandum" from Floyd E. Edwards, Regional Manpower Administrator, to Harold O. Buzzell, Deputy Manpower Administrator, Department of Labor, June 30, 1972.
30. The "Concentrated Employment Program" (CEP) is "a system of packaging and delivering manpower services in a clearly defined geographical area. Working through a single contract . . . the Manpower Administration provides a flexible package of manpower programs . . . to disadvantaged residents of the locally defined CEP area." The "Public Service Careers Program" provides "on-the-job training and supportive services to enable disadvantaged persons to qualify for jobs with Federal, State, and local governments, private non-profit agencies, and agencies that receive Federal grant-in-aid. Unemployed or underemployed persons 18 years or older are eligible for the program."

   The "Public Employment Program" seeks to "alleviate recent high unemployment by providing funds to State and local governments in a 2-year program to hire an estimated 150,000 to 200,000 unemployed persons for public service jobs. The jobs are to be transitional in nature, and the participants are to move to regular jobs as soon as possible."

   The "MDTA Institutional Training Program" provides "classroom occupational training and related supportive services for unemployed persons 16 years or older who cannot reasonably be expected to obtain employment with their present skills . . ." The "MDTA–OJT" programs provide "occupational training for unemployed persons who cannot reasonably obtain full-time employment without MDTA assistance. Such training is generally conducted through private industry in the regular work environment." General Accounting Office, "Federal Manpower Training Programs." Report to the U.S. Senate, February 17, 1972, p. 16.
31. Memorandum to Robert J. Brown, Director, U.S. Employment Service, from Merwin S. Hans, Deputy Associate Manpower Administrator, Office of Employment Development Programs, Dept. of Labor. Subject: "PVP-4th Quarter, FY 1972," July 21, 1972, p. 1.
32. *Ibid.*
33. "Monthly Program Analysis," June 31, 1972. President's Veterans Program.
34. U.S. Department of Labor, Manpower Administration. "Summary Enrollment and Termination Data By Program: Fiscal Year 1972." OFMIS, Manpower Administration, June 1, 1972.
35. See R. E. Hall, "Prospects for Shifting the Phillips Curve Through Manpower Policy," *Brookings Papers on Economic Activity*, 1971:3, pp. 659–701. See also "Evaluation of the Effectiveness of Institutional Manpower Training in

Meeting Employers' Needs," prepared for the Office of Policy, Evaluation, and Research, Manpower Administration. Olympus Research: June 1972.

36. Compared to other federal manpower training programs, PEP's turnover rates (only 25 percent per year, compared with the nearly 50 percent average rate recorded for other programs, and the 40 percent annual rate for all U.S. workers), starting wages (in FY 1972, $3.04 for PEP veterans), and operating efficiency (only a 1.6 percent overhead in FY 1972) indicate that it has been quite well-managed. Interview with Richard Wagner, Public Employment Program, July 24, 1972.

37. Manpower Administration, "Limitation on Grants to States for Unemployment Insurance and Employment Services: Proposed Amendment, 1972." July 1971, p. 6.

38. Training and Employment Service Program Letter No. 2678, "To All State Agencies: Subject: PVP." United States Employment Service, Manpower Administration, Department of Labor, August 20, 1971, p. 3.

39. President's Veterans Program, "Monthly Analysis," June 1972, p. 41. Interview with Herbert Rainwater, Director, Veteran Employment Service, October 20, 1972.

40. Glenda Lush, Labor Department Program Auditor, Detroit. "Study of Placement Process in an Automated Local Office. February 9, 1972, p. 3.

41. Letter from John M. Clark, Executive Director, Pennsylvania Bureau of Employment Security, to J. Terrell Whitsitt, Regional Manpower Administrator–Pennsylvania, U.S. Dept. of Labor, May 25, 1972, p. 1.

42. "Mandatory Listing: Response to Secretary Hodgson's Letter," Computer Printout, Manpower Administration, U.S. Department of Labor, June 26, 1972.

43. Memorandum, "Monthly Mandatory Listing Report, August 1972." From William U. Norwood, Jr., Regional Manpower Administrator, Atlanta, to the Manpower Administration, September 14, 1972, p. 2.

44. President's Veterans Program, "Monthly Program Analysis," June 30, 1972. Cf. "State Employment Service Activities," July, 1970–March, 1971, "MEHS Report," May 20, 1971, Manpower Administration, U.S. Department of Labor.

45. President's Veterans Program, "Monthly Program Analysis, ibid., p. 30.

46. Statement by Senator Vance Hartke, Hearings before the Senate Committee on Veteran Affairs, Transcript, September 28, 1971, p. 3.

47. Kirschner Report, p. 114.

48. "Monthly Program Analysis," supra, note 44.

49. Statement by Secretary of Labor George Schultz before the House Committee on Ways and Means, June 1969.

50. To measure the impact which PVP has had on veteran unemployment, we must look at the difference between the amount that veteran unemployment declined after PVP came into existence and the comparable decline in non-veteran unemployment. This will give us the maximum net decline in veteran unemployment that might be attributed to factors other than general economic improvements. Between the fourth quarter of 1971 and the fourth quarter of 1972, veteran unemployment (seasonally adjusted) fell from 8.3 percent (for veterans age 20–29) to 6.1 percent. But over the same year, non-veteran unemployment declined from 7.7 percent to 6.5 percent. This indicates that perhaps 1.2 percent of the 2.2 percent decline in veteran unemployment while PVP was operating at full capacity might be attributed to general economic improvement. This leaves a net change of about − 1 percent

for which PVP might be responsible. Data from Bureau of Labor Statistics, Department of Labor, "Employment Situation for Vietnam Era Veterans: Fourth Quarter, 1972." News Release, January 22, 1973.

51. *Ibid.*, Table 12: "Duration of unemployment of male Vietnam Era Veterans and Non-Veterans, annual averages, 1971 and 1972." Unfortunately, the BLS presents only a distribution of the periods of unemployment, from which it is impossible to compute a true mean. But 42.9 percent of all Vietnam era veterans were unemployed less than 5 weeks in 1972, and 30.5 percent were unemployed between 5 and 14 weeks. Only 26.6 percent were unemployed for periods of more than 15 weeks. This data is consistent with the notion of a rather unstable and quite active labor force.

52. News Release, January 22, 1973, Table 13. Again, BLS survey categories are not entirely appropriate for what is needed to understand the sources of veteran unemployment, and "young worker unemployment" in general.

53. "Data collected from manufacturing establishments shows that total accessions and separations have each exceeded 4 percent of the labor force per month since 1960." Feldstein, *supra*, note 7, p. 23. The Bureau of Labor Statistics estimates that for each worker who quits his job and fails to become employed immediately, four will quit and transfer to new jobs, in search for something better. Those who tend to wind up unemployed are, of course, those to whom the labor market has less to offer: the poor and the handicapped. In 1972, on the average, about 21 percent of all unemployed veterans who had held jobs just prior to being unemployed had become unemployed because they quit. If we take into account the short average duration of veteran unemployment— i.e., the fact that the unemployed veteran population "turns over" about once every four or five weeks—and also the ratio between "successful" and "unsuccessful" quitters (about four to one), then, using the data supplied by the BLS "News Release" of January 22, 1973, Table 13, it is possible to make a rough estimate of the incidence of job quitting among employed veterans during 1972. This turns out to be about 5.4 percent per month, or upward of 50 percent per year.

CHAPTER 9.   EDUCATION AND THE GI BILL

1. New York: Little, Brown, 1921, pp. 121–2, 130.

2. Louis Harris and Associates, Inc., "A Study of the Problems Facing Vietnam Era Veterans and Their Readjustment to Civilian Life." October 1971, p. 237.

3. U.S. Senate, *Education and Training for Veterans*, Hearings Before the Subcommittee on Veterans' Affairs of the Committee on Labor and Public Welfare, 91st Cong., 1st Sess., Part 2, p. 370. In presenting the participation rate for Vietnam veterans, the VA plays a rather pathetic little game. Under the most recent GI Bill, active duty servicemen are entitled to benefits after a minimum period of service (originally two years, later reduced to 180 days). In computing the participation rate for Vietnam veterans, the VA commonly adds the number of active duty servicemen who have used their benefits to the numerator, but fails to add the number of eligible servicemen to the denominator. Through this technique, the agency raises the participation rate several percentage points. Whenever we cite participation rates for Vietnam era veterans, we mean precisely that: the ratio of the number of veterans using

benefits to the number eligible. (Were we to include active duty servicemen on both sides of the ratio, the participation rate would be considerably reduced. To make fair comparisons with previous GI Bills, however, we naturally do not include them. Neither do we include the so-called Post-Korean veterans, those who served between 1956 and 1964 and were awarded GI Bill benefits only in 1966. For obvious reasons, they have a lower rate of participation in the program, and it would be unfair to include them in comparisons. Nevertheless, even with these exclusions, the participation rate under the current GI Bill has been lower.)

4. Veterans Administration, "Veterans Benefits Under Current Educational Programs," Department of Veterans Benefits, June 1972.
5. Harris Survey, *supra*, note 2, p. 240.
6. National Advisory Council on Extension and Continuing Education, *A Question of Stewardship: A Study of the Federal Role in Higher Continuing Education*. Washington, D.C.: Government Printing Office, 1972.
7. *Congressional Record*, August 4, 1972, at S12849.
8. Thomas C. Steinhauser, "Why Can't the VA Pay GI Students on Time?" *Armed Forces Journal*, April 1972.
9. *Ibid.*
10. Donald E. Johnson, "Text of Remarks," opening session, Veterans Administration National Task Force on Education and the Vietnam Era Veteran, January 10, 1972, Washington, D.C.
11. William Steif, "Viet Vets Ignoring GI Benefits," *The Cincinnati Post*, June 8, 1972.
12. *Ibid.*
13. In this chapter we are concerned only with benefits for education and training. Home loans are not discussed in this report, while unemployment compensation and job placement are treated in Chapter 8. Business loans and mustering-out pay have been discontinued under the current GI Bill.
14. *The Budget for Fiscal Year 1973, Special Analyses*. Washington, D.C.: Government Printing Office, 1972, p. 128.
15. See Keith W. Olson, "A Historical Analysis of the GI Bill and Its Relationship to Higher Education," Office of Education, Department of Health, Education, and Welfare, 1968.
16. Brent Beedin, "Veterans in College," *Research Currents* (ERIC Clearinghouse on Higher Education), March 1, 1972.
17. Michael S. Guy, "The GI Bill: Its Origins and Impact on Higher Education," paper presented at annual meeting, American Educational Research Association, April 4, 1972, Chicago, Ill.
18. Cited in David Ross, *Preparing for Ulysses* (New York: Columbia University Press, 1967), p. 108.
19. Robert Hutchins, "Threat to American Education," *Colliers* CXIV, December 30, 1944.
20. Cited in Olson, *supra*, note 15.
21. Cited in Guy, *supra*, note 17.
22. *Ibid.*
23. Seymour Harris, *A Statistical Portrait of Higher Education*. New York: McGraw-Hill, pp. 412–13. The statistics cited do not indicate what percentage ultimately went to college, but what percentage were in college at any given time. That is why they relate directly to the question of the size of the labor force.
24. See Norman Fredericksen and W. B. Shrader, *Adjustment to College—A Study*

of 10,000 Veteran and Non-Veteran Students in Sixteen American Colleges. Princeton, N.J.: Educational Testing Service, 1952.

Two claims are often made for the GI Bill that are probably unjustified. One is that it produced a 30 percent increase in the earnings of veterans over nonveterans (see, e.g., Guy, *op. cit.*). This is based on 1955 Census data that include no controls for race and other important variables. It may be that the median income of veterans in 1955 was higher than that of nonveterans primarily because few blacks served in World War II and were disproportionately represented in the nonveteran population.

A second claim often made for the GI Bill is that it helped reduce social and economic inequalities in the United States. Unfortunately, the evidence indicates otherwise. The distribution of income has shown no significant change since 1945. "The GI Bill of Rights," notes Colin Greer, "initiated the trend [toward seeing] higher academic achievement [as] increasingly essential for employment . . . 'The whole labor force has been upgraded but the relative position of various strata has evidently changed very little.' " See Colin Greer, *The Great School Legend*, New York: Basic Books, 1972, p. 34; Christopher Jencks and David Riesman, *The Academic Revolution*, Garden City, N.Y.: Doubleday, 1968, Ch. 3; A. H. Halsey, Jean Floud, and C. Arnold Anderson, eds., *Education, Economy, and Society*, New York: The Free Press, 1961; and Christopher Jencks *et al.*, *Inequality: A Reassessment of the Effects of Family and Schooling in America*, New York: Basic Books, 1972.

25. Veterans Administration, "GI Bill of Rights: 25th Anniversary, 1944–1969," Washington, D.C., p. 8.
26. *The New York Times*, February 6, 1950.
27. *Ibid.*
28. U.S. House of Representatives, *Report of the House Select Committee to Investigate Educational and Training Programs Under the GI Bill*, 81st Cong., 2nd Sess., 1951. Cited in Guy, *supra*, note 17.
29. Cited in Guy, *supra*, note 17. The data on veterans come from the Program Planning and Budgeting Service of the VA, while the data on the general population are drawn from American Council on Education, *Fact Book on Higher Education*, 1969 ed., No. 1, p. 9015.
30. *Air Force Times*, May 2, 1959.
31. *Air Force Times*, January 21, 1961.
32. Statistics cited on the current GI Bill usually refer only to Vietnam era veterans, meaning those who served after August 4, 1964, the date of the Tonkin Gulf resolution. The "Post-Korean" or "Cold War" veterans, who served between 1956 and 1964, represent a special category. Only when we label data as specifically embracing Cold War as well as Vietnam era veterans do we mean to include them.
33. A case can be made, however, for extending the term of eligibility for veterans who have received only part-time benefits. The low payments during the first few years of the GI Bill probably forced many students to go to school part-time while working full-time. They are now being caught by the thirty-six-month limit on eligibility, which ends before they can finish college.
34. 38 USC 1652 (b).
35. Frank B. Williams, "Basic Tenets: The Federal Government—The Veteran— And Education," prepared for National Task Force on Education and the Vietnam Veteran, January 10–12, 1972.
36. Veterans Administration, "Veterans Benefits Under Current Educational

Programs," Department of Veterans Benefits, June 7, 1971. Appendix Tables 14 and 16.

37. Cited in Guy, *supra*, note 17.
38. American Council on Education, *The American Freshman: National Norms for Fall 1971*, Office of Research, p. 40.
39. Howard E. Holcomb, "Comparison of Independent Colleges and Universities, 1947–48 vs. 1971–72, by Veterans Undergraduate Enrollment, Total Undergraduate Enrollment, and Increases in Total Costs," National Council of Independent Colleges and Universities. Reprinted in U.S. House of Representatives, *Education and Training Programs Administered by VA*, Hearings Before the Subcommittee on Education and Training of the Committee on Veterans' Affairs, 92nd Cong., 1st Sess., 1971, pp. 1693–1708.
40. Interview, Fairmont, W.Va., September 13, 1972.
41. Bureau of the Budget, "A Survey of Socially and Economically Disadvantaged Veterans," November 1969. The bureau's study is the best of a bad lot. Generally the quality of data in this area is extremely poor. The disadvantaged are almost always defined as those with less than twelve years of school. We have no data on GI Bill participation by family income, father's occupation, or any of the other standard indices of social class. The VA has been a bit shy about gathering such statistics. It would be interesting to know, for example, whether veterans from families with incomes in the lowest two fifths of the nation's population have significantly greater access to higher education than nonveterans from those same families. The premise of most public policy—the Moynihan Report, for example—is that this is true, but there is actually no data to support the position. One merely supposes it is true.
42. *Report of the President's Committee on the Vietnam Veteran*, pp. 8–9. The committee was called together in June 1969 at the suggestion of Moynihan, then a Presidential advisor, who was disturbed about the low use of the GI Bill. Moynihan, however, did not serve on the committee. Its chairman was Donald Johnson, at that time a new man in town, and its members included Secretaries Melvin Laird, Robert Finch, and George Schultz, as well as Donald Rumsfeld of OEO; Robert Hampton, Chairman of the Civil Service Commission; and Postmaster General Winston Blount. According to a staff member of the committee, its existence was resented by resident bureaucrats at the VA, who saw it as a threat to their authority. In the end, however, the report was brief—only thirty-four pages double-spaced—and the recommendations mild.
43. It should be noted that Congress also approved a "prepayment" measure that went into effect immediately. Under prepayment, a veteran receives money for the coming month instead of the month just completed. Under "advance" payment, he receives an extra month's allowance on the day of the registration to help him out with his initial expenses. It is the latter proposal that the VA had to put into effect in August 1973.
44. Interview, September 10, 1972.
45. *Congressional Record*, August 4, 1972, at S12849.
46. "The AAJC Program for Servicemen and Veterans 1971–72: The Second Annual Report to the Carnegie Corporation of New York," Summary Report, March 1, 1972, p. 27.
47. Office of Education, Department of Health, Education, and Welfare, Supplement No. 1 to the 1971–72 (TS/UB) Program Manual and the 1971–72 Part E, Education Professions Development Act for Institute and Short Term Training Programs, June 1972.

48. Andrew Hamilton, "Another Time at Bat for Vietnam Vets," *American Education*, March 1972.
49. Rosalind Loring and Edward Anderson, "The Considerations in Planning and Administering a College Prep Program for Veterans," *Adult Leadership*, September 1971.
50. Steward Feldman, "How an Individual College or Technical School Can Help Veterans Seeking Education," Veterans Education and Training Action Committee, August 1971. Oddly, the major thrust of the federal government's program on veterans' employment problems has been to encourage private institutions to take action, while its program on veterans' education has completely ignored private institutions. The irony is that in the area of employment, businesses have been limited in what they could do for veterans because of the overall economic situation: There just aren't enough jobs to go around. But in the area of education, colleges would not be similarly constrained. As the impact of the post-World War II "baby boom" on higher education has waned over the past few years, many colleges have found themselves with empty places in their freshman class. In demographic terms, Vietnam veterans represent a delayed input from the same cohort that inflated college enrollments during the mid-Sixties.
51. Letter from Olney Owen, Chief Benefits Director, Veterans Administration, October 2, 1972. Subsequent statistics reported in VA information bulletins show increases of about 10 percent which seem to be largely artificial. Because of the transfer of budgetary responsibility for in-service remedial education from the Defense Department to the VA's PREP program, the new statistics are showing large numbers of educationally disadvantaged servicemen. The VA adds these to its statistics for veterans, reports them together, and then claims to be making substantial progress.
52. President's Commission on Veterans' Pensions, Staff Report No. 9, Part B, pp. 113–14.
53. Veterans Administration, "Benefits Under Current Education Programs," Department of Veteran Benefits, June 1972, pp. 20–21.
54. Letter from Olney Owen, *supra*, note 51.
55. *Veterans of Foreign Wars Magazine*, June 1972.
56. Hearings Before the Federal Trade Commission on Proposed Guides for Private Vocational and Home Study Schools, December 1970, p. 523.
57. 38 USC 1652 (b).
58. Williams, *supra*, note 35.
59. National Systems Corp., Prospectus, June 10, 1971, p. 8.
60. Statement of Gerald O. Allen, former President, National Home Study Council, Before the Subcommittee on Readjustment, Education, and Employment, Committee on Veterans' Affairs, U.S. Senate, May 18, 1972.
61. Statement of Charles V. Chase, Special Studies Staff, Advance Schools, Inc., *ibid.*
62. Veterans Administration, "Veterans Benefits Under Current Educational Programs," June 1972, pp. 22–23.
63. Interview, July 17, 1972.
64. Comptroller General of the United States, "Most Veterans Not Completing Correspondence Courses—More Guidance Needed From the Veterans Administration," March 22, 1972.(Hereinafter cited as GAO Report.)
65. Letter to Mr. Ralph Nader, June 30, 1971.
66. Interviews with John Proffitt and Ronald Pugsley, Accreditation and Institutional Eligibility Staff, Office of Education, Department of Health, Education,

and Welfare, August 12, 1971; and with Henry Cabell, Federal Trade Commission, August 19, 1971.

67. Interview with James Taaffe, Director, Compensation, Pension, and Education Service, August 16, 1971. (Education has since been transferred into a department of its own in the VA.)

68. GAO Report, *supra*, note 64, p. 4.

69. Interview with David Lockmiller, National Home Study Council, August 1971. (Mr. Lockmiller has since retired.)

70. Records at the U.S. Office of Education.

71. Telephone interview with Henry Wellman, October 25, 1972.

    Indicative of the independence of the accrediting commission was a dispute in 1970 over the status of Lasalle Extension University, one of the large correspondence schools owned by Crowell, Collier and Macmillan. When the commission denied accreditation to Lasalle, CCM pulled all of its schools out of the trade association—not just Lasalle, but the Academy for Home Study, the Wayne School, Utilities Engineering School, U.S. School of Music, and the Washington School of Art. It then asked the Office of Education to end NHSC's recognition and took the council to court over a due process issue. According to Frank Dickey (in an interview on August 18, 1971), director of the National Commission on Accrediting, the court case would have cost NHSC several hundred thousand dollars and, having lost part of its membership, the council decided not to fight the issue. It settled out of court, and Lasalle got its accreditation. Peace and good will have reigned ever since.

72. Jessica Mitford, "Let Us Now Appraise Famous Writers," *The Atlantic*, July 1970.

73. National Systems Corp., *Annual Report 1971*. Revenues for that year were $18.7 million. Other costs were $5.4 million for "provision for doubtful contracts" and $2.6 million for general and administrative costs.

74. Quoted in Mitford, *supra*, note 72, p. 48.

    Jessica Mitford's article in *The Atlantic* was the first of a wave of troubles for FAS International. The following year (all by pure coincidence, according to the firm), its earnings plummeted, it was temporarily suspended by the New York Stock Exchange, its employees went on strike, and it was investigated by the Attorney General of New York, and required to give assurances it would not use any deceptive advertising in the future. Under pressure, FAS decided to restructure its marketing process and dropped the use of three-year enrollment contracts. Under its new approach it sells textbooks and education on a "pay-as-you-go" basis; i.e., students pay for lessons as they complete them. "No student is on the hook for more educational services than he wishes," says Gilbert Maurer, Executive Vice President. By eliminating long-term contracts, however, FAS incurred the wrath of the rest of the correspondence industry and in February 1972, the National Home Study Council discontinued its accreditation. "Their group," explains Mr. Maurer, "is committed to future-service contracts." FAS is now in bankruptcy proceedings. It is remarkable, though not surprising, that in all those years of deceptive advertising, the Famous Schools were able to retain their NHSC accreditation. It was only when they dropped the future-service contract that the council stepped in and cried foul.

    Asked specifically why NHSC had denied accreditation to the Famous Schools, Henry Wellman replied, "We can't give out the reasons." The council refuses to disclose or explain the results of any of its evaluations of individual correspondence schools. However, pressed as to whether the decision of FAS

International to abandon the future-service contract was a factor in the council's decision, Mr. Wellman stated, "That was certainly a part of it. The area of financial responsibility was certainly a part." Mr. Wellman also admitted that all schools accredited by the council employ future-service contracts. Telephone interviews with Henry Wellman, October 25, 1972, and Mr. Gilbert Maurer, Executive Vice President, FAS International, October 24, 1972.

75. GAO Report, *supra*, note 64, p. 13. Veterans were also asked whether they thought the VA should provide more information on correspondence courses. Over half the respondents stated it should.

76. GAO Report, *supra*, note 64, p. 12.

77. Statement of Gerald O. Allen, *supra*, note 60, p. 8.

78. GAO Report, *supra*, note 64, pp. 15–16.

79. Veterans Administration, "Veterans Benefits Under Current Educational Programs," June 1972, p. 8.

80. *The Chronicle of Higher Education*, Dec. 13, 1971.

81. *The Washington Post*, Aug. 26, 1972.

Index